Change in the International System

To Ole R. Holsti, who always helped along the way

Change in the International System

Essays on the Theory and Practice of International Relations

K.J. Holsti
University of British Columbia

Edward Elgar

Published by
Edward Elgar Publishing Limited
Gower House
Croft Road
Aldershot
Hants GU11 3HR
England

Edward Elgar Publishing Company
Old Post Road
Brookfield
Vermont 05036
USA

A CIP catalogue record for this book is available from the British Library.

A CIP catalogue record for this book is available from the US Library of Congress.

1 85278 381 8

Printed in Great Britain by
Billing & Sons Ltd, Worcester

Contents

Acknowledgements

I am grateful to the following publishers for permission to reprint, in edited form, the selections in this volume. MIT press, for permission to reprint 'Politics in Command: Foreign Trade as National Security Policy', *International Organization*, 40 (Summer 1986), pp. 643-71; Westview Press for permission to reprint 'Change in the International System: Interdependence, Integration, and Fragmentation,' in Ole R. Holsti, Randolph M. Siverson, and Alexander L. George (eds), *Change in the International System* (Boulder, CO: Westview Press, 1980), pp. 23-54; the Japan Association of International Relations, for permission to reprint 'International Theory: National or International?', *Kokusai Seiji*, 85 (May 1987), pp. 17-33; Butterworth Publishers, for permission to reprint 'Mirror, Mirror on the Wall, Which are the Fairest Theories of All?', *International Studies Quarterly*, 33 (September 1989), pp. 255-61; the Canadian Political Science Association, for permission to reprint 'Retreat from Utopia: International Relations Theory, 1945-1970', *Canadian Journal of Political Science*, 4 (June 1970), pp. 165-77, and 'The Necrologists of International Relations', *Canadian Journal of Political Science*, 18 (December 1985), pp. 675-95; the American Political Science Association, for permission to reprint 'Underdevelopment and the "Gap" Theory of International Conflict', *American Political Science Review*, 69 (September 1975), pp. 827-39; the International University of Japan, for permission to reprint 'Revolution in the Revolution: World Views and Foreign Policy Change in the Soviet Union', International University of Japan, *Annual Review*, 3 (1989), pp. 1-19; the Canadian Institute of International Affairs, for permission to reprint 'Along the Road to International Theory', *International Journal*, 39 (Spring 1984), pp. 337-65; Unwin Hyman for permission to reprint 'Restructuring Foreign Policy: A Neglected Phenomenon in Foreign Policy Theory', in K.J. Holsti et al., *Why Nations Realign: Foreign Policy Restructuring in the Postwar World* (London: George Allen and Unwin Ltd, 1982), pp. 1-20; and Macmillan Press Ltd, for permission to reprint 'The Comparative Analysis of Foreign Policy: Some Notes on the Pitfalls and Paths to Theory', in David Wurfel and Bruce Burton (eds), *The Political Economy of Foreign Policy in Southeast Asia* (London: Macmillan Press Ltd, 1990), pp. 9-20. Deepa Khosla, Marion Kaltenschnee and Karen Guttieri helped in many critical ways in the typescript preparation; I wish to acknowledge their assistance.

Introduction

1. Farming, Ranching, and Accounting: Perspectives on Change in International Relations

In a critical review of an evaluation of international theory, Susan Strange used the metaphor of farmers and ranchers to compare intellectual styles. Farmers, in Professor Strange's view, like to toil in well-defined disciplinary areas, within traditional paradigms and conventional methodologies. They 'want to put a neat boundary fence around International Relations, keeping out the roaming herds of social science irregulars'.[1] Ranchers, in contrast, are explorers. They look for new conceptual terrains to open up, indulge in unconventional methodological explorations, and generally expand the intellectual horizons of their followers. To extend her metaphor, I would argue that there is also a place for accountants. They are the stock-takers, the scholars who like to review the 'state of the field', to identify commonalities, lacunae, and perhaps point out ways that distortions and biases can be rectified. Accounting is not perhaps a noble endeavor, but it is necessary prelude to bringing some order and sense of coherence to the scholarly enterprise.

The essays in this volume represent a sample of all three types of intellectual activity. There is more farming and accounting than ranching, as the reader will quickly recognize. Yet, I hope the selections establish the value of all three kinds of activity. For in the academic study of international relations, as in most fields, there is a necessary interplay between them. Accounting underlines the importance of the traditions of the field, the predecessors to whom we owe a debt of gratitude for having been farmers and ranchers in their own time, creating the knowledge which serves as the foundation of this generation's activities. Farming is the necessary activity that slowly expands the body of knowledge, showing which practices - in our case, theoretical perspectives on the field - ultimately pay off, and identifying intellectual dead ends or non-productive curiosities. And ranching explores new ways of viewing and conceptualizing the world and developing approaches to integrating the diverse disciplinary and empirical sources of the field. Ranching also guarantees that the traditional does not attain mantra status, where it is merely repeated in celebratory fashion without examining its pertinence

3

to contemporary problems.

The theme that unifies the essays of this volume is change: change in international and foreign policy behavior - the substance of international politics - and change in the ways we approach and study the field. The two kinds of change are connected, for claims of scientific objectivity notwithstanding, how we see the world is often affected by what happens in it and how we theorize about it. On more than one occasion, analysts of international affairs have claimed that a war, peace conference, technological innovation, or revolution has created a 'new world'. These claims have often been premature, as other analysts respond that old patterns and habits of behavior seem to persist despite the dawning of a new era. We need to go back no further than the autumn of 1989 when the dramatic events in Eastern Europe and the Soviet Union prompted many to declare not only an end to the Cold War but also the emergence of a new world order, founded upon principles and modes of behavior more appropriate to an era of interdependence and global environmental problems. Saddam Hussein's conquest of Kuwait only less than a year later reminded us that security dilemmas, the use of force, and war remain endemic in the contemporary world and that the end of the Cold War has not fundamentally changed the international system, but only certain fissures and cleavages in it. How theoretical innovations and approaches to the field will develop over the next few decades will be strongly affected by our perceptions of such events. In our field, theory is inevitably driven, though not exclusively so, by changing events and trends.

There is an inherent tension between our desire for explaining and understanding international politics, and diplomatic change. To 'understand' this field means to develop generalizations that transcend time, location, and personality. Knowledge in our field necessarily incorporates the 'big picture', the identification of long-range trends and structural characteristics, patterns of behavior, and the classification of phenomena. The scholar's approach to the field must seek to achieve a certain level of generalization, otherwise we would be little more than reporters and critics of current events - of which there are already sufficient numbers. Explicitly or implicitly, we have some notion of what constitutes significant change from the more mundane or dramatic events of the daily headlines. Such events are examples of patterns (e.g., the recurrence of balances of power), significant anomalies (e.g., democracies do not war against each other), or emerging discontinuities (e.g., environmental degradation as a source of international conflict).

Yet, generalizations and theories may also be impervious to changes that are truly significant. To reduce all international

4

politics, for example, to a 'struggle for power' is to beg as many questions as to provide answers for them. Developments in technology, economic processes, the expansion of the international system, and the changing character of the state may have significant consequences on the structures and processes of international politics. It simply will not do to repeat the 'eternal verities' of international politics, identified and explained succinctly in many historical and theoretical works by thinkers such as Thucydides, Rousseau, Bentham, Morgenthau, and others, and to claim that these works are sufficient to understand all we want to know about international politics in the contemporary world. It is equally risky to assume that following some momentous event, everything is new and that, therefore, theorists must jettison past knowledge (generalizations based on reasonable empirical validation) and reconceptualize the world. In fact, most of the debates that abound among scholars of international relations revolve around the question of change: what is new, what is old, what continues, what is unique, and what conditions made changes possible?

Theoretical knowledge, I believe, must ultimately rest upon empirical foundations. The main challenge remains to develop statements that transcend time, location, and personality, recognizing, nevertheless, that each generalization or theoretical perspective will be only a representation of reality, and not a duplicate of it. The generalization gains authority, nevertheless, to the extent that it is founded on systematic evidence. Many patterns relating to the nature, characteristics, and incidence of international conflict, for example, have been discovered only through rigorous empirical work and data collection. The same holds for studies of international integration, collaboration, decision-making, dependency, and host of other areas that developed as a result of older theories or hypotheses. A number of perspectives and hypotheses, such as hegemonic stability theory, remained in the domain of speculation until historical evidence disconfirmed them. International theory necessarily involves the interplay of speculation and examination of the records created and left by diplomats, warriors, merchants, and scientists. But what are the sources of inquiry?

Generalizations are not easy to come by in a world of flux, but I do not believe we need to adopt the pessimistic posture that all theoretical enterprises are little more than the reflection of a political mood, or mere fig leaves for political purposes or ideological positions.[2] Many theorists write because they are intrigued by genuine intellectual puzzles, and not in order to fulfill some political agenda. Like mountaineers, they do their work because the challenge is there. Why scholars choose to pursue any

5

particular project cannot be answered simply. Certainly scholarship in our field does not follow strict canons of science, nor does it reflect only the events of the day. Problems and puzzles come to mind from many different sources. We may think that some previous theoretical statements or perspectives exclude important phenomena, or that they mask political preferences, or that they fail to explain numerous anomalies, or that they are simply unimportant or uninteresting. Or we may wish to develop new ways of examining/explaining persisting phenomena. There are numerous stimuli to inquiry.

The selections in this volume reflect many of these diverse sources. Rather than provide here a summary of each essay, it might be more interesting for the reader to have a biographical account of their origins. Why did I write each piece? What was I attempting to state or achieve? Where did my ideas come from? In what ways did they reflect the multiple and numerous sources of inquiry? What kinds of epistemological or normative positions are explicit or implicit in the analyses? How did theoretical puzzles stimulate empirical research and vice versa? Were the exercises primarily of a farming, accounting, or ranching character? How did the analyses reflect the continuing or changing character of international politics? And how do they reflect changing theoretical perspectives in the field of study?

The problem of change in international systems and foreign policy

'Underdevelopment and the "Gap" Theory of International Politics' had two significant sources. The first was my personal concern with the problem of war, the same problem that has motivated the inquiry of so many theorists of the field. What elsewhere I have called the 'classical tradition' in international relations[3] has centered around two fundamental questions: what are the causes of war and the conditions of peace? A concern with these problems needs no special explanation, much less an apology. I was a child during World War II and saw enough of the carnage as reported in various media to understand its horrifying aspects. As Finland's foreign minister (1936-1938) and ambassador to the League of Nations (1938-1941), my father was directly involved in the events that dashed hopes raised after the Great War and the launching of the League of Nations. The postwar revelations at Nuremburg - I was then old enough to understand them - and the onset of the Cold War helped to create in me an enduring interest in understanding the etiology,

6

character, and consequences of armed conflict. My undergraduate historical studies at Stanford University focussed on these areas and they were further extended during graduate studies at the time when the 'behavioral revolution' was just beginning to influence the field.

The second major source of the essay was a six week stay in Fiji in 1972. While hardly a paradigmatic example of an under-developed country, my stay there with a Fijian family in a slum and also in a rural village generated considerable curiosity about the state of underdevelopment and its sources. There was a notable discrepancy between what, in my opinion, was the conventional Western view about development, and what I saw. My conclusion was that the most painful aspects of underdevelopment are caused by the development process itself: environmental degradation; the strains on extended families and other traditional social units caused by Western psycho-materialism; the role of advertising in creating wants that cannot be satisfied given limited employment opportunities; the destruction of local arts, crafts, and other forms of employment by foreign imports and modern devices; the alienation of prime land for foreign tourist amenities; and the like.

Following up this experience, I spent a sabbatical year (1972-1973) reading the anthropological and sociological literatures on small communities in the Third World. In many cases, these confirmed my personal impressions: the processes associated with development are not neutral and the industrialized tutelary countries offer neither easy solutions nor adequate or appropriate models to be emulated. The next step was to link the development problematic to my traditional concern with international conflict and war. This was done in a paper presented to the International Political Science Association meetings in Montreal in 1974. The paper was effectively criticized by Alex Inkeles, one of this generation's foremost sociologists. He made many telling points, so I toned down the argument to accommodate the ones that struck me as valid. The main thesis, however, remained unaltered.

Of the selections in this volume, this is the most explicitly critical. It expresses views generated through original *in situ* experiences, but those perspectives were corroborated by an extensive literature in other fields. The personal impressions could hardly serve as the basis of generalizations transcending one particular country unless they were substantiated by comparative data and analyses. The linkage between development and conflict, I believe, is not misplaced or artificial. There have been, and remain, strong forces in the Third World that reject or question the Western modernization agenda and its commercial, diplomatic, and sometimes cultural expressions. Those reservations are occasionally expressed through various foreign policy behaviors, as in the cases of Burma and Iran, and in broader movements such as Muslim fundamentalism. It has also been seen in Third World scholarship. The literature on dependency, which was just beginning to appear in English or French translation, is just one example of an intellectual questioning of Western concepts of modernization.

While my purposes were partly didactic, I also thought that an unconventional and contrasting view of the typically anodyne understanding of the development problem in Western thinking would serve a legitimate intellectual purpose: to make the point that much of the theoretical literature on development and international politics is ethnocentric. For example, at this time the problem of war in the Third World was commonly seen as an outcome or reflection of the Soviet-American rivalry. While many conflicts had become internationalized through great power intervention, I wanted to make the point that some of the sources of conflict were indigenous and connected to the great 'modernization' problematic, rather than to questions of communist versus liberal ideologies. There is little to make me believe that today, twenty years later, the point is any less relevant. The end of the Cold War will not mean the end of armed conflict in the Third World. To understand the etiology of war there, we need to examine local conditions, and one of them is the social tensions created by development.

'Change in the International System: Interdependence, Integration and Fragmentation' did not result from personal experience, but the 'Gap' thesis was still firmly in my mind. I began writing this essay while spending part of a sabbatical as a visiting professor at the Hebrew University of Jerusalem, following a similar stint at Kyoto University in Japan. I had devoted some time earlier to studying some aspects of the Canadian-United States relationship. What struck me about this relationship was the strong Canadian resistance to integration between two very similar societies, a pattern of resistance that was different from the integration enthusiasm found throughout broad publics and elites in Europe. The literature on political integration of the 1960s and early 1970s was, in my view, based on some unexamined assumptions. Foremost was the implication of neutral or equal benefits and costs to the partners engaged in an integrative enterprise. For some integration theorists, the big prize was the end of war between states; for others it was wealth maximization. But researchers had failed to examine the resistance to integration that was expressed both within the integrating countries and from potential partners, such as Norway. In his seminal works, Karl Deutsch had asked the classical question: what are the conditions of peace? He developed theories and, along with his colleagues, impressive bodies of evidence to locate at least some of the answers.

But, as with development, the processes of integration are not without their costs and disadvantages. In highly asymmetrical relationships, as in the Canada-United States case, integration may indeed lead to greater economic efficiency, but it will also extract a high cost in terms of political autonomy, the preservation of local cultures and other values. And whereas integration theorists concentrated on the processes occurring in Europe (often anticipating that ultimately these would become universal), they ignored parallel processes that were driven by concerns of autonomy, independence, and greater distance between states - that is, by the forces of fragmentation. I wrote the piece, then, because I thought the optimistic and one-sided perspectives on integration - what we might call the benign liberal-pluralist view of international politics - needed to be confronted by the existence of other phenomena and patterns. The purpose of the essay was less innovative than compensatory. It was based on extensive research from several types of states, primarily Canada, but also from Burma and a few others.

There was perhaps a less explicit purpose to the essay. It was to give empirical grounding to a theme that recurred in other works written during the 1970s and 1980s: the value of pluralism in a world characterized by strong hegemonial and/or homogenization tendencies. I refer not so much to overt political hegemony (better termed domination) than to the predominance of economic, communications, and cultural projects that are largely but not exclusively associated with the American historical mission of universalizing its institutions. As a relatively small society with strong similarities to the United States, Canada is particularly vulnerable to the great sweep of American perspectives, tastes, ways of conducting public affairs, and political habits and institutions. I have always believed that there are great advantages to political, social, cultural, and economic pluralism. Most of those advantages have little to do with economic efficiency; indeed, they may be inconsistent with it. Yet, even in the commercial realm, I have never been convinced that there is a valid universal standard guiding 'market principles' or 'private enterprise' in general, or American practices thereof. Commerce is a historical-cultural construct, and how it is conducted varies between locales. Certainly no single society can suggest that its version of commercial practices constitutes a universal norm against which all other nations' practices must be measured. For a variety of historical and cultural reasons, Canadian business practices, social policy, national communications, and the like, differ from those of the United States, yet under the rubric of free trade, or appeals of greater efficiency, or 'adjustment' to global economic conditions, there is a presumption among many that these practices and policies must be made to conform to American standards. It goes without saying that the smaller partner in asymmetrical relationships will have to conform to the assumptions and practices of the larger, and not vice-versa. The essay was intended to highlight the robustness of and reasons for continued political fragmentation in an era of increasing economic and technological homogenization. Integration and fragmentation operate simultaneously, and therefore paradoxically.[4]

The next selection focuses most explicitly on the problem of change, but it is done at the level of the state rather than within dyads such as Canada-United States, or the system as a whole. The origins of my co-authored volume, *Why Nations Realign*[5] go back to the personal experience in Fiji and to its scholarly elaboration in the 'Gap' essay. I was interested in how some states respond to asymmetrical relationships and how they seek to protect themselves from a variety of external threats that are not primarily of the military kind. But this was the lesser concern.

The major source of the book, of which this selection is the introductory chapter, was my interest in comparative foreign policy studies. As a graduate student, I had been impressed with the decision-making approach to the study of foreign policy, an approach largely developed by Richard Snyder and his colleagues.[6] Not only did the approach offer a systematic way of analyzing the sources of foreign policy, but it opened the path for comparative studies of an analytical rather than purely descriptive nature. I had employed the Snyder framework in a dissertation study of Finnish foreign policy and located its strengths and weaknesses.

My main concern, as I looked at the sub-field, was a lack of conceptual consensus on the critical dependent variable, foreign policy. Snyder, and many who followed in his footsteps, went to great lengths to elaborate categories of independent, explanatory variables, but they could only use them to account for individual decisions. In my view, except for certain crisis situations or the launching of a major policy initiative, foreign policy cannot be reduced to single decisions.

Foreign policy analysis in the decades following Snyder's work, moreover, was predominantly static. Most studies described and/or explained particular countries' foreign policy decisions, usually at a given historical moment. They ignored foreign policy change, and particularly dramatic change. Here, perhaps, scholarship in the 1960s and 1970s reflected the static and repetitive nature of the great powers' foreign policies, and ignored the

10

policies of many other states. Thus, in organizing the volume, I wanted to achieve four interrelated purposes:

1) provide operational definitions and indicators of foreign policy as a concept;
2) explain foreign policy change;
3) develop a framework that would promote comparative analysis; and
4) sensitize readers and theorists to the importance of analyzing the foreign policies of non-great powers.

The source of inquiry, then, was discomfiture with the state of the field, and a sense of how some of its shortcomings could be overcome. The strategy was compensatory, building on the pioneering work of others such as Snyder and James Rosenau, but extending the analysis to offer a better conceptualization of foreign policy, and to move the field from a predominantly static and single-country posture to a more dynamic and comparative profile. To the extent that it succeeded, it had some affinities to the ranching endeavor.

The essay 'Politics in Command: Foreign Trade as National Security Policy' has a similar concern; it too is concerned with foreign policy change, and it too is based on comparative research. In this instance, only two cases, rather than seven, form the empirical basis for the generalizations. I undertook the comparative research on the basis of debates about a traditional issue in foreign policy analysis: guns versus butter. In the 1950s and 1960s, international relations theorizing raised security issues to the forefront and, as a consequence, relegated commercial issues to the realm of 'low politics'. Although most international relations textbooks contained chapters on international trade and finance they were seldom integrated into an overarching view of the field. All of this changed in the 1970s, as the OPEC oil embargo and a series of dramatic changes in the economic circumstances of the United States drove American, European, and Japanese scholars increasingly to devote attention to the economic and commercial underpinnings of international relations. International political economy was resurrected as a subfield of the discipline, and soon enough major theoretical statements, journals, newsletters, and networks of scholars sprang up. I did not join the race to this new cornucopia of theoretical possibilities, except to learn enough of it to use it for teaching purposes. However, it did strike me that some of the assumptions underlying the new debates were worthy of examination. One in particular was the idea - rather novel in the 1970s, if no longer so today - that commercial and security issues are separate domains.

In the United States and elsewhere during the Cold War, they had been. Concerned that international political economy study might reflect parochial (read American) biases, I wanted to explore the situation in some countries where trade policy was essentially and inextricably driven by security concerns.

I also maintained a continuing interest in the issues raised in the article on fragmentation. That study of Canadian-American relations had suggested to me that some societies are willing to forego economic opportunities and wealth maximization in order to preserve or extend other values. While Robert Gilpin[7] had suggested that states have shifting priorities between guns, butter, and other values, I wanted to see if there were not in fact hierarchies. Which is more important, given a necessary choice: security or wealth maximization? I did not think one could offer an answer in the abstract. The only way to find out was to research countries which have faced the dilemma. Equally important, I wanted to continue to emphasize the importance of studying how policies change over time. The question of guns and butter was therefore answered in developmental rather than static terms. Substantively, the results confirmed some of the statements in the 'fragmentation' argument that for many societies political autonomy is, as a value, more fundamental than wealth and efficiency.

'Revolution in the Revolution' was written in the summer of 1988 while I was once again in Japan. At this time, many skeptics maintained that Mikhail Gorbachev's foreign policies were merely updated and public relations-oriented versions of traditional Soviet foreign policies. Nothing fundamental had changed. The evidence that this was an untenable position was hardly overwhelming at that time, but it was beginning to pile up. I had maintained an abiding interest in foreign policy change during the 1980s, and this seemed a case where the explanation for change was largely, though not exclusively, intellectual. I wanted to chronicle the ideological reversals that had become increasingly apparent in the public statements of Soviet leaders in 1987 and 1988. It was these dramatically changing conceptions of the world, rather than individual foreign policy initiatives, that suggested that Soviet policies were being altered fundamentally. The jettisoning of traditional Soviet views of historical development, of the nature of the international system, and of that country's roles in it, suggested something more profound than mere cosmetic and tactical Cold War-inspired maneuvers. Henry Kissinger, among others, was during these times still proclaiming that the United States and the Soviet Union were destined to remain adversaries. Looking at the emerging evidence, by mid-1988 I was convinced that we were at the beginning of a historic

12

turning point. The purpose of the essay was to establish that position and, from a theoretical point of view, to show that change in policy can come as much from intellectual revolutions as from alterations of material circumstances such as declining power. It is for this reason that I included the essay in this collection.

Academic accounting: assessing the state of the field

The essays that make up part II of this volume are concerned with questions of 'how to' rather than 'what is'. Most of the selections are evaluations of particular approaches to the study of international politics and foreign policy, or to bodies of literature. They span twenty years, from the late 1960s, when analysts were beginning to make assessments of the achievements and short-comings of the great theoretical and methodological innovations that marked the 'behavioral revolution', to the late 1980s.

The essays reflect my adherence to some of the major tenets and aspirations of positivism: the search for valid generalizations transcending time, location, and personality; the foundation of those generalizations on systematic evidence; and the attempt to develop more consensus on the meanings of key concepts such as international system, subsystems, conflict, war, structures, processes, and the like.

I never accepted the more extreme claims of some 'behavioralists'. It does not seem to me that the field can be reduced to a series of law-like statements, that every hunch or hypothesis can be tested, as in laboratory procedures, with consensually-developed data, or that the aim of all analysis is prediction. I reject the assumption of many behavioralists that man is ruled by 'structures', class or group interests, or genetic dispositions. Human agency and its importance in the historical record lies at the heart of international relations studies. The essays nevertheless reveal admiration for many of the theoretical and empirical works of scholars working in the positivist framework. Whatever the shortcomings of this body of scholarship, I believe I know a great deal more, and more reliably, about behavior at the international level today than I did when I left graduate school in 1961. The field has been enriched by the theoretical and methodological innovations that took place during the 'revolution'. While there are many ontological and method-ological problems remaining - that of parochialism is particularly acute - I cannot agree that all of the scholarship of three decades was merely an apology for American hegemony, that it served only class or ideological interests, or that it was a mere epiphenomenon of some Cold War mood. While there are no doubt examples of all of the above, my estimation is that most of the work was driven by intellectual curiosity, by the need to improve upon or amend previous formulations and bodies of data (meeting the tests of reliability and comprehensibility), by a desire for greater precision in the handling of concepts, and many other legitimate sources of intellectual inquiry.

Certainly there has been faddism, the re-invention of theoretical wheels, a tendency to forget the works of our predecessors, and much theorizing that reflects little more than signal events in the world of diplomacy. There are many areas that remain in contention and warrant debate. But I do not share the pessimism of many critical analysts who imply that it has all been a waste of time, at best, and an apology for American imperialism at worst. Almost any topic of theoretical (and often practical) significance has been illuminated by the kinds of studies that emerged during and after the 1950s. These include war, conflict, escalation, misperception and miscalculation in policy-making, system transformation and dynamics, deterrence, comparative international systems, the sources and forms of international collaboration, and many others. Conceptual analyses - of sovereignty, international society, deterrence, and the like - are of equal importance. Nor do I agree that we have moved into a 'post-positivist' era of scholarship, except in the sense that we are more aware of the possible biases of evidence and the limitations of rigorous scientific models as applied to social phenomena. We are beginning to acknowledge the potential benefits of other modes of analysis, including critical theory.

Some have argued that we are in the midst of a third 'great debate' or even in a fourth one. I do not believe there has been more than one fundamental debate, and that one is taking place currently, represented by the 'dissidence' of post-modern critical theory. The idealism versus realism controversy of the 1950s focussed on policy prescription more than on approaches to scholarship. The acrid arguments between traditionalists and behavioralists in the 1960s concentrated on methods, conceptualization, and measurement, and not on the object or purpose of study. Like Rousseau, Bentham, Wilson, Carr, Morgenthau, and many others, most of the scholarship done under the behavioralist rubric has concentrated on the classical problematics of the causes of war and the conditions of peace/order/stability.

We are now entering an era of fundamental division and proliferation of 'schools' (in contrast to subject specialization) within the discipline. The cleavages are both substantive and meta-theoretical. The initial signs of theoretical dissent appeared in the early 1970s when scholars argued that the fundamental structures and processes of the world were changing significantly

14

and theory was not recording or explaining those changes or their consequences. Most notable as new trends were the alleged decline of the state, the rise of new kinds of international issues, the growth of interdependence and attending loss of autonomy, the melding of domestic and international politics, and the rise of new bases of international influence (technology and knowledge), replacing older techniques based on military threats. Old portraits of international politics as an eternal struggle for power no longer accorded with the observable world. The anomaly between theoretical characterizations of international politics and what was taking place in commerce, diplomacy, and grass-roots politics was too great to be glossed over by repeating the mantras of realism. Theorists had to develop new ways of looking at the world, and new kinds of phenomena had to be classified, compared, and explained. Much of the research agenda of the 1970s and 1980s was comprised of attempts to account for the rise and consequence of these significant changes. But the results did not replace realism. Rather, scholars now accept that there are many games of international politics, of which security dilemmas, self-help, and arms racing is only one. We therefore need different theoretical perspectives to illuminate critical core questions, such as war, peace, cooperation, and the problems raised by population, economic development, and environmental degradation. An elaboration and proliferation of theoretical perspectives is a reasonable reflection of the world's complexities. The 1970s and 1980s therefore saw theoretical growth, adjustment, and a certain amount of tolerance among practitioners of different substantive and methodological persuasions.

The first selection represents my view of international theory in the late 1960s. The thesis is simple enough: the search for a 'grand theory' of international politics is a chimera. This was an observation about the 'practice' of theory as it had developed in the 1960s. At the time, I thought a general theory was still a desirable project. I no longer hold this position. The world has become so complex that no single shorthand characterization of its structures, processes and dynamics, whether that of realism or any competitor, will be adequate. The field, as it was developing at the time, focussed on more limited phenomena, meaning that there was an increasing amount of scholarly specialization. International relationists were following the patterns found in other social sciences. The behavioral revolution gave further impetus to the process: now there were schools developed around methodologies as well as substantive issues. The proliferation of sub-fields also meant that one of the tenets of the scientific method - that research should be cumulative - was inaccurate. The research agenda of the 1960s had grown like a hydra. Few studies

15

duplicated or replicated earlier work to the point where a corpus of consensual 'truths' emerged. Middle-range theory - explaining limited ranges of phenomena - was the name of the game in that decade.

I undertook a similar exercise thirteen years later. The editors of the *International Journal* asked me to write a retrospective review and assessment of international theory for the twenty-fifth anniversary of that publication. In it, I attempted to identify the main approaches to the field, and bodies of knowledge where significant progress could be identified. I also noted areas of continuing concern. The trends which I had identified in the 1960s continued throughout the 1970s. The big debate over the virtues and inadequacies of realism was already underway, international political economy had become yet another sub-field in the discipline, and the proliferation of other specializations continued apace. The field appeared to be losing a core normative concern, and specializations were going their own ways, developing all the usual academic paraphernalia of intellectual ghettos: newsletters, separate societies, journals, vocabularies and jargon and, in some cases, arcane methodologies.

International Relations as a field of study and theorizing has always drawn upon the insights, methods, and data of other disciplines. But by the 1980s, it was no longer possible for an individual to keep on top of the proliferating schools of thought, technical studies, and bodies of data. Coteries of scholars developed their own research agendas, read only each other's works, and went off to tackle a variety of theoretical, normative, and data-collecting issues. Thus, while there had been considerable achievement and even signs of intellectual maturity by the 1960s and 1970s, the field now gave indications of flying apart. The selection 'Along the Road to International Theory' is the optimistic evaluation of achievements and compensates for the somewhat more problem-oriented and critical evaluation presented in *The Dividing Discipline*.

While I wrote the article in response to a request, the essay was at least partly biographical: I wished to acknowledge a number of people whose works I had read and re-read, admired, and taught over the previous twenty years. It struck me that we had all benefitted enormously from the pioneering efforts of people like Raymond Aron, Hedley Bull, Michael Brecher, John Burton, Karl Deutsch, Johan Galtung, Alexander George, Robert Gilpin, F.H. Hinsley, Stanley Hoffmann, Ole Holsti, Robert Jervis, Robert Keohane, J.D.B. Miller, Hans Morgenthau, Robert North, James Rosenau, J. David Singer, Richard Snyder, Susan Strange, Kenneth Waltz, Martin Wight, and Quincy Wright, just to mention some of the more obvious ones. Many of these individuals were intellectual innovators and explorers, real ranchers. They wrote works which have become a standard part of our intellectual equipment. We have internalized their ideas and insights to the point where they are part of our background. Their works have very successfully stood the test of time and I suspect a review of the field in another two decades will acknowledge their continuing importance. Their works remain significant because most successfully transcended time, location, and personality. They are not context-bound except in the broadest historical sense. For me, that is the surest signpost of quality scholarship.

The next selection represents my evaluation of one of the significant sub-fields of international politics. My interest in comparative foreign policy has not been confined to the problem of change. I believe the field continues to suffer some problems of conceptualization and, in particular, from the lack of an authoritative framework that can guide comparative inquiry. I was invited in 1986 by my Canadian colleagues, David Wurfel and Bruce Burton, to write a theoretical paper for a small conference on the foreign policies of Southeast Asian states. I took the opportunity to review some of the problems in the sub-field and to elaborate, however briefly, a project that could serve as an architectural guide to comparative research. While respecting the expertise of area specialists, I had been long convinced that their work was overly context-dependent, and could therefore serve only as sources of empirical materials for theorists. Foreign policy theorists, on the other hand, have seldom mastered the historical and contemporary details of countries other than their own. The conference was a major innovation, bringing together representatives of both camps and allowing them to learn from each other. The theorist can learn that facile and often ethnocentric generalizations do not fit well with the conditions of distant countries. And area experts can gain more insights by generalizing across countries and over time, rather than simply describing the latest events and trends in the country of their choice. It is also an opportunity for them to visualize how systemic and regional characteristics constrain and condition both the foreign and domestic policies of an individual country. Most important, they can come to appreciate the intellectual advantages of comparison.

My essay argues that perhaps we have been asking the wrong questions in the area of comparative foreign policy. Rather than identifying seemingly inexhaustible lists of independent variables to explain what no one has satisfactorily defined - foreign policy - why not start with a relatively simple question: what do all states, regardless of size, location, governing ideology, social makeup, and economic performance, seek to achieve in the modern world?

17

If we can identify common problems, then we are in a position to engage in comparative analysis.

I wrote this essay as an attempt to bring more coherence in a sub-field characterized by considerable disorder. By disorder I mean a lack of common analytical problems. It is a field that speaks to comparison across a broad range of countries but remains largely great-power oriented. It has featured methodological and conceptual innovation (and therefore uniqueness) rather than cumulation and comparison. This essay hardly solves all the problems, but it does offer some suggestions for improvement.

Returning to studies at the systems level, the essay 'The Necrologists of International Relations' is didactic. It has been a tradition of presidential addresses to the Canadian Political Science Association to take a position on contentious scholarly or policy issues. I therefore used the opportunity to offer observations on some of the ongoing debates in the field, and particularly on the role - or lack of it - of the state in international theory. My purpose was less to celebrate the staying power of this particular form of political community (although I have sympathy for groups that see the state as the primary guardian of their political autonomy and indigenous culture) than to raise questions about premature death notices. For it struck me at the time, and as I continue to believe, most renditions of 'global village', 'spaceship earth', 'growing interdependence', or 'demise of the state' hide certain assumptions. When analysts use such metaphors, they are not characterizing some blending or mutual reinforcement of diverse civilizations, languages, traditions, and cultures. They are really talking about the universalization of Western institutions and culture, where others will be celebrated as little more than sources of exotic cuisines and apparel fashions. We cannot talk about 'one world' or the demise of the nation-state without raising questions of its replacement(s) and upon whose model(s) they would be based. It would not be Indonesia, Japan, Bhutan, Burma, Saudi Arabia, or India, or dozens of other nations that represent civilizational forms of considerable merit. It would mean, for better and worse, the globalization of Western cultural, commercial, scientific, language and political traditions.

The main source of the essay, nevertheless, was academic. I do not believe there is sufficient evidence to warrant the conclusion that we can dispense *analytically* with the state as the primary - though not exclusive - actor in international politics. I also hold reservations about research programmes that are deterministic and provide little scope or intellectual interest in human agency. Studies of war and 'power cycles' in the international system have been particularly prone to structural explanations, ignoring the role of unique personalities and religious/ideological drives.

'International Theory: National or International?' confronts the problem of theoretical parochialism. It was written initially as an address for the thirtieth anniversary celebrations of the Japan Association of International Relations. Japanese scholarship in international relations has made great strides, but I thought it would be worth mentioning that its major theoretical aspects - some important Japanese Marxist studies aside - remain under the tutelage of anglophone and particularly American scholars.

This is one of the puzzles of the field. If there is any social science discipline that should be global in its perspectives, patterns of scholarship, communications, and generation of significant theoretical insights, it would be international relations. But the research reported in *The Dividing Discipline* confirmed my suspicion that the field encompasses only a small fraction of the world's international relations community. Most scholars become fascinated in the foreign policy problems of their own country or region and seldom emerge from that policy-relevant environment to see what is of distinct importance globally and theoretically. As the list of the 'greats' of the field in the 1960s through the 1980s indicates, theory remains the enterprise primarily of a small bastion of male anglophones, with only a few contributions from other academic cultures. So long as it retains this profile, it will necessarily reflect certain national, historical, and possibly gender parochialisms. Implicitly or explicitly, international theory is based on the European and Cold War historical experiences, a history that goes back, under the Westphalian system, less than 350 years. Is this experience adequate to base theories that are germane to a very different contemporary world? One may raise the question whether, for example, key concepts and assumptions of international theory are appropriate to the study of regional systems in the Third World where, in many cases, anarchy is the predominant condition *within* states and hierarchy *between* them. If this is the case, the empirical reality fundamentally reverses the assumptions of Realism and Neorealism, both of which emerged from the European historical diplomatic experience. It may not do simply to transfer the conceptual apparatus of one historical experience into different cultural milieux. What an international theory informed by the experiences of many communities throughout the world might look like is difficult to say. So far, only dependency theory has intellectual origins in the Third World, and while it has had an important sensitizing impact on scholarship, its structural and determinist characteristics raise reservations.

'Mirror, Mirror, on the Wall, Which are the Fairest Theories of All?' was written in response to a request by the editors of

International Studies Quarterly. They correctly judged that an important synthetic article by Yosef Lapid[8] raised a number of important issues about approaches to the field and the limitations of positivism. Critical (or post-modern) theory, as applied to international relations, is an offshoot of the more general post-modernist project of subjecting the Enlightenment's intellectual assumptions and habits to serious review. At the time I wrote the article (in the autumn of 1988), I was not sufficiently conversant with the new literature to make even temporary judgements of it. The purpose of the essay was, rather, to explain the various and varied sources of theorizing in the field, as I had seen it develop, to emphasize its eclectic rather than monolithic character, and to explain, again, why no 'grand theory' could account for all the things we might want to know. The essay is a plea for theoretical tolerance within a framework of discipline. While acknowledging some skepticism toward the version of intellectual 'freedom' that the 'dissidents' and 'exiles' (as two of the foremost innovators, Richard Ashley and Rob Walker term themselves[9]), they are making a case that requires serious consideration. Proponents of critical theory in international relations are not offering a few intellectual adjustments, or exploring new or supposedly new phenomena, or discovering lacunae in contemporary research agendas. They argue that all analytical models of the world, or theoretical statements about it, are historically-conditioned and (usually) politically-motivated constructs. Deeply flawed representations pass as 'knowledge' in the field. Dichotomies, such as anarchy-hierarchy, war-peace, sovereignty-populism cannot do justice to a world characterized by contradictions, differing concepts of time, space, and identity, and different understandings of the relationship between subject and object. Concepts such as sovereignty, the state, the state system, anarchy, structures, hegemony, great powers, and the like, have been 'privileged' in the discourses of the field. Critical theorists wish to know why they have they achieved such eminence, and what does their status mean in terms of developing alternative ways of contemplating and analyzing the world.

Will critical theory in its various forms significantly increase our knowledge of commercial, diplomatic, and military life at the international level? That remains to be seen. However, given its epistemological assumptions and explicit linkage of knowledge to *praxis*, the question itself is of dubious value. The purpose of inquiry, critical theorists argue, is *not* to 'increase' knowledge, but to lay the foundations for 'intellectual freedom', acknowledging the unresolvable paradoxes of political life, and paving the way for liberating political action. To accept paradox and ambiguity, to question all conceptualizations of time, space, and identity, and to de-memorialize conventional canons are just some of the features of critical theory as applied to international relations. Critical theorists are not interested in developing a new 'orthodoxy' or paradigm for the field. Its value to date lies in subjecting certain 'privileged' concepts and 'texts' to critical scrutiny and alerting analysts to treat as problematical ideas and traditions that have generally been 'memorialized' or accepted as 'givens' in the field.

Despite the novel elements of critical theory as applied to international relations, there are elements of *deja vu* in the new dissidence. Like the zealots of behavioralism three decades ago, many critical theorists rely on celebrated patron saints for their philosophical foundations. Instead of Weber, Kaplan, and Popper, it is Foucault, Habermas, and Derrida. The early writings have been replete with jargon, some of it unintelligible except to those who have exhaustively studied the founding fathers. Critical theorists' communications are often phrased in the manner of political exhortation to fellow converts rather than having the purpose of creating understanding among a broader audience. Like the early 'behavioralists', the leaders identify themselves as a dissident minority; anyone else is of the 'orthodox' school.[10] They appear indifferent or insensitive to the numerous philosophical, normative, and methodological themes that have constituted the field over the last three centuries. The 'orthodox', in their view, seem to include anyone between Aristotle and Waltz, which is about as accurate as describing Bach and Bruckner as similarly orthodox composers. Finally, like the positivist pioneers of the 1950s, the leaders of the movement in international relations, though relying on continental theorists, all come from the anglophone international relations community.

There is insufficient space to speculate on the implications of these similarities, but one might have hoped that as we enter the twenty-first century the theoretical aspects of the field could be nurtured and diversified by those coming from other cultures.

For some scholars, especially those interested in strategic and other policy-oriented studies, theoretical activity seems arcane and esoteric. Their criticism is that international theory is not relevant to 'real' issues. Critical theorists, in contrast, see it as an instrument of power, social control, and marginalization. To them, it has been altogether too relevant. Neither view, in my opinion, is justified, although there may be persuasive elements in each.

The essays in this volume demonstrate, I hope, the myriad sources of research and theorizing in international relations. Some were motivated by normative and political concerns; others were based on direct observation and experience at the grass-roots level; yet others were driven by theoretical and empirical concerns. Certainly all are colored by historico-cultural contexts, education, background, and all the other intellectual paraphernalia with which authors are typically burdened. Undoubtedly there were other ways to approach the subjects of investigation, but these are best identified with the benefit of hindsight.

I believe the metaphors in the title of this chapter better suggest what those purposes have been. These essays represent examples of intellectual accounting, farming, and ranching. The theme of change - including changes in my own interests and views - underlies inquiry. But there are also elements of continuity. These include a normative sympathy to the values of pluralism, political autonomy, and equality, and an academic sympathy to theoretical work that is empirically informed, that works to improve the efforts of predecessors, and that is sensitive to the importance of issues as the stuff of politics. Some of the essays may be mostly of archaeological interest, reflecting the kinds of questions that motivated theoretical work and debate during a particular historical stage of the field of study. Others, I hope, comment on problems and issues that remain current and that will remain with us for some time to come.

Notes

1. Susan Strange (1987), Review of K.J. Holsti, *The Dividing Discipline*, in *International Journal*, 42, Spring, p. 400.
2. These positions are taken, respectively, in R.W. Mansbach and J.D. Vasquez (1986), 'Values and Paradigm Change: The Elusive Quest for International Relations Theory', in M.P. Karns (ed.), *Persistent Patterns and Emerging Structures in a Waning Century*, New York: Praeger; and R.W. Cox (1986), 'Social Forces, States and World Orders: Beyond International Relations Theory', in R.O. Keohane (ed.), *Neorealism and its Critics*, New York: Columbia University Press.
3. K.J. Holsti (1985), *The Dividing Discipline: Hegemony and Diversity in International Theory*, London: Allen and Unwin.
4. Without implicating R.B.J. Walker as being a member of the 'orthodox' school of international relations, my views on the question of pluralism in political life are similar to his. See his thoughtful essay *One World/Many Worlds: Struggles for a Just World Peace*, Boulder, CO: Rienner, 1988.
5. K.J. Holsti et al. (1982), *Why Nations Realign: Foreign Policy Restructuring in the Postwar World*, London: Allen and Unwin.
6. R.C. Snyder, H.W. Bruck, and B.M. Sapin (eds), *Foreign Policy Decision-Making: An Approach to the Study of International Politics*, New York: Free Press, 1962.
7. R. Gilpin (1981), *War and Change in World Politics*, Cambridge: Cambridge University Press.
8. Y. Lapid (1989), 'The Third Debate: On the Prospects of International

Theory in a Post-Positivist Era', *International Studies Quarterly*, 33, pp. 235-54.

9. R. Ashley and R. Walker (1990), 'Reading Dissidence/Writing the Discipline: Crisis and the Question of Sovereignty in International Studies', *International Studies Quarterly*, 34, pp. 367-416.

10. As is argued in J. George and D. Campbell (1990), 'Patterns of Dissent and the Celebration of Difference: Critical Social Theory and International Relations', *International Studies Quarterly*, 34, pp. 269-95.

...antize data, on conflict interests, on wants and among the international interconnections than on the efforts to control or reduce them.

Global Interdependence

Interdependence, of course, is not an approach, framework for analysis, or metaphor distinct from those discussed above, although the concept of a global system, in which mankind is enmeshed, implies a high degree of interconnectedness among a variety of units. If there is no connection, there is no system; a global interconnectedness has certain surface qualities - transportation and communications - it can be measured by trading transactions and refers to sensitivity and vulnerability, where conditions in country A become critically influenced by decisions, trends, and events in countries B, X, Y, Z, etc... [illegible] it economically, interdependence, by joining needs, wealths, creates the closest ties of interconnected polities ...

[several illegible lines]

... vulnerability, that is, interdependence. Examining the rates of ... national from various countries, ... concluded that growth in transaction flows had approximately equal consequences ... all those engaged in the interaction ... transaction flows on the international ... [illegible]

following:

(1) Increased national sensitivity and vulnerability to decisions, trends, and events abroad - that is, increased interdependence - evolves.

(2) More cooperative endeavors and common problem-solving occur, which increases gains for all involved. No single nation can regulate any system characterized by rich transaction flows, and efforts to make decisions purely in terms of short-run national advantages - increasing national autonomy - will result in trade wars, currency instability, decline of investment, unemployment, and ultimately recession or depression.[11]

(3) The latitude of choice of governments in fashioning domestic economic and welfare programs is reduced.[12]

Part I

Foreign Policy Analysis:
The Problem of Change

2. Underdevelopment and the 'Gap' Theory of International Conflict

The diffusion of Western culture and economic patterns to other areas of the world has proceeded unabated for more than three centuries. Its forms, often violent and oppressive, have always been tempered by a faith in the ultimate benefits that the underdeveloped world would receive through the processes of cultural and economic interaction. While apologists for colonialism did not deny the strategic, prestige, and economic advantages accruing to the metropolitan states, they would point out simultaneously that the natives were also receiving benefits, including employment, stable government, Christianity, an end to local slave trade, and the introduction of education, democracy and modern health facilities. Nevertheless, the objectives of most colonial regimes were limited to securing advantages for planters, traders, the military and the church.[1]

During the past thirty years a greatly expanded view of the possibilities for the colonial territories has developed. The ultimate fate of the underdeveloped societies is to become fully developed. A common view is that these territories will have to become replicas of the highly industrialized states of Western Europe, North America and the Communist countries. There is no halfway station where a society can stop on the road to modernization. The 'gap' between the rich and the poor is growing, and the only solution is presumably for the poor to catch up and to become basically what the rich are. The end state of development is not the African or Asian version of late nineteenth-century Sweden (economically speaking), but the fully modern industrial urban society of 1995 or 2025. To suggest anything less is to deny the value of equal welfare and to perpetuate two classes of international citizenship.

The rationale for the egalitarian view of world development is to some extent humanitarian: everyone in the world should enjoy the blessings of the advanced countries. In other cases, economic considerations - the growing interdependence of the world - underlie the imperative for 'closing the gap'. Another important consideration is international peace and security. Many statesmen, politicians and academics have argued that neither domestic turmoil nor international wars can be avoided in a world of states many of whose populations suffer from poverty. The unrequited

27

goals of the 'revolution of rising expectations' in the underdeveloped countries will lead to frustration, domestic revolutions, political instability and messianic politics. These are likely to have spillover effects into the international system, causing regional rivalries at best and the intervention of the great powers at worst.[2]

Another view emphasizes the 'gap' between the rich and poor nations as a source of international conflict.[3] The powerful industrialized states constitute a model which the underdeveloped seek to emulate. Industrialization, mass consumption economies, modern military forces, high levels of technology and welfare-oriented politics stand as the indicators of worth in today's world. To the extent that the underdeveloped countries are not achieving anything resembling parity with those who have established these standards, or, put in another way, to the extent that they do not receive adequate proportions of the 'rewards' of the international system, frustration expressed through aggressive nationalism or adventurous foreign policies will result. Though few agree on the sources of the widening 'gap' (neocolonialism and imperialism are the causes according to writers of the 'New Left'; economic, social and cultural 'barriers' within the underdeveloped societies are the sources, according to more orthodox interpretations), there is a consensus that the condition left unresolved must lead inevitably to international conflict.

I shall subject this latter thesis to a critical scrutiny, not from the point of view of international conflict theory or a theory of the causes of underdevelopment, but from a perspective which emphasizes the impact of Western, including socialist, economic solutions on indigenous cultures and social structures.[4] From the perspective of future international relations, we can also inquire: if some underdeveloped countries adopt more nationalist economic policies, reject some forms of Western 'penetration', and isolate themselves more from international cooperative ventures, will the Western response be hostility or accommodation? The phenomenon of isolation or quasi-autarky is seldom noted in the development literature, I suspect primarily, because it challenges long-standing normative commitments to a world of increased international integration and communication. International relations scholars have also neglected the phenomenon because our ruling paradigm - the notion of an international system - does not lend itself to analysis of such normative problems as what sorts of influences (and what sorts of social consequences) permeate the 'nodes', 'networks' and 'linkages' of the system. In brief, while not rejecting the 'gap' theory of international conflict, I would like to explore an alternative scenario in which the international system becomes more fragmented and some underdeveloped countries selectively reduce their 'interdependence'.

The scenario derives from my critique of three components of the common Western image of underdevelopment. The first is the view that once having been influenced by modern communications, the people in the underdeveloped countries universally desire to change their life-styles and to adopt most, if not all, of the economic, cultural and technological advantages of the industrialized state. Thus, the main thrust for development comes from the grass-roots level, and local elites commit themselves to modernization in order to accommodate this 'revolution of rising expectations'. Second, our image of underdevelopment is based on considerable pictorial or written evidence of widespread poverty, despair, disease, lack of opportunity and cultural deprivation. If the picture of underdevelopment in our heads includes these characteristics as typical, then of course the 'revolution of rising expectations' seems a perfectly appropriate response. Third, given the first two components of the image, we often imagine that people in underdeveloped countries will quickly grasp the means by which their expectations can be met, readily accept the techniques necessary to lift themselves out of misery, and suffer few costs in doing so.

Many academic treatments of underdevelopment are more sophisticated than this description of these three components implies. Nevertheless, many fail to acknowledge the harmonious and satisfying aspects of the lives of non-industrialized peoples, the costs involved in many development schemes, and the inappropriateness of some aspects of Western-style economic activity to other value systems. This shortcoming becomes apparent when one compares the writings of economists with those of many anthropologists. Economists, accustomed to thinking in terms of aggregates and quantitative indicators, necessarily make inferences about individuals from aggregate data. Most economists believe that people earning $200 annually must suffer from extreme deprivation in all social, physical, economic and cultural dimensions. An anthropologist who has lived among people with such incomes, however, would see that that way of life typically includes close family ties, reasonable dietary standards (except in some countries such as Bangladesh, and during periods of natural catastrophe), cooperative work habits, effective, and often humane, social controls and intellectual stimulation through acquiring knowledge of the natural environment and skills relating to that environment.

Sources of the commitment to development

Given the strong resistance of many indigenous cultures to Western penetration[5] throughout the past centuries, it is somewhat surprising that today we should accept uncritically the thesis which portrays tribal peoples and peasants as grasping uncritically for the benefits of modern Western society and technology. Most political leaders in the world have referred to the 'revolution of rising expectations' as if this phenomenon were the sole source of the drive toward development. To be sure, few people reject all the benefits of modern technology, science and economic activity. With a modicum of demonstration, most people can easily see the benefits of better health or of decreasing dependency upon the vagaries of nature. No longer does everyone accept misfortune, poor housing, clothing, and diet as the will of God, and many aspire to improve themselves and their children through individual and collective action. But we have often confused these relatively simple aspirations for a better life with the assumption that everyone wants to adopt all Western institutions through Western-type economic activity. We have confused development with outright emulation; a reasonable standard of living with large cities, heavy industry, mass consumption, personal mobility, rejection of agriculture as an appropriate 'way of life', high per-capita income, personal ownership of an automobile and the like.

Evidence that many people in underdeveloped countries do not accept all aspects of the 'developed' society as an end state of human activity is not overwhelming but appears regularly. In Kenya, South Africa, Zambia, Sicily and Thailand, for example, many go to cities and towns to work for wages, but a high proportion return eventually to the rural areas.[6] They want the wages that offer them some increased economic opportunities, but the major social, psychological and emotional supports of their lives remain in rural areas.[7] Migration back to the country occurs despite the notable bias of economic development plans (Cuba, Taiwan, and Tanzania excepted) favoring urban over rural programs.[8]

This is not to deny strong grass-roots impetus for the betterment of life. But a case can also be made that the strongest thrust for modernization conceived as industrialization, urbanization and consumerism derives from the aspirations of a relatively small, Westernized elite whose members have been educated and trained in the West or have pursued career opportunities which are closely linked to Western economic institutions and international organizations.

Another important source of the development thrust is national security. Nayar[9] shows that rapid industrialization in Japan, the

Soviet Union, China and India has related less to public welfare considerations than to the requirements of military security and national independence. The leaders of these countries, through their speeches and actions, have argued that modernization is a necessary condition for securing and maintaining independence in an international or regional system of hostile states. Even in some smaller underdeveloped societies, such as Thailand, Western economic techniques were borrowed as a means of reducing Western economic penetration.[10]

Closely related to the perception of external threat and the desire to secure national independence are considerations of prestige. Once the leaders of underdeveloped states become integrated into the international system, they adopt the measures of worth of that system.[11] Jacobs, for example, points out that a prime stimulus for economic modernization among the Thais is not the felt needs of the people, but the needs of the patrimonial leadership, which include the desire to be 'politically respected in the halls of the developed Western powers'.[12] Hence, as has been noted often in the literature, many visible indicators of modernity - commercial urban centres, national airlines, heavy industries, middle-class suburbs, and a plethora of private vehicles and consumer goods - are promoted less to assuage popular economic expectations than to bring diplomatic influence and prestige to the nation.

It is difficult to assess the relative weights of these sources of the drive for modernization. Undoubtedly they vary greatly from country to country, and in many instances large proportions of the population support their leaders' quest for international recognition and securing independence. Taken together, however, socialization, national security and international prestige probably provide as plausible an explanation for the commitment to create a replica of the industrial states as does the hypothesis of a grass-roots revolution of rising expectations.

Some leaders, of course, do not see their nations as potential miniatures of Britain, the United States or the Soviet Union. They have deliberately created alternative welfare models and pursued development strategies reasonably consistent with indigenous social and economic patterns. Julius Nyerere of Tanzania, for example, saw the goal of development as a reasonably independent economy based on local ownership, little direct dependence upon the major powers for capital or technical assistance, and a more or less egalitarian social structure in which the major segment, the peasants, work communally and cooperatively in accordance with, not contrary to, traditional social patterns.[13] Thai political leaders, despite their rhetoric in favor of economic rationalization and industrialization, maintain a

31

firm commitment to political and economic forms which are based on patrimonial personal relations and which incorporate uniquely Thai ideas of moral goodness.[14] Other exceptions could be cited; but most leaders of underdeveloped states have adopted the Western developed state (including variations of socialism) as their goal or model, as well as Western analyses of their social and economic problems, and Western strategies for overcoming them.

Their goal is *economic growth*. United Nations reports indicate that although most governments also talk about social progress, equality and advancement of culture, their budget allocations and administrative performances are geared primarily to a particular type of economic development.[15] These and other reports make it clear that the philosophy of Western-style economic development has spawned strategies favoring industry over agriculture, urban over rural areas, the modern over the traditional sector and large capital-intensive projects over smaller labor-intensive initiatives. Income is distributed primarily toward urban middle classes, thus encouraging migration to cities and discouraging agricultural development.[16] The priorities of development policies thus seem to reflect short-run considerations of security and prestige, as well as a rather uncritical acceptance of Western definitions of development.

Western images of underdevelopment: the sources of bias

There are frequently contradictions between popular Western images of underdevelopment (including assumptions about the pervasiveness of the revolution of rising expectations), and the social and economic realities some investigators find in underdeveloped societies.[17] Most striking is the strange conservatism among vast populations: many simply will not act according to Western conceptions of rational economic behavior. The resistance to urbanization, mechanization, capital savings, regular work schedules, achievement criteria, production of surplus and to many other facets of Western commercial behavior is often noted in the literature, but less often taken seriously as evidence that some Western development goals and strategies are simply inappropriate for other value systems. The literature, moreover, makes no effort to link these resistances to foreign policy or to the overall character of relations between developed and underdeveloped countries. The 'gap' theory of international conflict rests squarely on the notion of economic growth as the primary goal of underdeveloped societies and on the hypothesis that failure to reach the economic levels of the developed states will lead to frustration and aggressive nationalism. It is less often acknowledged that development itself may create strains and turmoil that will spill over into the international system.

A number of reasons could be put forth to explain inconsistencies between images and realities. Given graphic details of the worst aspects of lives of people in underdeveloped societies - the street people of Calcutta or the *favelas* of Latin America - we assume that it is only natural for others to want what we have. We are seldom told, however, that often the worst social blights in the underdeveloped world are the *results of development policies* which place highest priority on urbanization, heavy industry and 'growth' in economic indicators, while simultaneously neglecting agricultural and rival problems.[18]

Others have looked at the problem of underdevelopment primarily in terms of the Cold War and have seen only two paths or models of development - socialism and free enterprise. The possibility of some entirely new strategies for development, or goals which realistically fall far below a per capita income of $800, are simply not considered; an economy based on farming, fishing, handicrafts and some light industry and commerce just does not add up to a socialist or Western image of being 'developed'.

The main reason for failure to understand indigenous resistance to development may be, however, common Marxist and liberal assumptions about the worth of economic activity. Development analysts for the most part carry these assumptions into their images of the underdeveloped world, into the goals they project and into the strategies they propose for achieving those goals. We need to go back at least to Bentham to find the intellectual source of our contemporary preoccupation with economic growth. His simple assumption was that the maximization of wealth led to the maximization of happiness ('each portion of wealth has a corresponding portion of happiness...'). Not only does Bentham describe the basically appetitive nature of man in economic terms, but he is among the first to argue that acquisitiveness is both rational and morally commendable in its consequences for private and public welfare. His view of the economic mainsprings of human activity still characterizes Western images of development. It is his version of 'economic man' which most developers are trying to mold or create; they cannot see how people who do not share Bentham's view of human motivations can be rational or happy. The prime prerequisite for aid programs is thus to instill a respect for materialism and to overcome all those aspects of a culture which impede economic activity.[19] Economic sectors composed of producers who meet only immediate needs are labelled 'stagnant'. If there is no economic 'growth', there can be no cultural progress.[20]

Take one example. Norman Jacobs presents an interesting analysis of modernization and development in Thailand in which he laments the fact that values other than economic maximization are rampant in the society. While Jacobs cannot entirely hide an admiration for the Thais' proverbial propensity to enjoy life - even to the point where they would rather go to a party or ceremony than show up for work - his overall conclusion rests squarely in the tradition of Western writing on underdevelopment: no matter how one may enjoy life through non-economic activities, it is better to work hard and create institutions which encourage savings, long-run investment, production beyond immediate needs, strict work schedules and the like.

Now if development (defined by Jacobs as 'maximizing the economic potential of the environment')[21] is the most important personal and national goal, then of course conventional analyses of the problem of underdevelopment may be valuable. But many discussions of development fail to demonstrate that economic maximization is a superior value for the individual, even if it is important at the aggregate level. In some societies, of course, overpopulation forces governments to act as if production were the first national and individual priority. In those areas where there is still considerable land available and where some people prefer not to adopt Western-style value structures, should they be condemned or urged to act to the contrary? The unwillingness to save, to increase output, or come to work according to a rigid schedule should indicate something about the preferences of people about their life-styles, rather than being portrayed as 'irrational' behavior, the consequences of superstition, or plain stubbornness.

But, it can be argued, most of the people we are discussing live in such pitiful conditions that they must be shown how to become economic maximizers. If we go to the extreme of cultural relativism and accept all traditional practices as 'functional', we are overlooking the problem of some objective minimum standard of general welfare. Growing populations, urbanization and the requirements of international politics do not allow us the luxury of respecting traditional values and pursuits. Modernization can only come about through breaking up traditional social and economic patterns.

There is merit in this reply, particularly if we agree that in all cases population pressures allow no alternatives, and uncritically accept the assumption that a precarious economic existence must cause intellectual and cultural poverty as well. These positions may be substantially correct in countries such as India, Egypt, Pakistan and in regions subject to natural disasters. Even in moderately developed countries such as Mexico, recent studies describe rural life in a manner to substantiate Hobbes's characterization of man in the state of nature.[22] Oscar Lewis's scenarios show a life with no reprieve from economic insecurity, a life of constant fear and distrust of friends and neighbors and of virtually no opportunities for self-betterment.[23] In southern Italy and Sicily, too, peasant life is known for 'La Miseria'. Edward Banfield's classic study, *The Moral Basis of a Backward Society*,[24] leaves little doubt that some sort of economic development is essential if the people of the region are to enjoy even a modicum of opportunity and a diminution of distrust, suspicion, and miserliness.

Yet when we realize that many of these studies portray societies undergoing rapid economic and social change, or describe characteristics that are also prevalent in developed societies (gossip, insecurity, and the like), then other portrayals take on more credibility. Robert Redfield, after years of field research in Mexican peasant communities, came to appreciate many aspects of peoples' lives in an underdeveloped community.[25] He not only pointed to the integrative and satisfying aspects of small community life, but implied that mental balance cannot be sustained in a society undergoing rapid change. While Redfield was not opposed to change, he saw that raising expectations which cannot be fulfilled only creates frustration, and that a great deal of so-called development creates wants 'whose satisfaction brings no satisfaction'.[26] More important, '[the peasants'] way of life, the persisting order and depth of their simple experiences, continue to make something humanly and intellectually acceptable of the world around them'.[27] More contemporary observers of peasant communities are similarly impressed by, and respectful of, traditional cultures and sensitive to the problems created by technological innovation, industrial development schemes and the general penetration of relatively isolated communities by Western values and mores.[28] Redfield's observations are by no means exceptional. Thus, the wretchedness of most underdeveloped peoples' lives should be viewed as a hypothesis, not as a universal fact. At the very least, the first component of the common Western image - widespread economic and intellectual poverty - needs to be spelled out in much greater detail. The urban slum-dweller of Bogota cannot be equated with the South Pacific islander or the Thai subsistence farmer. Per capita income figures reveal little about happiness or misery among such diverse people, much less about the importance of economic activity to their welfare. Indeed, the whole notion of 'development' needs to be broadened to include more profound objectives such as esteem, self-actualization,[29] justice and the maintenance of emotional communities. Economic growth may have only slight impact on these forms of development, and in some cases it is actually inconsistent with them. A brief review of some of the non-financial costs of economic development policies will help explain why resistance to development exists, and why the 'revolution of rising expectations' provides a questionable basis for the theory that international conflict will result from the 'gap' between developed and underdeveloped countries.

The costs of development

George Foster's analysis of underdevelopment and his solutions to it are reasonably typical of the literature. The requirements for inducing development include reducing the strength of conservative forces or neutralizing their results, while simultaneously strengthening the forces of change.[30] How is this to be done? Among other things, all cultural and social 'barriers' to development must be overcome. These include 'the basic values of [a] group, its conception of right and wrong...[and] the "fundamental fit" or integration of its parts....'[31] Barriers such as the social structure of groups and the prevailing type of family relationships must also be amended so that economically maximizing behavior can result. In short, social and cultural patterns which are incompatible with industrialization, 'community development', and many other favored Western notions of what constitutes a good society, must be eradicated. While Foster does not endorse the 'stern measures' advocated and practiced by developers in the socialist countries,[32] it is not hard to see why people who have any pride in or attachment to their culture, folkways, and social patterns might react negatively to such prescriptions for 'growth'.

One of the foremost analysts of underdevelopment, Gunnar Myrdal, appears no less impatient of those 'barriers' to systematic national planning and Western-style economic activity and institutions. His major work in the field, *Asian Drama: An Inquiry into the Poverty of Nations* (1968), is replete with disparaging references to language and ethnic differences among peoples, to religious traditions and customs which go back several thousand years, and to other social institutions which seem incongruent or incompatible with drastic land reform, heavy industrialization and above all, with nationwide planning programs that move people in the same manner that one moves non-human resources. Myrdal is not reticent in urging compulsion where growth is inhibited by non-economically maximizing behavior - in short, he believes

36

man should be forced to become more wealthy.[33]

Most economists and anthropologists note that there are costs to be paid in programs which involve breaking down traditional social pattern and practices. But they seldom dwell on these costs, and very few indeed have acknowledged that certain forms of development are not worth the price they extract.

Consider some of the development costs listed by Foster and others.

1) Destruction of the 'extended family'. By breaking down traditional family patterns which emphasize mutual obligation, a productive man is liberated so that he can become part of a mobile labor force. He casts off his family obligations (presumably to be taken over by the state) in order to maximize his economic and, perhaps, career possibilities. The destruction of the extended family is directly attributable to the demands and opportunities of modern economic organization and of technology.[34]

2) Destruction of traditional rural cooperative work patterns. Although communal work may not be as productive as individual enterprise, it fulfills social needs that cannot be met through private labor. The introduction of cash crops and money are directly linked to the demise of communal work in rural areas.

3) As peasants become integrated into a commercial economy, dietary standards often decline. According to various studies cited by Foster,[35] a significant proportion of malnutrition in the world can be attributed to the substitution of packaged foods for traditional dietary sources. People purchase packaged foods primarily for their prestige value, the efficacy of advertising, or aesthetic rather than dietary reasons. (This phenomenon raises the question of measuring primary need satisfaction. Most development planners would identify increased cash spent on food as indicating growth and progress, whereas from a dietary point of view, needs might be met less adequately than previously. The availability of packaged foods, like many other commodities, is also linked to escalating definitions of primary needs among populations; once obtained, they tend to become necessities.) Another study discloses that many mothers in agrarian societies, imitating middle-class patterns in the West, have given up breast feeding their babies, with resulting undernourishment and protein deficiency.[36]

Many other costs could be cited. Perhaps chief among them is the rise of class distinction. In villages which are patterned on communal labor and mutual help, introduction of larger incomes and the availability of Western-style consumer goods creates status distinctions that are disruptive to cooperation, political decision-making, and to inter- and intrafamily harmony.[37] But what is most deficient about the notion of economic 'growth' as measured by increased per capita income is that it reflects little about the sense of well-being. Various studies show that there is no apparent connection between the massing of consumer goods - even home comforts - and happiness. Development breeds new wants and the perception of new needs, but when these have been met, the people do not feel they are better off.[38] At the same time, one investigator, reflecting his American values, was surprised to find a great amount of contentment among rural Filipinos living at subsistence or near subsistence levels.[39] Such contentment did not in the least suggest to the researcher that perhaps the people in question should be left 'underdeveloped'.

Finally, there are the indicators of social stress resulting from rapid cultural change. These do not appear everywhere, of course, but the question of people's ability to undergo change involving destruction of traditional economic and social patterns is not yet understood well enough. (Even in the United States, government officials have resisted the idea of an annual 'social state of the union' report. The traditional 'State of the Union message' is concerned mostly with economics, as if all other 'states' depended upon the rise and fall of economic indicators.) Consider the following report upon the consequences of a well-intentioned Danish program to offer training, economic opportunities and the cultural benefits of town life to native Greenlanders. According to a Greenlander member of the Danish parliament, many benefits have resulted from these programs, 'but we young Greenlanders find that the creation of a modern social pattern has not been accompanied by human growth, mental stability, psychological balance - in short, human well-being - in the new environment. Families are breaking up, crime is increasing, alcoholism is spreading even to the very young. The number of psychological disturbances is increasing, also among school children. Many people discern an inner confusion and disillusion. The social privation of the past is being replaced by human disintegration'.[40] Similar observations have been made about Fiji, the Philippines and the aborigines of Australia.[41]

Recognition of these and other costs have not, for the most part, reduced the zeal with which many governments and some populations pursue the road to modernization. Apparently most have agreed that on balance the costs are worth the advantages, or, without looking around for alternative images or strategies of development, they have assumed that the degree of need allows no other course of action. Most, however, simply do not make an assessment of the relative balance between the costs and advantages. The latter are assumed to be obvious and preponderant. Yet, we would expect that as some of the costs become more obvious and painful, some governments, supported by people facing cultural stress, will begin to acknowledge the political benefits of resisting further westernization. It is then that we could expect to see more 'buffers' erected by the governments of underdeveloped states against the penetration of foreign influences.

The 'maldeveloped' societies

Most of the literature on development assumes that the paths we have trod must serve for others as well, give or take a few national peculiarities.[42] But it is becoming increasingly apparent that as our own growth continues at astonishing speed, increases in indicators of social stress are occurring with disturbing regularity. The British government's recent 'official social commentary' on the state of England shows impressive economic gains over the past decade but reveals that in the same period violent crimes have almost trebled and that many other indicators of serious social problems are rising at a rate much faster than population growth. The number of women employed part- or full-time in the world's oldest profession has increased at an alarming rate in Italy and Israel, while in the United States, murder, assault and burglary rates have doubled in most cities during the past decade. The number of people hospitalized for mental illness is growing proportionately much more rapidly than is the general population - one-half of all beds in American non-Federal hospitals are occupied by people suffering from mental disorders[43] - while child beatings are reported to be increasing dramatically. Alarmed physicians note that child beating usually serves the needs of the attacking adult seeking relief from uncontrollable anger and stress.[44] For their part, the young in many countries are contributing to an ever-swelling juvenile delinquency rate. While all these phenomena cannot be attributed to a single cause such as social change or urban density, it is significant that their highest incidence is commonly found in urban areas.[45]

It may be that the worst physical aspects of rapid industrialization, so precisely described by Dickens and Zola, are behind us. What may lie ahead of us is social stress and possible breakdown. The other manifestations of the maldeveloped society - pollution, destruction of wilderness, waste, depletion of resources, and the like - are too well-known to require further comment. In the face of these physical and social consequences of rapid change, we must begin to wonder if our prescriptions for others are really well-advised. The model of the 'developed' state seems increasingly tarnished. When elites or others already subject to the strains caused by development begin to learn of our difficulties, they may well question whether they are willing to undergo similar consequences. Disillusionment with the 'developed' model may thus become another source of policies which attempt to isolate underdeveloped areas from certain forms of Western penetration.

Avoiding conflict between underdeveloped and 'maldeveloped' states: some solutions to the 'gap' problem

The Pearson Report, government statements in support of private investment and foreign aid, and academic treatises as well agree basically with the view expressed by former Under-Secretary of State U. Alexis Johnson in 1972 that the growing gap between the rich and poor is a 'fundamentally unacceptable situation [which is] explosive in a political sense'.[46] The solutions offered to this problem have been mostly continuations and expansions of past approaches: more trade, lower tariffs in the industrial countries, more private investment and more international cooperation. For Mr. Johnson, the solution is greater international cooperation and increased interdependence. The 'foundation bricks' of his image of a more egalitarian world order are being laid by private citizens, and particularly by private businesses and multinational corporations. The gap will be closed to the extent that these private networks of association grow. While Mr. Johnson is expressing a private opinion, his view is consistent in its fundamentals with the solutions proposed by many governments and international agencies.

Another view, expanded at length by Denis Goulet in *The Cruel Choice*, argues that the gap can never be closed until the developed states allow the other areas of the world to share in their decision-making power and wealth. All the exploitative aspects of contemporary international economic relations must be ended, and the small states suffering from underdevelopment, status inconsistency, or whatever, must be made into active partners in the formulation of world monetary, trade, and aid policies. But the main ingredient of the solution must be a willingness by the 'maldeveloped' states to decrease their levels of consumption in order that others may have more. There must be a fundamental redistribution of political power and economic resources in the world.

40

Mr. Johnson's solution contains several immediate problems. It assumes, first, the availability of infinite resources in the future. While Johnson may recognize some of the shortcomings of advanced societies, his plea for more interdependence - more trade, private investment, tourism and extraction of natural resources - does not reveal how it attacks such fundamental problems as overpopulation and the present distribution of energy use. Edward Woodhouse has argued recently that given finite resources, we can no longer adhere to the view that economic development should be the primary goal of all states, or that 'unlimited urbanization, industrialization, and GNP growth...are in fact possible or worthy any longer.'[47] In his opinion, development as it has been defined by most economists is a chimera. The dwindling availability of resources, in addition to the pollution problem, simply will not allow the world to be composed of 160 or more highly industrialized collectivities. More 'interdependence' as proposed by Mr. Johnson sounds as if there should simply be more 'growth' in all economic dimensions.

There is little reason to believe, moreover, that the governments of underdeveloped countries will continue to accept uncritically those relationships which Western governments and multinational enterprises define as 'interdependent'. To an increasing number of observers, these relationships are being defined not as 'cooperation', but as dependence (at best) or imperialism (at worst). The continuation of present economic trends in the world is not likely to allay these fears; quite the contrary. More trade, for aid, more private investment, more tourism and more private contacts - the traditional ingredients of the liberal view of internationalism - are all implied in Johnson's formula, but he fails to take into account that the consequences of these types of interactions often create feelings of resentment, racial antagonism, and perceptions of exploitation.

The solution offered by Goulet seems attractive. It acknowledges the problems of dwindling resources, and unequal decision-making power and economic rewards in the international system. But there is little evidence that any government in a 'maldeveloped' state is even beginning to think in his terms. While many governments have begun to organize anti-pollution programs, none has yet instituted a regime of rationing in order to reduce pollution or to save resources... even for its own population. That it would do so to redistribute the world's resources in favor of the underdeveloped states seems highly unlikely in the foreseeable future.

The underdeveloped states reject the 'maldeveloped' states: an alternative view of the source of international conflict

Although academic researchers show little agreement on the correlation between the state of the underdevelopment and the propensity to engage in aggressive foreign policy,[48] we cannot dismiss entirely the 'gap' theory of international conflict. There might well be more military crises triggered by domestic turmoil in the underdeveloped countries, and the 'have nots' may, as revealed in the Arab oil embargo of 1973, undertake aggressive policies toward the 'haves'.

Many governments, of course, have probably gone too far down the path of industrialization, urbanization and consumerism to change their course significantly. Many will continue to pursue Western-type development for reasons of national security or international prestige, or because their westernized elites (including Marxists) remain cut off from their roots. Most of the Latin American countries are already heavily urbanized and, despite large population increases, have shown impressive economic growth rates. India, Egypt and some of the other more overpopulated countries will probably continue industrialization programs enabling them to maintain regional leadership roles, prevent overdependence on great powers for military supplies, or avoid the consequences of not having adequate arable land to sustain rapidly growing populations in rural areas. The alternative scenario, then, would refer primarily to some of the smaller states in Africa, Southeast Asia, the South Pacific and possibly the Middle East. These are the states already on the periphery of the international system, least touched by Western influences and thus perhaps most vulnerable to cultural dislocation caused by increased penetration from outside.

These states, rather than accepting greater interdependence, would seek to reduce the penetration of external societies. Tourism would be discouraged; foreign aid turned down; aid experts expelled; foreign corporations nationalized; and new multinational enterprises denied opportunities for exploitation of natural resources or development of markets. While not all forms of contact would cease - trade, normal diplomatic contacts and some international cooperative programs would remain - those which were identified as 'endangering' the local culture or creating undue dependency on outside states would be curtailed or terminated. The models of Burma under General Ne Win and contemporary Iran come to mind.

What sorts of evidence might be put forth to support even a minimal confidence in the scenario as a possibility? There is no systematic evidence yet, much less an identifiable trend, but some indicators of the rejection of liberal nostrums for the 'gap' problem are beginning to appear. First, at the grass-roots level, there is the persistence of millennial movements in many African and some South Pacific societies. Lanternari[49] shows that almost all of these movements and their early twentieth-century predecessors are a response to extreme external disturbances to indigenous ways of life. The people seek relief from their frustrations and sufferings in religious ways, usually before they turn to political means. It is thus possible to speculate that many of the adherents of millennial movements today might someday constitute a fertile ground for strongly anti-Western political leaders. The religious prophets of these movements could also adopt political roles.[50]

Second, most of the current generation of leaders in the underdeveloped countries are highly 'westernized'. But what of a new generation of leaders, some of whom will be less personally familiar with the West and whose careers might be founded on a populist base that contains anti-Western attitudes? Is President Amin of Uganda - a man whose career includes few of the experiences his African counterparts had in Western societies - an exception, or might others of his persuasion and tactics follow? If nativist political groups begin to flourish, will the external sources of the commitment to development - prestige, security and socialization patterns - remain so potent?

It has been argued, third, that part of Allende's appeal in the 1970 elections in Chile was based on his handling of the issue of foreign influence in the Chilean economy. Aside from the well-known American corporations operating in the country, there was a rapid growth of foreign ownership of Chilean manufacturing in the late 1960s.[51] While the Chileans were by no means rejecting Western patterns of economic organization in general, the popularity of appeals against foreign economic penetration was undeniable. Chile will probably not be the last country which decides to accept the costs of decreasing foreign economic influence in order to enhance governmental control over the direction of development.

Fourth, the notion of mutual benefits accruing to underdeveloped countries through capital transfers and the operations of foreign-based corporations is being increasingly scrutinized. Except among Marxists, it has been commonly assumed until recently that private investment from the industrialized countries brings significant economic gains to the host underdeveloped countries. The transfer of technology and of managerial skills, along with the training of a skilled work force, is a positive consequence of this activity. And a good case can be made that foreign investment and production which lead to import substitution help the host country's balance of payments position.[52] Yet there are also tangible and intangible costs to the host country. Some studies show, for example, that over the long run, the flow of capital tends to reverse itself; remitted profits, royalties, and management fees become greater than the amount of new capital flowing into the host country. In the period 1950-1965, remittances of Latin American subsidiaries of American parent companies exceeded new private investment by 7.5 billion dollars, and for the period 1965-1969 the gap was an additional three billion.[53] When we consider that many subsidiaries of multinational corporations provide their own managerial talent, that they import components from parent companies (rather than purchase them locally), and that in many ways they reduce the possibilities for local firms to survive,[54] the benefits accruing to the host country begin to pale. Even employment benefits may be much less than is often assumed. Capital-intensive projects simply do not provide the opportunities for employment that, let us say, investment in agriculture would.[55]

Moreover, most foreign-owned manufacturing enterprises in underdeveloped countries must work assiduously to shape Western-style consumption habits among people becoming part of the market economy. Yet it is precisely these habits which are inimical to many preferred development strategies. People are encouraged to acquire tastes which, while perhaps meeting prestige needs, make little contribution to the general welfare or to community development. As Illich has pointed out, every automobile manufactured and sold in Latin America implies that more rational mass-transportation policies are less likely to be developed. As cars are purchased, national resources will have to be (and have been) devoted to the construction of mass highway systems, benefiting primarily the modern urban middle class. Correspondingly less will be spent, we can assume, on high capacity systems of urban and rural transportation. Every private refrigerator sold makes it less likely that villages will want to organize community freezers.[56]

The presence of foreign-owned firms whose existence and expansion depend upon fostering Western-style consumption patterns can seriously limit the ability of a government to shape development strategies with a maximum social impact. The pattern of saving and the pattern of consumption, to name only two aspects of economic behavior, can be significantly distorted by the advertising and blandishments of foreign manufacturers and their local emulators.[57] Yet most observers predict a dramatic rise in the numbers and size of multinational firms within the next several decades. The majority of contemporary multinational enterprises focus their productive and marketing activities in the industrialized countries. But in the future they can be expected to seek many new ventures in the Third World. The evidence about their impact on underdeveloped societies is by no means entirely negative, but the traditional view that their activities bring substantial benefits, with no attending costs to host countries, has come under increasing attack.[58] Given the increasing awareness of the negative consequences of their activities, it would not be rash to predict that some governments will adopt more stringent and, in some cases, exclusive policies against Western economic interests.

The growth of tourism by Westerners in underdeveloped countries has had a number of consequences not originally anticipated by those who see travel and personal interaction as important sources of building 'international understanding'. While American- and European-built and -owned tourist facilities provide some local employment, taxes and beneficial effects to the host country's balance of payments,[59] they also tend to create ghettos for the rich, places of amusement which display ostentatious wealth and which alienate prime land. The behavior of many tourists is no less conducive to bad impressions and to social tensions: at its worst, it can be vulgar and racist; at its best it tends toward the paternalistic. According to L.E. Braithwaite[60] the situation in the Caribbean is already dangerous: the peculiar characteristics of North American tourists simply breed resentment and antagonisms. Pollution, the rapid growth of prostitution and many other menial 'service' trades to comfort the Northerners, and alarming increases in delinquency involving tourists as victims are all byproducts of this developing industry. While one would not want to argue in all cases that the disadvantages outweigh the costs, this aspect of 'interdependence' may also come to face limitations and restrictions imposed by some governments in the underdeveloped countries.

Finally, in a few countries, receptivity to bilateral aid programs is diminishing. The main objective of the American aid program in Brazil has been to promote a good 'climate' for American investment. One byproduct of this objective is that today the more dynamic American firms dominate most of the modern parts of Brazilian industry. Both Brazilian intellectuals and government officials are becoming increasingly suspicious of the consequences of American aid.[61] No government is likely to look with favor upon a situation where important sectors of their country's economy become dominated by foreign interests. To the extent that foreign aid programs are used as a vehicle to promote private investment, we could expect some diminution of enthusiasm to participate in them. Moreover, there is some evidence that economic aid does not promote economic growth and, indeed, in the case of Latin America, that aid may retard growth.[62] Trade and private investment rates between the United States and Latin America, according to another study, also correlate negatively with economic development: the greater the economic dependency of South American countries, the lower their growth rate.[63]

Bits and pieces of evidence such as those listed above do not constitute in any sense verification of a hypothesis. They do suggest that many of the traditional liberal assumptions about the development of a world order through increased interdependence are being questioned.

The responses of the developed countries to autarky or isolationist policies are difficult to predict, but it is tempting to assume that in the short run they will be more hostile than indifferent or supportive. Governments of developed states have usually retaliated in instances where important economic interests were expelled, nationalized, or even restricted in their activities. Moreover, the economic charitableness typical of the great powers in the postwar years may be waning as concentration on economic problems and safeguarding economic interests replaces fixation on the Cold War and issues of national security conceived in military terms. Underdeveloped states which undertake to restrict investment opportunities or the marketing activities of multinational firms thus may invoke not only the attention of Western governments and populations, but hostile responses as well. (Of course when a relatively uninvolved state such as Burma acts individually, few international repercussions will ensue.) But if the scenario described in the paper involves a reasonably large number of states within a fairly short period of time, the consequences to the interests of industrialized countries might be much more severe.

An alternative response, perhaps more likely in the long run, is indifference. The governments of many industrialized states, deeply concerned about social trends in their own countries, may understand that all of the orthodox solutions to the problems of underdevelopment have to be re-examined. In the meantime, aid policies would be reformulated by both donors and hosts to concentrate more on social development, agriculture and population control and less on heavy industrialization and activities which bring advantages primarily to the modernized urban middle classes.

Whatever the hypothetical responses, there is little in the present literature on international conflict to suggest probabilities. We know a great deal about decision-making behavior in crises, the relationship between national attributes and conflict behavior and the actions and reactions of governments in an arms race. Our conflict studies are based for the most part on the interaction of

46

parties who are locked into a system involving high densities of verbal and symbolic communication. We know a great deal less about isolationist impulses, about situations where one state is attempting to break away from dependence upon others, or in other ways to decrease the degree of integration with the outside world.

Our visions of future international systems generally assume greater transaction flows, an increase in non-governmental associations and a burgeoning 'international culture'.[64] But before we can accept these models as possible norms for the future, we should ask many empirical and normative questions. How are the benefits of increased transactions being distributed? What are the sources of values in the 'international culture'? Is the international system tending toward cultural and material homogeneity or toward acceptance and promotion of pluralism? Is homogeneity of life-styles, economics and views of man and human activity something to be promoted or deplored? Is increased international economic integration or interdependence consistent with the preservation of the most meaningful parts of indigenous cultures? Are the networks of communication and economic activity that surround the globe capable of promoting and sustaining two-way movement, or have the networks developed in such a manner as to assure the predominance of Western and socialist states over the Third World? These and many other questions have not yet been raised by systems theorists of international relations or by those who are concerned with development problems. If the scenario in this paper has validity, then questions such as these should begin to command our attention.

Notes

1. Richard D. Wolff (1974), *The Economics of Colonialism: Britain and Kenya, 1870-1930*, New Haven: Yale University Press and Ngo Vihn Long (1973), *Before the Revolution*, Cambridge, MA: Massachusetts Institute of Technology Press.

2. This common view is proposed in *Partners for Development: Report of the Commission on International Development* (1969), Chairman: Lester B. Pearson, New York: Praeger, p. 7; see also Robert S. McNamara (1968), *The Essence of Security*, New York: Harper and Row, pp. 145-146.

3. A.F.K. Organski (1968), *World Politics*, 2nd ed., New York: Knopf and McNamara, pp.146; Angelos Angelopoulos (1972), *The Third World and the Rich Countries*, New York: Praeger, p. 7. For a critique of the statistical biases and fallacies in measuring the 'gap', see P.T. Bauer (1971), *Dissent on Development*, London: Weidenfeld and Nicolson, chap. 1.

4. Throughout this paper the term 'Western' includes most of the developed socialist states. Literature on the causes of underdevelopment is largely fostered by the pioneering work of Andre Gunder Frank (1969), 'The Development of Underdevelopment', in A. G. Frank (ed.), *Latin America: Underdevelopment or Revolution?*, New York: Monthly Review Press. A summary and critique of the underdevelopment-dependency literature is in Benjamin J. Cohen (1973), The *Question of Imperialism: The Political Economy of Dominance and Dependence*, New York: Basic Books.

5. H. A. C. Cairns (1965), *Prelude to Imperialism*, London: Routledge and Kegan Paul; Edmund Stillman and William Pfaff (1964), *The Politics of Hysteria*, New York: Harper and Row; Ignacy Sachs (1974), *La decouverte du tiers monde*, Paris: Flammarion, chap. 4.

6. See respectively, Colin Leys (1971), 'Politics in Kenya: The Development of a Peasant Society', *British Journal of Political Science*, 1, July, pp. 307-37; Sheila T. Van der Horst (1965), 'The Effects of Industrialization on Race Relations in South Africa', in Guy Hunter (ed.), *Industrialization and Race Relations: A Symposium*, London: Oxford University Press, pp. 112; Norman Long (1968), *Social Changes and the Individual*, Manchester: Manchester University Press, chap. 9; Johan Galtung (1971), *Members of Two Worlds: A Development Study of Three Villages in Western Sicily*, New York: Columbia University Press; Norman Jacobs (1971), *Modernization Without Development*, New York: Praeger, p.178. Nevertheless, the growth of urban population in Africa, even if unstable, has been phenomenal. Most cities doubled their populations during the 1960s. For statistics, see Donald G. Morrison, Robert C. Mitchell, John N. Paden, and Hugh M. Stevenson (1972), *Black Africa: A Comparative Handbook*, New York: Free Press, part 2.

7. The transfer of tribal customs and social relationships into an urban environment is possible. See Peter C.W. Gutkind (1969), 'African Urban Family Life and the Urban System', in Paul Meadows and Ephraim Mazruchi (eds), *Urbanism, Urbanization, and Change*, Reading,MA: Addison-Wesley, pp. 215-22.

8. This bias is acknowledged in (1972), 'International Bank for Reconstruction and Development', in *World Bank Operations: Sectoral Policies and Programs*, Baltimore: The Johns Hopkins University Press, p.418. For a study of the antirural bias of development planners in India, see M. Lipton (1973), 'Urban Bias and Rural Planning in India' in Henry Bernstein (ed.), *Development and Underdevelopment: The Third World Today*, Hammondsworth: Penguin, pp. 235-53; for Africa see Gerald K. Heleiner (1971), 'Structural Change in Africa', in Barbara Ward, J. D. Runnals, and Lenore D'Anjou (eds), *The Widening Gap*, New York: Columbia University Press, p. 92.

9. Baldev Raj Nayar (1971), 'The Political Mainsprings of Economic Planning in the New Nations: The Modernization Imperative Versus Social Mobilization', paper presented at the conference 'Asia in the Seventies', Carleton University, Ottawa.

10. Jacobs, *Modernization without Development*, pp.131-33.

11. Denis A. Goulet (1971), *The Cruel Choice: A New Concept in the Study of Development*, New York: Atheneum, p. 80.

12. Jacobs, p. 126.

48

13. See paper 'Ujamaa - The Basis of African Socialism', in Julius K. Nyerere (1967), *Freedom and Unity: A Selection of Writings and Speeches*, London: Oxford University Press, pp.162-71, 183-88. The Arusha Declaration of 1967 explicitly rejects a Western consumption-oriented society for Tanzania.

14. Jacobs, chap. 5, pp. 314-16.

15. Goulet, p. 70.

16. *World Bank Operations*, pp. 96-7. Until the late 1960s, India's priorities lay clearly with heavy industry. Although 80 per cent of the population was employed in agriculture, only 20 per cent of public development expenditures went to this sector. See *Partners for Development*, pp. 287-88.

17. Dan Usher describes finding that an early conception of living conditions among the Thais, based on economic studies, was greatly at odds with the reality he experienced living among them. The low per capita income figures indicated virtually nothing about material welfare or sense of well-being. See his (1968), *The Price Mechanism and the Meaning of National Income Statistics*, Oxford: Oxford University Press.

18. For an account of the depressing effects of unbalanced urban industrialization on a rural population, and the distortion of government expenditures in favor of the modern sectors, see Robert H. Bates (1973), 'The Policy Origins of Migration in Zambia', presented at the meeting of the American Political Science Association, New Orleans, September.

19. Among the many examples in the literature, see the attitudes expressed implicitly and explicitly in George M. Guthrie (1970), *The Psychology of Modernization in the Rural Philippines*, Quezon City: Ateneo do Manila University Press.

20. Virtually all commentators characterize non-industrializing and non-high-growth economies as 'stagnant'. For one example, see E. K. Fisk (1970), *The Political Economy of Fiji*, Canberra: Australian National University Press. Fisk praises the Indian community in Fiji for its aggressive economic advancement, while criticizing native Fijians for their lack of interest in large-scale economic pursuits.

21. Jacobs, *Modernization Without Development*, chap. 5.

22. For a summary of the debate on characteristics of peasant societies, see George Foster (1970), 'Interpersonal Relations in Peasant Society', in Monte Palmer (ed.), *The Human Factor in Political Development*, Boston: Ginn.

23. Oscar Lewis (1959), *Five Families: Mexican Case Studies in the Culture of Poverty*, New York: Basic Books.

24. Glencoe, IL: Free Press, 1958.

25. See (1934), *Can Kom, A Maya Village*, Washington: Canegie Institution of Washington; (1930), *Tepoztlan: A Mexican Village*, Chicago: University of Chicago Press; and (1960), *The Little Community*, and *Peasant Society and Culture*, Chicago: University of Chicago Press.

26. *The Little Community*, p. 63.

27. Redfield (1956), *Peasant Society and Culture*, Chicago: University of Chicago Press, pp. 132-33.

28. For others, see John Greenway (1972), *Down Among the Wild Men*, Boston: Little, Brown; Aliczia Iwanska (1971), *Purgatory and Utopia*, Cambridge, Mass: Shenkman; Lisa Peattie (1968), *The View from the Barrio*, Ann Arbor, MI: Universtiy of Michigan Press; Colin M. Turnbull (1966), *Tradition and Change in African Tribal Life*, Cleveland, OH: World Publishing.

49

29. Goulet, *The Cruel Choice*, chap. 2.
30. George Foster (1962), *Traditional Cultures and the Impact of Technological Change*, New York: Harper, p. 59.
31. *Ibid.*
32. The ethnocentrism of analysts of underdevelopment in the socialist countries is remarkably explicit. All local customs which inhibit industrialization and the development of an urban proletariat must be destroyed, no matter at what cost. There is only one route to modernization, namely heavy industry and collective agriculture, based on the Soviet pattern. V.G. Solodovnikov (1970), *Afrika vybirat put*, Moscow: Hayka.
33. For a critique of Myrdal's approach to economic development, see Bauer, *Dissent on Development*, chap. 5.
34. Foster, *Traditional Cultures...*, pp.30-40; Hafeez M. Said (1970), *The Village Culture in Transition*, Honolulu: East-West Center Press, pp. 140-43.
35. Foster, *Traditional Cutures...*, pp. 33-7.
36. An FAO study cited in Conrad M. Arensberg and Arthur H. Niefhoff (1971), *Introducing Social Change*, Chicago: Aldine, p. 126.
37. For other costs, see Herbert Blumer, 'Industrialization and Race Relations', in Hunter (ed.), *Industrialization and Race Relations*, p. 226; V.H. Joshi (1966), *Economic Development and Social Change in a South Gujarat Village*, Baroda: University of Baroda Press, pp.101-13; and James M. McKendry et al. (n.d.), *The Psychological Impact of Social Change in the Philippines*, Science Park, Penn.: H. R. B. Singer, Technical Report 857-R-2, pp. 66, 72.
38. Goulet, *The Cruel Choice*, p. 80; Redfield, *The Little Community*, p.62. Quantitative evidence supporting this statement is found in Guthrie, *The Psychology of Modernization...*, pp. 90, 96.
39. McKendry et al., p. xii.
40. George Boultwood (1972), 'Danish Plan for Greenland Too Fast', *The Montreal Star*, Oct. 12.
41. Statement of Fiji minister of tourism to a meeting in Djakarta, reported in *The Sun* (Vancouver), Sept. 4, 1974, p. 34; 'Civilization Brings Grief to Aborigines', *The Sun* (Vancouver), Sept. 19, 1974, p.42; McKendry et al., p.18.
42. Possibly this assumption is being questioned more frequently today. See, for example, the testimony of U. Alexis Johnson, former Under-Secretary of State in the United States, before the House Subcommittee on National Security Policy and Scientific Development. Johnson claimed that the concept of development needed to be redefined to eliminate the worst effects of industrialization as experienced in the advanced countries. US, House of Representatives, Committee on Foreign Affairs, Subcommittee on National Security Policy and Scientific Development (1972), *National Security and Changing World Power Alignment*, 92d Cong., 2d Sess., pp. 372-94.
43. Noted in Robert C. Wood (1966), 'The Future of Modernization', in Myron Weiner (ed.), *Modernization*, New York: Basic Books, p. 49.
44. *The Globe and Mail* (Toronto), Aug. 18, 1971, p. 8. The rising figures on child abuse may be accounted for, on the other hand, by new legislation requiring physicians to report incidents to police authorities.
45. A study by W.M.S. and Claire Russell demonstrates the positive correlation between urban density and crime rates, reported in *The New York Times*,

Aug. 16, 1970, sec. 1, p. 53. Care must be taken in interpreting crime and mental health statistics, as these may be manipulated for political purposes, or they may reflect better detection methods.

46. *National Security and Changing World Power Alignment*, Johnson's testimony on Aug. 7.

47. Edward J. Woodhouse (1972), 'Re-visioning the Future of the Third World: An Ecological Perspective on Development', *World Politics*, 25 Oct., p. 9.

48. For example, Rudolph J. Rummel (1968), 'The Relationship Between National Attributes and Foreign Conflict Behavior', in J. David Singer (ed.), *Quantitative International Politics: Insights and Evidence*, New York: Free Press, pp. 187-214. See, however, the chapter by Michael Haas in the same volume.

49. Vittorio Lanternari (1963), *The Religions of the Oppressed: A Study of Modern Messianic Cults*, New York: Knopf.

50. Other forms of protest that have been linked to the disruptive effects of modernization are social banditry and some guerrilla movements. See Eric J. Hobsbawm (1959), *Primitive Rebels: Studies in Archaic Forms of Social Movements in the Nineteenth and Twentieth Centuries*, Manchester: Manchester University Press.

51. Richard N. Cooper (1972), 'Economic Interdependence and Foreign Policy in the Seventies', *World Politics*, 24 Jan., pp.172-73.

52. Raymond Vernon (1971), *Sovereignty at Bay: The Multinational Spread of U.S. Enterprises*, New York: Basic Books.

53. Peter B. Evans (1971), 'National Autonomy and Economic Development: Critical Perspectives on Multinational Corporations in Underdeveloped Countries', *International Organization*, 25, Summer, p. 678.

54. For a discussion of some of the negative consequences of American firms operating in the Canadian economy, see Kari Levitt (1970), *Silent Surrender: The Multinational Corporation Canada*, Toronto: Macmillan. See also Fouad Ajami (1972), 'Corporate Giants: Some Global Social Costs', *International Studies Quarterly*, 16, Dec., pp. 511-29.

55. *World Bank Operations*, p. 418.

56. Ivan Illich (1969), 'Outwitting the "Developed" Countries', *New York Review of Books*, 13, Nov. 6, 1969, p. 20. For a more general discussion of the negative cultural consequence of multinational firms operating in underdeveloped countries see David Osterberg and Fouad Ajami (1971), 'The Multinational Corporation: Expanding the Frontiers of World Politics', *Journal of Conflict Resolution*, 25, Dec., especially pp. 461-68. Concerned with the problem of distorted consumption, the government of Tanzania has the importation of automobiles for private use. See Woodhouse, 'Re-visioning the Future of the Third World', p.28. In February 1973, Tanzania began prohibitions against effectuation of certain Western dress habits, such as long hair for males and short skirts for females.

57. For a discussion of the negative cultural impact of American televison advertising in Latin America, see Jack N. Barkenbus (1973), 'Communication and Cultural Change: Experience in Latin America', paper presented to the meeting of the International Studies Association, New York, March.

58. Disenchantment among some non-Marxist economists with many of the liberal solutions to underdevelopment is discussed briefly in Cohen, *The*

Question of Imperialism, pp. 169, 218.

59. The net foreign exchange earnings brought by tourism vary greatly from country to country. But in many of the underdeveloped countries, the foreign owned tourist industry must bring in management, building supplies, and many operating items, including food and beverage. In these countries net foreign exchange earnings are usually from 45 per cent to 60 per cent of gross receipts.

60. 'Race Relations and Industrialization in the Caribbean', in Hunter (ed.), *Industrialization and Race Relations*, pp. 39-45.

61. Samuel P. Huntington (1970-71), 'Foreign Aid for What and for Whom?' *Foreign Policy*, 1, Winter, pp. 186-88.

62. Keith Griffin (1969), *Underdevelopment in Spanish America*, London: Allen and Unwin, p. 124.

63. Lawrence R. Alschuler (1973), 'Satellization and Stagnation in Latin America', paper presented at the European Consortium for Political Research, Mannheim, West Germany, April.

64. For example, John Burton (1968), *Systems, States, Diplomacy, and Rules*, London: Cambridge University Press; George Modelski (1972), *Principles of World Politics*, New York: Free Press.

3. Change in the International System: Interdependence, Integration, and Fragmentation

Observers of contemporary international relations have used a variety of terms to capture the essential characteristics of global interaction and politics. Many have emphasized detente, dependency, neocolonialism, or the development of multipolarity. Even Luard, in his comparative analysis of historical international systems, calls the 1914-1974 period an 'age of ideology', in contrast to most of the nineteenth century, which was an 'age of nationalism'.[1] But whatever the relations between the major powers, the distribution of power and influence in the international system, or the forces that motivate foreign policy, most would argue that *interdependence* is the most pervasive and fundamental result of rapidly growing *transaction* rates between societies. The development of closer and multidimensional contacts between societies thus constitutes one of the fundamental forms of system change in the twentieth century.

Few have argued that another prominent feature of our world is disintegration and international fragmentation. The dramatic growth of means of transportation, communication, and exchange of goods, money, and ideas has helped bring about an unprecedented 'interconnectedness'[2] between societies. It has thus been fashionable for commentators to claim that in these circumstances, the 'shrinking world' has superseded nationalism. Nationalism reached its zenith in nineteenth century Europe and in the anticolonial movements of this century; to most observers, it is now declining as an international phenomenon.[3]

This view is largely incorrect either as a description of current reality or as a prediction for the future. Analysts have been so impressed by growing interdependence that they have ignored a simultaneous or parallel process that results in increased international fragmentation. While transactions between societies have indeed grown dramatically throughout this century, nationalism, separatism, and international disintegration have also been prominent. Walker Connor may exaggerate when he claims that 'the centrifugal forces of national aspirations are growing more powerful than the centripetal forces of transnationalism'.[4] Yet, the two trends of integration and disintegration or fragmentation are taking place concurrently, and in some cases the latter is the consequence of, or reaction to, 'too much' interdependence or integration. Both represent different types of system change.

Nationalism can be defined both as attitudinal attributes of individuals - strong primary or exclusive loyalties to the ethnic group, nation, or to its legal embodiment, the state - and also as governmental policies that are designed to control, reduce, or eliminate a wide range of foreign influences and transnational processes on a society.[5] This essay uses the term in the latter sense. Such policies reflect a search for autonomy in a world of interdependence, amalgamation, and homogenization. A government that raises tariffs to protect a particular industry and its employees is not necessarily expressing either mass sentiments of national loyalty or a search for autonomy. Seeking greater economic benefits may be involved in nationalist behavior, but psychological benefits and threat/vulnerability reduction appear more significant. A government that simultaneously imposes barriers to foreign investment, censors incoming publications and films, expels foreign aid advisers, bars a wide range of imports, inculcates a distrust of foreigners, and places restrictions on the activities of foreign firms or diplomats likely does these to minimize or reduce threats it sees emanating from overly profuse links with the outside world. Deliberate and comprehensive reduction of transactions between any pair of states results in international fragmentation. In cases where two political units have achieved a high level of formal political or economic integration[6] and one subsequently attempts to establish increased autonomy, disintegration is the result. In both cases, the transaction 'distance' between societies has been increased, resulting, presumably, in a decline of interdependence or, in asymmetrical dyads, of dependence.

To my knowledge, no major approach to international relations theory has emphasized the prominence of nationalist behavior as an important characteristic of the contemporary international system. And only a few have examined the nature and sources of autonomy-seeking behavior at the foreign policy level.[7] The glitter and dazzle of growing interdependence have caused a degree of myopia in both academic speculation and diplomatic rhetoric. When we examine the popular contemporary portraits of the international system, it becomes easier to understand why nationalist phenomena have received so little attention. There is insufficient space to provide a full analysis of current characterizations of the international system; hence, the systems image will be reviewed only briefly, with more elaborate explorations of the literature on interdependence and integration.

The world as a system of transnational relations

Many authors have rejected the image of international politics as a game played by sovereign, impermeable states. They argue that the archaic conception of power politics does not take into account the fundamental consequences of modern technology, the close interconnection between domestic and foreign policy, and the permeability of societies to outside forces. To accommodate the new facts of international life, the world must be seen as a system of patterned interaction in which the main units of action are individuals and a variety of functional groups, as well as national and subnational government units. All these actors 'process' issues; somehow political and economic outcomes feed back and create new 'states' of the system. The world, then, looks like millions of spider webs superimposed on each other, with individual filaments symbolizing various types of transaction flows.[8] For a system to survive, adaptation to new technological, political, and economic trends is necessary. This view seems based on an assumption that as interactive processes grow and expand, as people increasingly interact across state frontiers, they will be more prone to adjust their differences rather than resort to lethal violence which might destroy the system. A further assumption holds that as technology increases the opportunities (some imply necessity, rather than opportunity) for interaction, people, groups, and states will want to take advantage of them and will seldom suffer losses from so doing. Interactions, transactions, networks, nodes - all of these terms apply to processes going on in a genuine international community.

The systems metaphor has the advantage of placing the state in a setting that is broader than the traditional one in which only diplomats, heads of state, and military forces interact. We are alerted to the importance of subnational foreign policies, to the influence of international organizations, and to the role of transnational groups that have an impact on states and societies. But except for studies on the economic and political impacts of MNCs on developing countries, little attention has been directed to the efforts of many governments to control, reduce, and sometimes even to eliminate the influence of transnational groups and processes on their societies and politics. While the growth of transnational organizations may appear inevitable, it is by no means inevitable that governments will merely 'adapt' to them. Some will perceive them as threats to a variety of national values and will deal with them accordingly, even at considerable economic cost. Attempts to enlarge autonomy, to reduce external penetration, and to control transnational organization may involve the construction of national 'moats'. To date, however, the systems image has promoted more research and writing on international interconnections than on the efforts to control or reduce them.

The world of interdependence

Interdependence, of course, is not an approach, framework for analysis, or metaphor distinct from those discussed above; indeed, the image of a global system, in which profuse transnational relations take place, implies a high degree of interconnectedness among a variety of units. If there is no connection, there is no system. Global interconnectedness has certain sources (technology, transportation, and communication), it can be measured by looking at transactions, and it leads to sensitivity and vulnerability, where conditions in country A become critically influenced by decisions, trends, and events in countries B...X. As Cooper defines it economically, 'interdependence, by joining national markets, erodes the effectiveness of [domestic] policies and hence threatens national autonomy in the determination and pursuit of economic objectives.'[9] Interconnectedness often, but not necessarily, creates interdependence. Much of the early literature on interdependence measured growth or fluctuations in transaction flows without exploring the problem of sensitivity and vulnerability, that is, interdependence. Confining their analyses primarily to statistics from industrial countries, the authors often assumed that growth in transaction flows had approximately equal consequences for all those engaged in the transactions.[10] Only recently have studies begun to explore the consequences of varying transaction flows on the international system and the foreign policies of countries. Among the more important consequences noted or hypothesized by some authors are the following:

1) Increased national sensitivity and vulnerability to decisions, trends, and events abroad - that is, increased interdependence - evolves.
2) More cooperative endeavors and common problem-solving occurs, which increases gains for all involved. No single nation can regulate any system characterized by rich transaction flows, and efforts to make decisions purely in terms of short-run national advantages - increasing national autonomy - will result in trade wars, currency instability, decline of investment, unemployment, and ultimately recession or depression.[11]
3) The latitude of choice of governments in fashioning domestic economic and welfare programs is reduced.[12]

4) Governments are growing incapable of effectively controlling transnational activities.
5) 'Complex interdependence' grows, tantamount to a new type of international politics. It is characterized by the importance of nonstate actors in setting the international agenda and determining bargaining and conflict outcomes, no permanent hierarchy of issues on the agenda, and the irrelevance of military power and threats in issue processing and bargaining outcomes.[13]
6) At the system level, status hierarchy declines as interdependence grows. The relatively weak tend to obtain more favorable outcomes and the major powers are less able to attain desired ends. They increasingly have to lead by example and persuasion rather than by dictation or coercion.[14]
7) As international communications develop and spread out, knowledge and information of others increases, which in turn augments mutual understanding and tolerance. Reduced levels of international conflict are a likely outcome of international exchange.

Most of these hypothesized consequences are undoubtedly correct in many contexts. But some need to be subjected to scrutiny and not accepted uncritically. For example, because it measures aggregate transaction flows, the literature implies that interconnectedness is a condition affecting equally all parties involved. Thus, we often hear that the *world* is increasingly interdependent, as if growing interconnectedness affected everyone in the same way. Once we begin looking at pairs of states rather than at regional or global trends, however, the realities of great differentials in vulnerability, dependency, influence, and coercive capacity become much more apparent. The world may indeed be more interdependent, but that fact has not radically altered the position of, for example, Czechoslovakia or Chile when they attempted to break away from the hegemony of the Soviet Union and the United States. If anything, the extensive interconnection between the client states and their mentors prevented the former from achieving policy-making autonomy and generated conflict, not mutual tolerance or empathy.

Statements such as 'the world is increasingly interdependent' are generally nonilluminating except in the banal sense that what people do today has greater impact on others abroad than was the case six centuries ago. Even if the comment contains some face validity, it can be applied with complete accuracy only to the relations between the industrial countries and possibly between them and members of the Organization of Petroleum Exporting Countries (OPEC). The fact is that important transaction flows are not growing at equal rates across different regions. The proportion of less developed countries' (LDCs') exports to total world exports, for example, continues to decline. Except for the OPEC countries, there is virtually no investment from the LDCs into the industrial countries, and only a limited amount from a few communist countries into the West. What Tanzania does economically has little or no impact on economic fortunes in Kenya, Uganda, or England. Except for contacts through international organizations, the relations between most Latin American and Southeast Asian countries are virtually nonexistent.

The argument that increased interdependence is likely to reduce international conflict is also open to serious question.[15] As diplomatic relations in Africa have grown more complex, the number of diplomatic quarrels appear to have increased. It would be well to recall also that the marked growth of European interconnectedness and interdependence throughout the nineteenth and twentieth centuries did not prevent the outbreak of the two most destructive wars in human history. To sum up: the fact of increasing interconnectedness is undoubtedly correct. Its consequences remain problematical, however. Increased transaction flows can lead to dependency, exploitation, conflict, and violence as well as to more collaboration and mutual knowledge. To find out the actual consequences of interconnectedness, one must examine pairs of states to avoid the ecological fallacy of arguing that a system property pervades the relationships in all dyads.[16] The *patterns and qualities* of transactions are more important than quantities and growth rates. Nationalist policies, secession, and international fragmentation and/or disintegration are likely to occur exactly in situations typified by asymmetrical patterns of sensitivity and vulnerability, unequal exchange, unidirectional flows, and attempts by the strong to penetrate the political, economic, and cultural life of the weak.

The world of integration

Few postwar diplomatic developments have excited as much intellectual enthusiasm as has the regional integration of Western Europe. Integration theorists have undertaken a massive cumulative effort to explain why formerly independent units come together to create supranational bodies. While the movement for European unification gave the impetus to the inquiry, most of the theories and models of integration have been developed with an eye to universal application. This body of literature has sought to identify necessary and sufficient conditions for integration, has developed techniques for measuring degrees of integration, and has speculated at great length on which variables explain what aspects of the integration process.

What types of independent variables are relevant? Virtually any condition between proximate societies has been mentioned. In some of Deutsch's work, transaction flows, mutual responsiveness, shared values, and the like are posited as necessary conditions for the creation of 'security communities'.[17] As in the interdependence literature, communication between societies is also essential. Yet in later work, Deutsch speaks of transaction flows as *indicators* of integration or political cohesion - that is, as dependent rather than independent variables.[18] The dependent variable - integration - has caused no less confusion. To some, public attitudinal support for supranational bodies is tantamount to successful integration. For others, supranational policymaking is the critical indicator. At the other end of the spectrum, a mere willingness to enter into transactions appears sufficient to indicate a high degree of community.[19]

Debates on methodological questions have prompted investigators to examine many of their assumptions, develop better techniques of measurement, and come to understand that a consensus on definitions of independent and dependent variables is unlikely to be achieved. Yet, many of the normative proclivities of authors have remained immune from scrutiny. While research on integration has generally followed many canons of scientific inquiry, there is little question that authors have been 'for' integration - hence the problem has been approached in a particular way, namely, locating the necessary and sufficient conditions for *successful* integration. Conditions militating *against* integration - particularly political opposition to integration - have received little attention.

Why the great concern - or hope - for political amalgamation? Most authors implicitly, and sometimes explicitly, assume that integration reduces international conflict. Hence, to study integration is to study the conditions of peace. Although this notion borders on a tautology, it is ultimately the search for peace that has justified the extensive intellectual endeavor. Deutsch's earliest formulations on integration were motivated by a desire to explore the fundamental problem of international politics and organization, 'the creation of conditions under which stable peaceful relations among nation states are possible and likely'.[20] According to the early Deutsch, 'if the entire world were integrated into a security community, wars would eventually be eliminated'.[21] To Amitai Etzioni, 'The most compelling appeal of regionalism is that the rise of regional communities may provide a stepping-stone on the way from a world of a hundred-odd states to a world of a stable and just peace. Such an achievement seems to require the establishment of a world political community'.[22] Although Etzioni approaches the subject of integration from a scientific perspective, his values are clearly revealed in his disappointment, for example, that the Scandinavians have not taken the final step into full political amalgamation. Integration, however defined, is thus the ultimate answer to the problem of war. Why should we assume that decreasing the number of sovereignties decreases the incidence of lethal violence?

The most obvious answer is that people who share a common identity and political loyalties do not quarrel as often or as lethally as those who are separated by language, ethnic, religious, and political frontiers. In the work of Deutsch and his colleagues, for example, transaction flows assume central importance as a foundation for successful integration. As people communicate, they become salient to each other. Mutually rewarding transactions help develop mutual trust, confidence, and similar perceptions of international problems. While Deutsch more recently has acknowledged that communication and interpersonal contacts can be 'negative',[23] most of the literature posits a causal relationship between increasing transactions, integration, and ultimately, less conflict. Integration theory rests squarely upon the old idea that the better people know each other the more they will like each other. This 'birds of a feather flock together' thesis is a critical normative dimension in much of the literature, one which is more often assumed than demonstrated.

Many authors have criticized early writings on integration for their air of inevitability and universality. In particular, they have pointed out that conditions in the developing countries today are so different from those in Europe during the 1950s and 1960s that the successful European Economic Community (EEC) experience can provide few clues to the possibilities of success in other geographic contexts. If one had to wait for the richness of transaction flows found in Europe, even prior to the Rome Treaty, to be duplicated in the LDCs, the chances of successful integration in the Third World would be virtually nil today. Transaction flows within most Third World regions have not yet even reached the levels found in Europe in the nineteenth century.

But it is more than a question of comparative transaction flows, or even the economic gains that can be achieved by the creation of large markets. Conditions in Europe after World War II were unique in ways other than those that can be easily quantified. To what extent were these conditions important in helping make the EEC a success? If the judgment is that they were important or critical, then we must ask whether or not their absence in other regional settings would preclude successful integration. First, on the eve of economic rationalization in Western Europe, the region had just emerged from the most destructive war in human history. One of the prime lessons of that experience was that the ancient Franco-German enmity must be resolved. One way to accomplish the task was to create institutions - the European Coal and Steel Community (ECSC) - that would lock the two economies into a system of mutual dependence. Second, a real pan-European movement, particularly appealing to the young, developed in part to underline Europe's separate identity from the United States. The emotional commitment to 'Europe' was an important part of the milieu in which plans for the Common Market were launched. Third, many accounts give considerable personal credit to Jean Monnet and Maurice Schuman for developing the blueprints for the ECSC and for their many years of lobbying to sell the conceptions to the various national capitals. Fourth, nationalism throughout Europe in the late 1940s and early 1950s was probably at its historical nadir - a condition that exists in few other regions today and one that has changed even in Europe in the past decade. Finally, part of the motivation for the Common Market was to decrease dependence upon the United States and to create economic institutions that could compete effectively with US enterprises and exports. To a certain extent, then, the Europeans accepted integration in order to disintegrate (or at least to create more equality) from a hegemon.

With the exception of the last condition - which has been a relevant consideration in the formation of economic groupings such as the Andean Pact - the others have not been duplicated elsewhere. This is not to argue that customs unions and common markets in Southeast Asia, Africa, and Latin America are doomed to failure, but we must be aware that success in Europe could not be predicted *solely* from the growth of pro-European public opinion or from broadening transaction flows. Much of the theoretical literature, in its attempts to operationalize variables that can be both measured and compared, by necessity overlooks unique historical circumstances, some of which may be critical. For example, the ephemeral phenomenon - leaders' political will - is crucial to integration. If there is no desire to amalgamate, then it does not matter how much mail, trade, tourism, telephone calls, student exchanges and compatibility of values flourish. The examples of Canada-United States, Australia-New Zealand and Scandinavia should make this clear.

Political or economic integration should not be expected to occur, moreover, where there is a basic asymmetry in the pattern of transactions and in expected economic gains between the parties. Asymmetrical 'interconnectedness' between two societies or groups is likely to lead the smaller and weaker to perceive threats to its national identity and possibly to cultural survival. There may be only a fine line between integration and absorption. The 1972 Norwegian vote against ratifying membership in the EEC was in part based on widespread fears that economic integration would lead to the destruction of traditional small farming and fishing sectors. Promises of future economic gains were insufficient to offset fears that certain life-styles would be destroyed through decisions taken by Europeans who have little or no knowledge of Norwegian traditions and social values. A significant portion of British opponents of EEC membership argued along the same lines. Yet, the literature has mostly ignored the phenomenon of opposition to integration.[24] If authors explored the issue, perhaps they would not so easily dismiss nationalism as some declining relic of previous centuries. By asking the fundamental question, 'Why, or under what conditions, does integration succeed?' commonalities are likely to be emphasized. Were researchers to approach the subject in terms of 'Why has there been no movement to integrate in areas characterized by rich transaction flows and cultural similarities?' or 'Why didn't integration fail in Europe?' they would focus on different phenomena, including the peculiar conjunction of circumstances that led many Europeans *not* to fear absorption.

Why didn't the opponents of integration prevail? Perhaps it is, as Caporaso has put it, 'because the new community system has ... made it possible for Europeans to enjoy the fruits of a large market and customs union while at the same time sacrificing neither cultural identity nor political autonomy'.[25] But in many other areas of the world, where transactions and other types of relationships are characterized by asymmetry, vulnerability, and conflict, amalgamation would be perceived as a threat to a variety of national values. In their longing for successful integration, and hence peace, many academics have easily slipped into the position of seeing Europe not as an exception to the course of history and the near-universal persistence of nationalism, but as a harbinger of the future and as a model for others to emulate.

Others have made the observation that processes leading to increased interdependence and fragmentation may occur simultaneously.[26] But is there a connection between the two processes? My argument is that in some cases, disintegration and fragmentation are *responses* to asymmetrical integration and to certain profiles of transactions in dependent and interdependent relationships. They are the reactions of those who see greater interconnectedness not in terms of greater opportunities or benefits, but rather as resulting in inequitable distribution of rewards or as posing threats to national, ethnic, language, or religious identity. In brief, the 'shrinking world' may result not in greater consensus and internationalism, but in heightened nationalism and drives to extend or protect autonomy.

Five general types of policies resulting in international disintegration or fragmentation can be outlined. Governments or groups claiming governmental status may:

1) Terminate practices of joint policy-making, problem-solving, or policy coordination; they may also withdraw from, or reduce participation in, institutions having supranational characteristics.
2) Construct mechanisms systematically to reduce or terminate the free flow of goods, people, funds, and ideas between two or more societies. Those fearing absorption or loss of autonomy attempt to reduce external penetration of their government, economy, and society by building walls to reduce access. In its extreme form, it can be termed isolationism.
3) Alter asymmetrical relationships by significantly diversifying external contacts, building regional coalitions, or entering into regional integration schemes as a way of escaping domination by a hegemon.
4) Organize, at the national level, a secessionist movement which seeks to secure or protect autonomy by establishing independent statehood.
5) Resist further integration but not seek to disintegrate or secede. This would be a marginal category.

Governments may pursue several of the policies simultaneously. Whether singly or in combination, the underlying objective is to create more distance between governments and societies and/or gain national control over transnational processes. In the brief outline of the nationalist behaviors in Canada and Burma in recent years, we will see that the results of greater transaction flows and increased interdependence (or dependency) were not those predicted in most of the literature. The inexorable forces of interdependence in these cases did not result in more integration, more mutual empathy and understanding, or less international conflict. If anything, the reverse was the case.

Canada-United States

No two separate societies in the world better fulfill the assumed necessary conditions to amalgamate politically than do those of

63

the United States and Canada. For most of this century these two countries have constituted a pluralistic security community, where no military forces have been arrayed against each other and where no government has contemplated the use of force to resolve bilateral conflicts. Using some of Deutsch's variables in which high rankings on indicators of social assimilation predict successful integration, Canada and the United States could have been expected to amalgamate long ago.

Proximity. Not only are Canada and the United States neighbors, but they have the longest unguarded frontier in the world. Moreover, approximately 90 per cent of Canada's population lives within 100 miles of the border, a distribution which is unique among the territorially large states of the world.

Social Homogeneity. With the exception of Quebec's six million French-speaking residents, and the Negro and Hispanic population in the United States, the composition of these two countries' populations are similar in terms of ethnic background (predominantly English, Scots, and Irish), language, social mobility, educational level, literacy, and political and social values.

Transactions. The transaction indicators clearly reveal that there are more transactions annually between these two societies than any others in the world. It is not possible to obtain separate figures on mail flows and telephone calls between the two countries because Canada and the United States already constitute a fully integrated communications network with the border having no practical impact on flows. In the early 1970s, Canadians and Americans annually made an average of 12 million visits to each other's country; no other pair of nations begins to approach such magnitudes of personal exchange. Seventy per cent of Canada's exports go to the United States, a figure which constitutes approximately 22 per cent of Canada's GNP, while the United States provides nearly that figure as a source of imports. While US trade with Canada constitutes a much lower percentage of its total trade, Canada is still the largest single foreign market and source of supplies for the United States.

Money flows freely across the border as well. Until the mid-1960s, Americans had invested more funds in Canada than in Latin America and Europe combined. Likewise, virtually all of Canadian foreign investment was directed to the United States. Until petrodollars began flowing into the United States, Canadians owned more of the US economy - although the percentage of total economic activity was miniscule - than did any other national group. In addition to these figures we could cite the fact that throughout the 1950s and 1960s Canadians watched more US- than Canadian-originating television programs, a large proportion of Canadian university graduates went to the United States for graduate studies, and there was almost unrestricted migration between the two countries.

Mutual Knowledge. Here asymmetry is the rule: Canadians know a great deal about the United States - indeed some Canadians know much more about US politics and history than they do about their own country. Americans, while on the whole perceiving Canadians with strong positive regard,[27] have little substantive knowledge of the country.

Previous Integrative Experience. Through enterprises such as agreements on trade in farm implements, the St. Lawrence Seaway, North American Air Defense (NORAD), the North American Automotive Product Trade Agreement - all of which contain integrated characteristics - both countries have gained appreciably. These schemes have applied criteria of economic and security rationality in order to maximize joint gains, and for the most part have succeeded. The Automotive Product Trade Agreement of 1965, for example, has made North America a single production and marketing zone. This has vastly increased Canadian production of cars, provided substantial employment and tax benefits for Canada, and slightly reduced price differentials of cars between the United States and Canada. The Defense Production Sharing Agreement has created free trade in arms bidding and manufacturing, thereby sustaining a Canadian defense industry which would not be viable if its market were confined to the small Canadian armed forces.[28] NORAD has created an early warning and antibomber defense system that would have cost much more and been less effective had each country proceeded on its own.

Integration of Policy-making Institutions. There are some nineteen permanent joint US-Canadian institutions. Most of them meet occasionally for discussions and consultation, but a few of them have some of the characteristics of supranational authority. Perhaps equally important is the vast network of transgovernmental relations, where elements of the two countries' bureaucracies deal directly with each other, far removed from central control. The manner in which government business was conducted between Ottawa and Washington almost suggested the irrelevance of the international border. In some policy areas, collaboration and coordination reached very high levels (e.g., between the US Federal Bureau of Investigation [FBI] and the Royal Canadian Mounted Police [RCMP], or between the defense establishments), if not total integration. While Canada and the United States would not score as high on Nye's integration indicators[29] as would the EEC members, by the mid-1960s the two countries indulged in considerable policy consultation and coordination. One could argue that if the trends of the 1950s and 1960s had been allowed to continue, a fully integrated continental economy would have emerged by the 1980s or 1990s and if the spillover hypothesis was correct, this would subsequently lead to political integration.

Such predictions were, of course, the problem. By the mid-1960s, many Canadians were becoming increasingly concerned that if natural market forces were allowed to continue between the two countries, Canada eventually would be *absorbed* by the United States. Although the scope and breadth of transactions between the two societies was unparalleled in the world, the flows were basically asymmetrical. Hence, many Canadians came to regard them as threatening to Canadian culture and identity, and ultimately to political autonomy. What a neutral observer (particularly a theorist of integration) might see as an extraordinarily rich relationship in terms of empathy, shared values and transactions, many Canadians came to see as overextensive US penetration into Canadian society.[30]

Whether or not one sympathizes with various manifestations of Canadian nationalism, it is not difficult to understand why a negative response to asymmetrical transaction structures would arise. For example, on the average during the 1960s, Americans owned or controlled 55 per cent of Canada's manufacturing capacity, constituting more than 20 per cent of Canada's GNP; over 90 per cent of unionized Canadians belonged to US labor organizations. With a majority of the Canadians living within the broadcast range of US television stations, most Canadians were watching US material most of the time. The Canadian entertainment industry, with its market only 10 per cent that of the United States, could not compete successfully. Although Canadian newspapers and magazines were locally owned, virtually all news of the outside world came via United Press International (UPI) and Associated Press (AP), or from *Time* magazine. Finally, in many Canadian universities, some departments were heavily staffed by Americans, and in more than one instance US department heads would hire fellow nationals without even looking for qualified Canadians.

Under these circumstances - as well as the Canadian view of the Vietnam War and domestic disturbances in the United States - Canadian nationalists were able to select from a wide menu of issues and argue that if trends in economics, communication, education and culture were allowed to continue, Canada would eventually lose what remained of its political autonomy. While public opinion polls of the period clearly showed a rising concern about the problem of US investment and influence in the country, at the leadership levels many prominent figures of all political

66

persuasions united to express demands for placing controls on the free flow of goods and investment between the two countries.

Between 1968 and 1973 the Canadian federal government - reacting to, rather than leading, public opinion - instituted a variety of measures to alter the pattern or structure of transactions and to halt certain integrative trends. This included a notable decline in the use of some of the many Canadian-US institutions for policy coordination. At the cultural level, the Canadian Radio and Television Commission imposed minimum Canadian content requirements on all broadcasting facilities; developed a set a regulations forcing advertisers to produce their commercials in Canada rather than importing them from the United States; and required Canadian broadcasting companies to divest themselves of US ownership to the 20 per cent level. The Canadian secretary of state's office placed considerable pressure on US-owned theater chains to show Canadian films. It also acted several times to prevent US firms from buying out Canadian publishers. After years of debate the Canadian federal government also set up a foreign investment review board with the task of assuring that foreign investment and takeover bids of existing Canadian companies would bring 'significant benefits' to Canada.

Starting in 1972 the government also reorganized its policymaking procedures with the United States. Its general philosophy was to create a more 'arm's length' approach, to accept higher levels of conflict with the United States, and to impose more central control over transgovernmental relations.[31] The days of the 'special relationship' and 'good partner' diplomacy came to an end. Moreover, the Canadian government politely turned down US proposals to establish more institutions for policy coordination and joint problem-solving. The political atmosphere in Ottawa and the country was such that any proposals smacking of 'continentalism' (the Canadian expression for arrangements containing integrationist characteristics) were quietly rejected. A detailed Economic Council of Canada study on trade between the two countries, which emphasized the economic gains accruing to the country from a free trade arrangement, never saw the light of public or parliamentary debate.

At the level of foreign policy, the Canadian government set out to diversify its diplomatic and trade contacts as a means of reducing Canada's vulnerability to US economic decisions, such as Nixon's import surcharge and dollar devaluation in August 1971. The major thrust of the program was to use the EEC and Japan as counterweights to the overwhelming trade reliance upon the United States.

Measures to reduce penetration and to reverse integrationist arrangements were not confined to the federal government level.

Many provincial governments passed legislation prohibiting the sale of crown lands to nonresidents and a few even considered banning sales of private property to foreigners. The Canadian trade union movement began systematically untying itself from US organizations: by the mid-1970s more than one-half of Canada's unionized labor belonged to independent Canadian unions; a decade earlier the figure had been only 30 per cent. The universities agreed upon regulations requiring all academic positions to be advertised in Canada, and a number of departments unofficially began to give preference to Canadian applicants.

Taken together, all these policies were designed, sector by sector, to monitor and control, or alter the profile of Canadian-US transactions, to build up local institutions more effectively to compete with Americans, and to erect filters or screens on some forms of US penetration such as private investment. Programs were also designed to create more distance in diplomacy, to turn the border into a reality as far as cultural relations were concerned, and in a few cases to abandon or modify certain Canadian-US arrangements and institutions that contained integrated characteristics. The policies represent a combination of types 1, 2, 3, and 5 listed earlier. The Canadian example - which lasted well into the 1980s - shows clearly the linkage between increased transaction flows, interdependence (or dependence), and the rise of nationalism.

Burma

Burma is an example of an even more extreme reaction to foreign penetration and asymmetrical interdependence. From 1963 to 1966, the Burmese government constructed an extensive set of mechanisms to reduce foreign penetration and to establish a greater degree of policy-making autonomy.[32]

The U Nu government, from 1948 until its overthrow in 1962 by the military, generally opened up the country to a number of foreign influences and adopted the typical strategy of development through foreign tutelage, learning from others, seeking foreign investment and aid, and importing modern technology.

The military regime under General Ne Win adopted exactly the opposite approach: total autarky and isolation, with development achieved through self-reliance. Burma is an extreme case, of course, but it does illustrate how the typical postcolonial pattern of contacts between industrial and developing countries can lead to a fear of being overly penetrated and ultimately losing all cultural and political autonomy.

The Ne Win government systematically began expelling foreigners in 1963: missionaries, foreign professors teaching at the University of Rangoon; all foreign researchers, from agricultural specialists to anthropologists; and medical personnel. Cultural exchange programs such as Fulbright, Ford Foundation, and British Council were terminated, aid programs were not renewed, and foreign travelers were provided with only twenty-four hour visas, thus ending tourism. The government imposed strict censorship on foreign books, films and magazines - not so much to control political thought as to prevent the 'pollution' of Burmese culture from 'degenerate' foreign materials. Foreign advisors, who in the U Nu days had been operating at all levels of society from small villages throughout the bureaucracy to assisting cabinet ministers, had all departed by 1964. The country had become effectively sealed off from foreign penetration within two years after the coup.

In its foreign policies, the Ne Win government also shunned external contacts. It scrupulously avoided any involvement in Southeast Asian regional economic and technical undertakings. Its delegates, once active in United Nations affairs, were prominent primarily by their absence or by the number of times they abstained from voting. Once a leader of the nonaligned movement, by the 1960s and 1970s Burma attended only in a perfunctory capacity. And in the Geneva disarmament committee, the Burmese delegate - supposedly a representative of the nonaligned states - stopped attending.

Ne Win's attempt to turn Burma into a hermit nation was motivated in part by security considerations - relations with China and the problem of domestic rebellions - but also by the judgment that Burma would eventually lose its autonomy if it continued the U Nu strategy of development through foreign tutelage. Important sectors of the Burmese elites wanted to end a situation that they defined as one of foreign penetration and domination, where the country was in effect run by outsiders who know little about Burmese history and culture. Interdependence, if that meant slavishly copying foreigners and indiscriminately adopting their cultural habits, was, in the government's view, a condition that could only lead to the destruction of all that was good, pure, and moral in the Burmese culture. Modern communications, transportation and publications because they were primarily running in one direction - into Burma, but not from Burma abroad - would eventually turn the Burmese into second-rate carbon copies of Westerners - just as Burmese civil servants had become under British colonial rule. In Ne Win's judgment, Burma could not achieve true independence if Burmese politicians and civil servants took their political (cold war) cues, their consumption habits, their cultural values, and their life aspirations from others. Interdependence (or as the Burmese would define it, overdependence) thus led to an extreme, almost xenophobic response. Isolationism seeks not just to create greater 'arm's length' from a former or actual hegemon, but to reduce *all* contacts with the outside world to a bare minimum.

Many have argued that isolationism is no longer feasible in today's interdependent world. Indeed, if growth in national wealth is the criterion of national success or failure, isolationism in most cases - including Burma - leads to economic decay. But as theorists of interdependence and integration seldom acknowledge, economics is not everything. Other values - in the Burmese case, national pride and fear of loss of autonomy - are also relevant. Economic gains may be forsaken in order to maximize other values.

Some may object that the Burmese case is so atypical that it hardly constitutes evidence for the assertion that processes of fragmentation resulting from 'too much' interdependence and/or integration constitute an important trend in the *system*. How much of any phenomenon is required in order to establish a trend is of course an arbitrary matter. With the exception of the EEC there has not been much successful economic integration in other regions of the world, and virtually no political amalgamation anywhere. Yet, if measured by trade, investment, and communications, interconnectedness has dramatically increased since World War II.

On a highly judgmental basis - since there are no reliable data - we can list those countries which in the past decade or so have built significant walls around them to reduce foreign penetration, have taken steps to undo integrationist programs or institutions, or in the marginal case, have resisted attempts to create more integrated mechanisms. The list would include Albania, Bhutan, Burma, Canada, Chile (1971-73), Cambodia, Iran, Iraq, Norway, Peru, Tanzania, some Council for Mutual Economic Assistance (COMECON) members, and perhaps others. In each of these cases, governments sought by various means to fundamentally alter the interdependent - or dependent - relationships they had become enmeshed in during the 1950s and 1960s.

Secessionist movements and international fragmentation

International fragmentation may result also from the myriad of contemporary secessionist movements. There are no collected longitudinal data on the incidence of secessionist movements during this century, so it is not possible to determine whether or not there are trends. Nevertheless, ethnically based nationalism is highly visible today and is not confined to the developing nations. Table 3.1, which is not exhaustive, illustrates the pervasiveness of nationalism at the substate level, and suggests that desire for group independence persists strongly in our age of interdependence.

Table 3.1
Active Secessionist Movements, 1973-1980

Movement	Location
Movements employing violence on a significant scale:	
Basques	(Spain)
Canary Islands	(Spain)
Corsica	(France)
Eritrea	(Ethiopia)
Kachins	(Burma)
Kurds	(Iraq, Iran)
Muslims	(Philippines)
Nagas	(India)
Ogaden Somalis	(Ethiopia)
Polisario	(Morocco, Mauritania)
Shaba	(Congo)
Shans	(Burma)
South Moluccans	(Indonesia)
Ustashi	(Yugoslavia)
Active, non-violent secessionist movements:	
Azores and Madeira	(Portugal)
Bretons	(France)
Catalonia	(Spain)
Karens	(Burma)
Nepalese	(Bhutan)
Pushtoos	(Pakistan)
Quebec	(Canada)
Scottish National Party	(United Kingdom)
Transylvania Magyars	(Romania)

If increased interdependence is supposed to create bonds of community between peoples and societies, why does the search

71

for autonomy and separateness continue at the national and international levels? Several hypotheses might be advanced.[33]

The necessary condition for most secessionist movements is the existence of more than one ethnic language or religious community occupying the same state territory. This condition exists in a majority of the world's states. Connor writes that of 132 states (in the late 1960s), only 12, or 9 per cent, can be described as basically homogeneous in ethnic makeup. In 32 states, the largest single ethnic group does not comprise even 50 per cent of the population, and in 53 states, the population is divided into more than five significant groups.[34] In such nations increased communications between ethnic, language, or religious groups may underline uniqueness, cause greater group solidarity, promote stereotypic thinking, and ultimately increase intergroup cleavages. Connor[35] has argued that the optimistic predictions about the results of increasing social communication are taken from the US or European nineteenth-century experience and are not borne out in other milieus. In many developing countries, the first extensive contacts between minority groups and central government authorities or the dominant cultural communities lead to conflict, not assimilation. Leaders of many secessionist movements are not those who have remained isolated; on the contrary, most have had considerable experience with the majority population and central government agents.[36] They have rejected offers to assimilate and even to share political power, and chosen the path of armed struggle for independence. Increased communication has fostered separatism, not integration. Contrary to much popular thinking on interdependence and political development, we might hypothesize that the faster the rate of growth of communication between distinct social groups or societies, the greater the probability that autonomy-preserving or -seeking behavior will result.[37]

A second avenue for exploration would focus on the *profile of social transactions* between groups or states. Our examples suggest that where transactions are highly asymmetrical and contacts between societies involve unidirectional penetration, perceptions of nonmilitary threats (e.g., threats to autonomy, continued independence, cultural survival, religious purity, and the like) are likely to arise, resulting in demands for controlling international transactions and instituting policies to establish greater 'distance' between groups within a state, or between states. When some see their community or society has become highly penetrated by outsiders - even by good friends - common knowledge, broad communication, and empathy are not likely to prevent demands for protecting or reestablishing autonomy. The Quebec independence movement grew apace as French-speaking Canadians were required to speak English in English-Canadian firms, as the flow of non-French-speaking European immigrants into the province continued to rise, and as the birth rate of French-Canadians continued to decline. The nationalists drew the obvious conclusions from these trends: if allowed to continue, French language and culture in North America would no longer exist after several generations. Few in Quebec could ignore these facts, even if they were bilingual, felt national loyalty to Canada, conducted extensive transactions with English-Canadians and 'understood' them. Quebecois have argued that the flow of transactions and communications, increasing throughout the 1960s, was predominantly in one direction: from English-Canada into Quebec. While Anglophone Canadians were worrying about the US 'threat', Quebecois were worrying, not about Yankees, but about Anglophone Canadians. The parallel in each language group's concern with autonomy and cultural preservation is striking.

If we combine the variables of communication growth rates and degrees of transaction asymmetry, the probabilities of autonomy-seeking behavior as an outcome might appear more like an inverted U than linear. Robert Keohane has suggested that as very high levels of communication increase, combined with great asymmetry in transaction flows, autonomy is extremely difficult to achieve. The small state or nationalist group in all probability has been successfully absorbed or thoroughly dominated by the hegemon. He points out, for example, that anticolonial movements were much more vigorous in Indo-China than among the small weak states of Francophone Africa. Similarly, nationalist policies in Argentina, Chile, Brazil and Mexico are significantly more prominent than in Costa Rica, Guatemala and Honduras, where asymmetrical ties and fast-growing communications with the United States are particularly pronounced.[38]

A third line of explanation would emphasize hardheaded economic calculations: disintegrative and secessionist movements are likely to arise when certain groups perceive that they are not receiving an adequate and/or fair share of economic gains, resulting from interdependence, or are paying an inequitable share of government or supranational burdens. The East African Community dissolved in 1977 over disagreements on both costs and rewards.[39] Small secessionist movements in Western Canada argue that Alberta and British Columbia pay taxes to the federal government way out of proportion to the services they receive from Ottawa.[40] Finally, Chile withdrew from the Andean Pact after 1974 because the Pinochet regime did not want to apply the restrictions on foreign investment called for in the treaty.

Fourth, demands for disintegration or secession may arise

where loss of decisionmaking autonomy has become intolerable. Interdependence and integration exact a high cost in freedom of choice. The reasons for collaborative undertakings and integration are no doubt compelling - particularly maximizing joint gains - but frequently some are going to believe that supranational policy-making bodies do not take into account sufficiently the unique needs of certain partners. The Canadian attempt to return to a more classical diplomatic relationship with the United States was in part formulated on the grounds that use of joint institutions locked Canada into agendas set in the United States and induced a presumption of collaborative behavior that mitigated against the vigorous pursuit of Canadian national objectives.

Finally, the doctrine of self-determination, a genuine transnational ideology or value, has become one of the most important sources of political legitimacy, the most potent propaganda symbol used to raise the consciousness (and conscience) of both nationals and foreign audiences. A national liberation movement, no matter how authoritarian its leadership and bloody its tactics, can obtain significant international attention, sympathy, and occasionally material support by portraying itself as fighting a colonial regime or seeking to obtain independence for a distinct ethnic, language or religious group. In the early twentieth century, the notion of self-determination was closely linked to democratic principles. Its application to the defeated powers after World War I was based on the assumption that the new states would adopt reasonably pluralist political institutions. Today, in contrast, a national liberation movement does not have to establish democratic credentials in order to claim legitimacy. Merely to speak in the name of a minority is usually sufficient. Thus, as long as there are states whose boundaries do not coincide with ethnic divisions, we can expect to see the continued development of secessionist movements, invoking the doctrine of self-determination to justify their struggles.

Consequences

If we acknowledge that nationalism continues to be a potent force in national and international politics, and that increased interdependence may foster nationalism and instability as well as integration and harmony, what consequences can we expect in terms of the structure and processes of the international system? At first glance, the prevalence of secessionist movements might suggest that the number of sovereign units in the system will continue growing, with perhaps as many as 200 members in the United Nations by the end of the century. If such were to be the

74

case, the system would be numerically one of the largest since the early spring and autumn period during the Chou dynasty in China of the eighth century B.C. Many of the microstates would be highly dependent upon outsiders for economic and defense support, but they would still possess voting power in international organizations. Since many of the new states would come from the developing areas, we would expect them to lend additional weight to the LDCs on north-south issues. The industrial countries would thereby become an even smaller minority in global organizations, maintaining influence primarily by the size of their financial contributions rather than by their numbers. We could predict as well that if the number of violent secessionist movements continues to grow, new arenas of international conflict would appear, as the major powers would likely involve themselves either to promote the forces of national liberation or to protect the territorial integrity of the mother nation - as the Soviets and the French have done in Ethiopia and the Congo.

Numerous predictions about the consequences of increasing the size of the international system by about 25 per cent over the next decades could be made, but for such an exercise to be worthwhile there must be a reasonable probability that the predicted trend will in fact occur. Despite the universal popularity of the self-determination principle and the widespread sympathy secessionist movements manage to generate abroad, experience of the past suggests that many of the movements will not succeed in obtaining full independence. Whatever their sympathies, most governments have opted for the principle of territorial integrity over minority independence when confronted with the choice.[41] The ethnic rebellions in Burma have been continuing for almost three decades, with little probability of ultimate success, and with little outside support. In Biafra, the Congo, the Ogaden, and elsewhere, most foreign governments have ended up on the side of the central authorities in their contests with secessionist movements.[42] In the United Nations, members have voted consistently to emphasize that the principle of self-determination applies to territories and not to peoples. For example, during the fifteenth session of the General Assembly the members strongly supported a resolution that stated: 'Any attempt at the partial or total disruption of the national unity and territorial integrity of a country is incompatible with the purposes and principles of the United Nations Charter'.[43]

Secessionist movements in the industrial countries seem to have few possibilities for obtaining full independence. Both local arrangements involving greater autonomy and protection of ethnic, language or religious traditions and/or repression seem more likely outcomes. In brief, the probabilities of a significant increase - say 25 per cent - in the number of new states are quite low. This is not to say that the number of secessionist movements is likely to decline, however. If increased communication in multiethnic societies results in greater conflict, as often seems to be the case, we could expect continued fragmentation, particularly in the developing countries where many central governments are only beginning to foment 'crises of penetration' as they seek to establish jurisdiction and economic programs in the hinterlands. Domestic instability and occasional insurrection remain distinct possibilities, but dramatic increases in the rate of international fragmentation appear unlikely.

The incidence of international disintegration or more 'moat-building' foreign policies in the future remain problematic. Weak and vulnerable societies involved in highly asymmetrical relationships no doubt find strategies of self-sufficiency and autarky politically, if not economically, appealing, if only to break down dependency and to reduce foreign penetration of their institutions. On the other hand, development strategies such as those pursued by Saudi Arabia and the Shah's Iran, where extensive foreign investment and penetration are accepted, may have greater appeal because of the visible and rapid economic results. The lack of research on isolationist and autarkic impulses makes it difficult to predict which types of societies, under which sorts of domestic and international conditions, will attempt to disengage themselves by turning inward.

Conclusion

This excursion into the international ramifications of modern nationalism has been undertaken in an attempt to compensate for some of the distortions found in contemporary conceptions of the international system, as well as in much current diplomatic rhetoric. Themes such as a 'shrinking world', 'growing interdependence', 'regionalism', or 'international system' often imply inevitable processes leading to desirable outcomes, affecting all equally. While there are undoubted benefits accruing to human societies from their greater interconnectedness, there are costs that must be considered as well. Concerned about the impact that US military presence in Iceland has had on the local culture, Sigurdur Magnusson has written:

Nationalism is not the most highly regarded sentiment in this age which has been accustomed at least to think that international cooperation and understanding are worthy ends. But there are various kinds of nationalism, and for tiny nations like Iceland nationalism is in reality a pre-condition for the

76

continuous growth of native culture and the preservation of political independence.[44]

Weak, vulnerable societies and communities are not likely to favor schemes of economic or political integration if they predict that their implementation will lead to extensive foreign penetration, inequitable distribution of costs and rewards, and submerging of local life-styles. To argue abstractly that integration increases the possibilities of peace is not likely to make much impact on those who see their language, religion, customs or occupations threatened by foreign penetration.

The statistics demonstrating increased transaction flows throughout most of the world cannot be denied. But as this essay has sought to underline, this growth can have numerous consequences, not all of which contribute to international peace and stability or integration. An accumulating body of evidence suggests that in many instances as interconnectedness increases, so does nationalism (in the sense of more 'moat-building'), and interethnic and international conflict. If our conceptions of the international system are to be reasonably consistent with realities, we must not confuse the European with a universal experience, assume that the consequences of increased communications are always positive, or argue that processes that are developing primarily among the industrial states extend to other areas of the world as well. This is not to argue that the manifestations of nationalism outlined previously lead to desirable consequences either. Ultimately the costs and gains of integration or fragmentation can only be assessed according to one's value preferences.

Taking a long-range historical perspective, we are seeing the playing out of European-oriented nationalism to its logical conclusion. Our international system has grown from 23 members in the Napoleonic period to more than 160 today. The increase in numbers has occurred in fits and starts (the addition of the Latin American republics during the early nineteenth century was as much a quantum leap in the size of the international system of the time as was the addition of more than 30 African states in the 1950s and 1960s), but the trend line is clear. And the forces which helped create the new nation-states of the nineteenth century are basically similar to those that still operate today: the drive to establish the state on the basis of a distinct ethnic, language or religious group.

What is least unexpected is the continuation or resurgence of nationalism in areas where considerable integration (defined as the existence of a 'security community', vast transaction flows, or institutionalization of bilateral diplomatic and technical relationships) has already occurred. North America, Scandinavia,

Australia-New Zealand, Eastern Europe and perhaps Latin America do not represent change as much as they are living demonstrations that growing transaction flows and mutual empathy do not result inevitably in integration. The balance between the search for continued autonomy and efforts to create supranational institutions clearly lies on the side of the former.

Notes

*   I am grateful for the many useful comments and suggestions offered by Peter Busch, David Haglund, Ole Holsti, Roff Johannson, Robert Keohane, Saadia Touval, and John Wood.

1. Evan Luard (1976), *Types of International Society*, New York: Free Press.
2. Alex Inkeles uses the term to signify transactions and interactions between societies in (1975), 'The Emerging Social Structure of the World', *World Politics*, 27, July, pp. 467-495.
3. Walker Connor (1967), 'Self-Determination: The New Phase', *World Politics*, 20, October, p. 45; Zbigniew Brzezinski (1970), *Between Two Ages*, New York: Viking Press, esp. p.275. A notable exception to this view is Robert O. Keohane and Joseph S. Nye Jr. (1977), *Power and Interdependence: World Politics in Transition*, Boston: Little, Brown and Co., esp. p. 4.
4. Connor, 'Self-Determination: The New Phase', p. 46.
5. Nationalism translated into foreign policy has also been viewed as involving aggressive behavior, embodied in imperialism or efforts to expand territorially. This essay does not use the term in this sense.
6. There are numerous definitions of integration and the phenomenon has been measured in many different ways. For a review of the various conceptualizations, see Joseph S. Nye Jr. (1971), *Peace in Parts: Integration and Conflict in Regional Organizations*, Boston: Little, Brown and Co., chap. 2.
7. Richard Cooper (1972), 'Economic Interdependence and Foreign Policy in the Seventies', *World Politics*, 24, January, pp.159-81.; Connor, 'Self-Determination: The New Phase', Arnfinn Jorgensen-Dahl (1975), 'Forces of Fragmentation in the International System: The Case of Ethno-nationalism', *Orbis*, 19, Summer, pp. 652-74; and the argument that interdependence is now giving way to a new mercantilism, Gregory Schmid (1975-76), 'Interdependence has its Limits', *Foreign Policy*, 21, Winter, pp. 188-97.
8. John Burton uses the metaphor in his (1968), *Systems, States, Diplomacy and Rules*, Cambridge: Cambridge University Press, p. 8.
9. Cooper, 'Economic Interdependence', p. 164.
10. K.J. Holsti (1987), 'A New International Politics? Diplomacy in Complex Interdependence', *International Organization*, 32, Spring, p. 517.
11. Cooper, 'Economic Interdependence'. He acknowledges that some small states can flout the system and get away with it. Examples include countries granting flags of convenience and tax havens.

12. Edward L. Morse (1972), 'Crisis Diplomacy, Interdependence, and the Politics of International Economic Relations', in Raymond Tanter and Richard H. Ullman (eds), *Theory and Policy in International Relations*, Princeton: Princeton University Press, pp. 123-50.
13. Robert O. Keohane and Joseph S. Nye Jr. (1977), *Power and Interdependence*, Boston: Little, Brown and Co., chap. 2.
14. *Ibid.*, esp. chap. 8.
15. Morse, 'Crisis Diplomacy'. He predicts increased incidence of crises and conflict resulting from interdependence. Other newer writings on interdependence also acknowledge that interdependence and conflict do not necessarily vary in the same direction. See Keohane and Nye, *Power and Interdependence*, chap. 5, pp. 8-11.
16. Holsti, 'A New International Politics?', p. 520.
17. Karl W. Deutsch et al. (1957), *Political Community and the North Atlantic Area: International Organization in the Light of Historical Experience*, Princeton: Princeton University Press, esp. pp. 70-78.
18. Karl W. Deutsch (1964), 'Transaction Flows as Indicators of Political Cohesion', in Philip E. Jacob and James V. Toscano, eds., *The Integration of Political Communities*, Philadelphia: J. B. Lippincott Co., chap. 3.
19. For example, Roger W. Cobb and Charles Elder (1970), *International Community: A Regional and Global Study*, New York: Holt, Rinehart and Winston.
20. Deutsch et al., *Political Community and the North Atlantic Area*, p. 5.
21. Seventeen years later, however, Deutsch wrote: 'This notion that groups that do not integrate must destroy each other is a widespread but false belief. Luckily it is not true', 'Between Sovereignty and Integration: Conclusion', in Ghita Ionescu (ed.) (1974), *Between Sovereignty and Integration*, London: Croom Helm, p. 181.
22. Amitai Etzioni (1965), *Political Unification*, New York: Holt, Rinehart and Winston, p. x. Ernst B. Haas stated forcefully that the search for peace justified the intellectual pursuit in (1970), 'The Study of Regional Integration', *International Organization*, 24, Autumn, pp. 608-09.
23. Deutsch, 'Communication Theory and Political Integration', in *The Integration of Political Communities*, p. 67.
24. The importance of preserving autonomy while accepting regional policy coordination and some economic free trade arrangements in Scandinavia is discussed in Toivo Miljan (1977), *The Reluctant Europeans: The Attitudes of the Nordic Countries Toward European Integration*, Montreal: McGill-Queen's University Press. This is one of the few studies that seriously examines opposition to integration.
25. James Caporaso (1971), 'Theory and Method in the Study of International Integration', *International Organization*, 25, Spring, p. 231.
26. See Geoffrey Goodwin 'The Erosion of External Sovereignty', in Ionescu (ed.) (1974), *Between Sovereignty and Integration*. Robert Gilpin has discussed the causal relationship between increased integration and the rise of economic nationalism in the smaller party in (1974), 'Integration and Disintegration in the North American Continent', *International Organization*, 28, Autumn, pp. 851-74. Anti-integrationist tendencies are acknowledged in Ernst B. Haas (1976), 'Turbulent Fields and the Theory of Regional Integration', *International Organization*, 30, Summer, pp. 185,

195-96.

27. See John H. Sigler and Dennis Goresky (1974), 'Public Opinion on United States-Canadian Relations' in Annette B. Fox, Alfred O. Hero, and Joseph S. Nye Jr. (eds), *Canada and the United States: Transnational and Transgovernmental Relations*, New York: Columbia University Press, pp. 45-7.

28. For a discussion of the economic gains accruing to Canada from the automotive and defense arrangements, see Canada, Standing Senate Committee on Foreign Affairs (1978), *Canada-United States Relations, Vol. II: Canada's Trade with the United States*, Ottawa: Queen's Printer, pp. 89-107. More recent academic evaluations have suggested net trade losses for Canada, however.

29. Nye, *Peace in Parts*, chaps 2, 3.

30. The increase of Canadians perceptions if threat emanating from US presence - particularly economic - in Canada is clearly revealed in public opinion polls. For example, in 1964, 46 per cent of the respondents believed there was enough US investment in the country. In 1978, the figure had risen to 69 per cent. See *Vancouver Sun*, 12 August 1978, p. D-1. Responding to the question, 'Do you think the Canadian way of life is, or is not being too much influenced by the United States?' 39 per cent replied in the affirmative in 1961, and 53 per cent in 1966. See Sigler and Goresky, 'Public Opinion', pp. 64-5.

31. The most comprehensive treatment of Canadian policy formulation to alter the pattern of Canadian-US relations is by John Kirton (1977),'*The Conduct and Co-Ordination of Canadian Government Decisionmaking Towards the United States*', Ph.D diss., Johns Hopkins University.

32. A detailed description of Burma's isolationist strategy and at attempt to explain the reasons it was chosen is in K.J. Holsti (1982), *Why Nations Realign: Foreign Policy Re-structuring in the Postwar World*, London: Allen and Unwin, chap. 7.

33. A thorough discussion of the preconditions and necessary conditions for the rise of secessionist movements is in John R. Wood (1978), 'Toward a Theory of Secession', paper presented to the American Political Science Association meeting, New York, September. Only a few of the conditions that are relevant both to secession and international disintegration are discussed here. Multiethnicity is an important source of disintegration only at the national level.

34. Walker Connor (1972), 'Nation-building or Nation-destroying', *World Politics*, 24, April, pp. 320-21.

35. *Ibid.*, pp. 346-48.

36. Jorgensen-Dahl, 'Forces of Fragmentation', p. 664.

37. In a statistical study of secessionist movements, Church and his colleagues demonstrate a positive relationship between the degrees of social mobilization and separatism. Social mobilization, of course, involves a notable increase in communication flows. Roderick Church et al. (1978), 'Ethnoregional Minorities and Separatism: A Cross-National Analysis', mimeo, pp. 20-1.

38. Correspondence with the author, 27 November 1978.

39. See Nye, *Peace in Parts*, p. 33.

40. The Quebec government has used data to demonstrate that the province has

done poorly in terms of taxes and government benefits under confederation. This argument rationalizes separation and is not a cause for it.

41. Various considerations underlying external powers' generally conservative stance regarding support for secessionist movements are discussed in Wood, 'Toward a Theory of Secession', pp. 26-7.
42. The successful breakaway of East Pakistan, with Indian assistance, is the significant exception to the generalization.
43. Cited in Jorgensen-Dahl, 'Forces of Fragmentation', p. 669.
44. Sigurdur A. Magnusson (1978), 'Iceland and the American Presence', *Queen's Quarterly*, 85, Spring, p. 83.

4. Restructuring Foreign Policy: A Neglected Phenomenon in Foreign Policy Theory

Between 1963 and 1965 the government of Burma undertook a series of domestic measures and foreign policy decisions which fundamentally altered its orientation toward the outside world. Except for maintaining essential trade and participating in several minor foreign aid projects, the Burmese government drastically reduced its external contacts and imposed a variety of measures which were designed to end external penetration into Burmese society, economics and politics. Foreign aid officials, missionaries, foreign academics and researchers, correspondents and tourists were expelled from the country. Foreign-owned enterprises were nationalized and the government established strict censorship over incoming mail, films and magazines. The Burmese government shunned all invitations to join various regional economic and functional undertakings, vetoed a proposal to build the India-Singapore highway through its territory, became inactive in international organizations and, with a few minor exceptions, took little part in the meetings and diplomacy of the non-aligned states. These actions constituted a radical departure from Burma's traditional foreign policy undertakings which had been actively involved in the non-aligned movement in the United Nations, and in various programs of regional cooperation.

Burma is only one of many interesting cases of a government undertaking to reorient its foreign policy. This essay examines this important foreign policy phenomenon, a type of political behavior that has been largely neglected in international relations theory, and only recently alluded to in analyses of Third World states' foreign policies.

We are concerned with a type of foreign policy behavior where governments seek to change, usually simultaneously, the *total* pattern of their external relations. The changes usually occur both in the pattern of partnerships (for example, Cuba's trade shifts from the United States to the Communist bloc in the early 1960s) and in the type of activity (for example, a country withdraws from an international organization). The sectors, in brief, may be either geographic or functional. The countries have sought to create essentially different or new patterns of relations in both sectors.

83

Where the intent (reorientation) has been followed by alteration of the total pattern of external actions and transactions, we can say that a country has successfully restructured its foreign policy. We thus distinguish normal foreign policy change, which is usually slow, incremental and typified by low linkages between sectors (for example, a change in foreign aid policy would not be reflected in foreign trade policies), and foreign policy restructuring, which usually takes place more quickly, expresses an intent for fundamental change, is non-incremental and usually involves the conscious linking of different sectors.

The method, while not free of data problems, is basically simple. It describes each nation's pattern of foreign relations at t^1 and the actions taken to establish new patterns. A second 'photograph', at t^2 indicates the degree of change. The more difficult task is to explain why, given the considerable costs often involved, governments undertake to restructure their foreign relations. This is a particularly important question for developing countries, because in today's world it is primarily these countries that display the most dissatisfaction with the structures and patterns of relationships that they inherited after World War II and the early post-colonial experience.

Foreign policy reorientation is certainly no new phenomenon in international politics. Balance of power theory requires governments to align themselves militarily only so long as a particular distribution of capabilities exists. If that distribution is threatened, governments must be willing to establish new commitments. Military threats were historically the common condition underlying such alterations. The famous 'renversement d'alliance' of 1756 ensued from a variety of incompatible interests - and Kaunitz' wiles - but at the core of the diplomatic revolution was Austria's earlier loss of Silesia to Prussia and its elaborate plan of retribution against King Frederick. One hundred sixty years later the United States abandoned its policy of non-involvement in European quarrels and joined the Entente against Germany. The subsequent decision not to join the League of Nations - the return to 'normalcy' - demonstrated that American isolationism had been abandoned primarily because of a military emergency. Perhaps the most dramatic recent historical example of foreign policy restructuring occurred in 1939, when the Soviet Union abandoned its anti-Nazi foreign policy in order to sign the Non-Aggression Treaty with Hitler's regime. Prior to that agreement, the Soviet Union had played a reluctant, though not destructive, role in the League of Nations, collaborated with France in guaranteeing Czechoslovakia's independence, generally eschewed revolutionary policies abroad, and identified Nazi Germany as the main threat to the Soviet Union's security and to world peace. Though Russia's trade was small, its destinations were diverse.

After August 1939, the Soviet Union completely reversed its previous patterns of activity. Attacks on the Baltic States and Finland (sanctioned in the secret protocols of the Non-Aggression Pact) led to the Soviet Union's expulsion from the League of Nations; Soviet trade was drastically redirected toward Germany, and propaganda tirades became directed predominantly against the Western democracies. Within a matter of weeks, the Soviet Union had altered the role of champion of anti-Nazism and international peace to one of military aggressor and accomplice in Germany's grand design to carve up Europe.

The reasons for this dramatic change are not difficult to pinpoint. Basically, Stalin's disillusionment over British and French appeasement, the Western democracies' vacillation over a proposed alliance with the Soviet Union, and Poland's stiff refusal to allow Soviet troops to transit its territory in case war broke out over Czechoslovakia, led the dictator to conclude that Russia's security interests could best be assured by buying time with the main threat, which was Nazi Germany. In brief, security consideration dictated foreign policy restructuring.

The examples of post-World War II foreign policy restructuring are more difficult to analyse. While military and strategic concerns are underlying factors in some, most have resulted from, or have been responses to, more complex domestic and external conditions. Economic vulnerability, the social consequences of modernization, dependence, ideological disputes between factions, xenophobia, neocolonialism and nationalism are relevant. China's turn toward self-sufficiency and break with the Soviet Union occurred long before security issues and territorial disputes came to the fore. Similarly, Burma's turn toward isolationism during the mid-1960s can be understood more adequately as a response to extreme foreign penetration and domestic turmoil than to a Chinese or general cold war threat. Canada's attempts to diversify trade and cultural contacts and to regulate the amount of American penetration during the 1970s had nothing to do with military concerns. If threats are perceived, they are of a distinctly economic and cultural character.

A typology of foreign policy restructuring

Types of reorientation and restructuring can be distinguished on the basis of significant changes in:

a)   the *levels* of external involvement

b) the policies regarding types and sources of external penetration
c) the direction or pattern of external involvement and
d) the military or diplomatic commitments.

While these criteria do not cover all aspects of foreign policy, they should indicate the major directions of actions, transactions and commitments. The following types, with distinguishing characteristics, result.

Isolation. Characterized by a extremely low level of external involvement, combined with comprehensive exclusionist policies. All military and diplomatic commitments are avoided. Since externally directed transactions are few, direction is relatively unimportant, and there are few discernible patterns in actions and transitions.

Self-reliance. Trade, diplomatic and cultural contacts are diversified, but levels of transactions are generally low. Any patterns suggesting dependence or vulnerability are scrupulously avoided. Some selective exclusionist policies - usually in the form of import substitution programmes - are instituted. Military commitments which involve dependence conditions (for example, great vulnerability to cessation of arms shipments) or support for other states' interests which are not similar to one's own, are avoided.

Dependence. Externally directed actions and transactions are at a fairly high level, and are characterized by high concentration toward another state or group of similar states (for example, EEC). Essential economic, technical, communication and military requirements come from abroad, usually from a single country. The state is highly penetrated by outside actors, in the form of government advisers, foreign investment, tourists, educators, communications and possibly military personnel. Security is provided by a mentor power, often in return for base rights.

Non-alignment-diversification. This type is characterized by extensive externally directed actions and transactions, but they are well scattered among many states and groups of states. External penetration is often notable, but the government attempts to maintain balance of diversity between numbers and types of foreign agents. The government strictly avoids military commitments to any actual or potential mentor.

When one surveys the state of the contemporary world, it is clear that few fit these types perfectly. The categories are based on continua of involvement, diversification, commitments and exclusion of foreign penetration. Hence, it is possible that states could rank high or low on some of them, but not on all. But there are also examples of states that rank high or low on all dimensions simultaneously so that they typify the otherwise arbitrary categories. Burma in the mid-1960s and Bhutan until the late 1950s certainly are examples of isolated states, for they rank extremely low on all continua. China in the early 1960s fits the self-reliance type reasonably well. The Ivory Coast since independence perhaps epitomizes the dependent state, while Tanzania since at least 1967 has systematically sought to reduce its ties with the former mentor to diversify its external contacts and sources of aid, and selectively to exclude foreign agents or processes which might re-establish patterns of dependence or somehow threaten the ruling party's domestic priorities. Most other states could not be so easily categorized.

The problem, however, is not only to delineate state A's pattern of foreign relations at time X, but to describe and explain change from one type, even if it does not fit perfectly, *toward* another type. By combining the four ideal types, there are twelve theoretical possibilities for change. Figure 4.1 outlines these. One is hard pressed to find post-World War II examples of each type of change.

Figure 4.1
Possible types of foreign policy restructuring

from-to	isolation	self-reliance	dependence	diversification
isolation	X			
self-reliance		X		
dependence			X	
diversification				X

It might be interesting, nevertheless, to present a non-exhaustive list of post-World War II cases of foreign policy restructuring. In addition to the twelve theoretical possibilities of change, a further category of abortive attempts is included. Changing from one dependence to another ('switching partners') is also added. Table 4.1 does not include foreign policy restructuring which resulted from victory or defeat in World War II (for example, Finland since 1944), or from the postwar communist revolutions in East Europe.

The provisional list indicates that a majority (sixteen of twenty-eight) of the actual or suspected cases involves countries that are normally defined as belonging to the Third World. Conspicuous by their low numbers are countries in the 'First World'. Only France - a debatable case - and Canada appear in the list. No particular inference can be drawn from this fact, but it does suggest either that the developed countries are more 'satisfied' in the basic pattern of their foreign relations than are the developing states, or that the costs of restructuring are inordinately high for industrial countries. Why the developing countries should be dissatisfied with their lot is now well-known; among the reasons are concern over a situation that contains many characteristics of neocolonialism. Thus, foreign policy restructuring is not only directed toward establishing a *new* set of relationships, but often requires the destruction of old patterns.

Table 4.1
Foreign Policy Restructuring, 1945-1979

Type of change	Countries	Approximate dates, begin and complete
From isolation to:		
1) self-reliance	none known	
2) dependence	Nepal	1948-1950
	Bhutan	1964-1967
3) diversification	China	1970-1973
From self-reliance to:		
1) isolation	China	1966-1969
2) dependence	none known	
3) diversification	none known	
From dependence to:		
1) isolation	Albania?	1977-1979
2) self-reliance	China	1959-1966
3) dependence		
('switching partners')	Guinea	1958-1960
	Iraq	1958-?
	Albania?	1960-1976
	Cuba	1960-1963
	Indonesia?	1962-1965
	South Yemen	1971-?
	Ethiopia	1977-1978
4) diversification	Yugoslavia	1948-
	Rumania	1960s
	France	1962-1968
	Tanzania	1967-1972
	Libya?	1967-?
	Iran	1970-1974

	Guyana?	1970s
	Canada	1972-1978
From diversification to:		
1) isolation	Burma	1963-1965
	Iran	1979-
2) self-reliance	none known	
3) dependence	Israel?	1948-1950
	Brazil	1965-
Abortive attempts:		
	Guatemala	1953-1954
	Hungary	1956
	Chile	1971-1973

? denotes marginal case or lack of data

Prelude to foreign policy restructuring: disengagement

In many cases, countries that adopt a new foreign policy orientation systematically destroy old patterns of diplomatic, commercial, cultural and military relations. For some, it is forced upon them by the boycotts, embargoes and expulsions of mentor powers. For example, the reorientation of Yugoslavia and Cuba, and to a lesser extent Guinea, was partly a necessary response to the mentor power's step to cut traditional ties. The old relationships had been terminated for them by the Soviet Union, the United States and France. As Canada's relations with the United States in the 1970s reveals, restructuring can be attempted by selective measures to reduce penetration and vulnerability, combined with vigorous actions aimed at establishing balancing economic, diplomatic and cultural links abroad - all without fundamentally altering or severing ties to the mentor.

Where disengagement does precede restructuring - or takes place simultaneously - it can usually be understood as a response to perceptions of dependence and/or to extensive external penetration. By dependence, we mean a situation where the 'smaller' state can act in its domestic and/or external policies only with the implicit or explicit consent of another state, and where the capacity to threaten or reward in the relationship is highly asymmetrical. To put it another way, the major power - what we call the mentor - establishes the parameters for the political and economic actions of the dependent state, and has the means to ensure conforming behavior. Although there has been considerable controversy over the precise meaning of dependence and the types of indicators that should be used to measure it,[1] this working definition should adequately suggest the essential nature of a dependent relationship. Highly asymmetrical patterns of transactions between two states (for example, 70 per cent of A's trade goes to B, but only 5 per cent of B's trade goes to A) provide clues to the potential availability of coercive instruments; in this example, B possesses economic leverage and a capacity (though not necessarily intention) to threaten or carry out economic pressure against A. Such patterns also imply asymmetrical vulnerabilities. Vulnerability is one consequence of a dependent relationship; not only does the mentor possess coercive capabilities, but if they are applied, the costs will be asymmetrical. B can hurt A, while the reverse is not possible. Moreover, because of a high degree of economic integration, B's domestic polices may significantly harm A's interests, without B even intending such harm. Efforts to restructure foreign policy often have as a major objective the reduction of vulnerability.

Disengagement may also be a policy response to extensive external penetration. Characteristically, the bureaucracies of penetrated states are supervised by hordes of foreign advisors and, in many cases, high civil service positions are actually held by foreign nationals. Industrial, educational and cultural organizations are often owned or staffed by non-citizens, as are the media. Also, the political process in the penetrated states is often subject to manipulation, bribes and pressures from foreign agents. Not all these characteristics exist simultaneously, but they are widespread enough in many states to cause nationalist responses in the form of demands for exclusionist domestic policies and termination of asymmetries. Leaders may conclude, for example, that despite the economic benefits of foreign aid or private investment from a mentor power, the structural constraints imposed by such programmes are not compatible with sovereignty, national dignity or some other value. Such calculations, along with the sense of vulnerability and perceptions of other types of threat, combine to produce demands for terminating penetration and/or dependence.

International relations theory and foreign policy restructuring

We may ask, then, why such events - often dramatic, and often generating intense international conflict - have not commanded attention. Numerous answers could be advanced, but three intellectual perspectives in recent international relations literature deserve attention in particular:

1) emphasis on the Cold War and its associated problems,
2) narrow interpretation of the concept of threat in diplomacy,

and
3) concentration on 'interdependence' and integration as
    inevitable and progressive trends, with a concomitant
    neglect of nationalism and disengagement.

Much of the literature on international relations during the last
three decades has focussed on the cold war and problems
associated with it. Our 'maps' of the world have commonly
featured only three kinds of states: the Communist, Western and
non-aligned. Movement from one type to the other was almost
impossible because of the sanctions bloc leaders could impose on
the wayward or recalcitrant. Indeed, it was not until the 1960s that
the concept of non-alignment met with any enthusiasm in
Washington or Moscow. The world, then, was rigidly structured
into patrons and clients, with non-aligned states being assiduously
courted by the superpowers. Underlying these analyses of
international politics, whether studies of deterrence, bargaining,
alliances or economic development, was a pronounced, if often
unstated, concern for values, namely, the preservation of freedom
against the onslaughts of revolutionaries and subversives. The
defections of Yugoslavia and Cuba from their respective mentors
caused much discussion, but these were seen as significant
aberrations from the normal diplomatic line-ups, and certainly not
events upon which to theorize.
A literature with a particularly Third World outlook has
developed only recently. As detente has become a relatively fixed
feature of international life, international theory has become
increasingly concerned with the problem of inequality.
Dependence may have been an acceptable state of affairs in a
world confronted with military threats and possible nuclear war. It
is no longer accepted with equanimity today. The quest for greater
equality and drives to end dependent relationships are important
characteristics of contemporary diplomatic life. Dependency
theory, appropriately, developed initially in Latin America in the
1950s and 1960s but did not become a standard perspective in
international relations theory until the 1970s. Its popularity among
North American social scientists is symptomatic of growing
concern over the plight of the small and weak state. Only very
recently have writers begun to explore foreign policy change as a
response to conditions that have no connection with the Cold War.
Emphasis on military and subversive threats has been a second
important bias of our maps of international relations. The
international system has been portrayed as basically benign except
for the fulminations and plots of communists, or the military
build-ups of the two major communist states. Writers have
commonly assumed that once these threats were dispelled through

preventative war, nuclear supremacy, stable deterrence, alliances, arms control or even through unilateral disarmament, the world could return to a condition of peace and stability with an orderly growth of interdependence. Western academics and statesmen have ignored until recently the idea that small, weak and or vulnerable states could also face a variety of *non-military threats* from the external environment, threats that have little to do with the Cold War in general or the moves of great powers in particular.

However, spokesmen from the developing world have made the point that their countries' political independence, cultural integrity and economic fortunes are threatened by a variety of non-military conditions in the international system, including new developments in technology, communications and business enterprise. Despite all the talk in Western industrial capitals about the mutually beneficial consequences of growing international interdependence, about the potential for development through private foreign investment, aid and tourism, and the advantages accruing to all through a truly global communications system, many radicals in the developing countries have interpreted these institutions, trends or processes as posing treats to a variety of local values. The claims of these radical nationalists have won the support of even some conservative regimes in the Third World. The list of actual or potential threats, as seen from the vantage of the developing countries, is lengthy. It has been discussed in detail through a variety of publications and conferences over the past two decades. We do not need to dwell on them here.

Much of the dependency literature has reflected the ideological zeal of individual writers more than the perceptions of those who are responsible for public policy. Nevertheless, as the officials view the world around them, the actual and potential threats that loom on the horizon are often not of a military nature, but involve economic and social phenomena. All types of interactions with the industrialized countries extend vulnerabilities and often involve risks, frequent maldistribution of benefits and occasional exploitation. Even where dependent relationships bring notable economic benefits - as in the case of several of the former French colonies in Africa - some factions may find it politically expedient to demand the sacrifice of those advantages in order to gain more political, economic and cultural autonomy. In their campaigns, they frequently portray the foreigners as posing a variety of threats.

For many industrial countries, non-military threats are perceived only intermittently. Europeans have worried about America's technological invasion, Canadians constantly complain about the economic and cultural effects of the American presence in the country, and the Arab oil embargo forced some Americans to acknowledge that control over vital resources by hostile governments could constitute a serious threat to United States' security. Some influential Americans have even urged the government to broaden the concept of national security, and to begin monitoring the international system for all sorts of potential and actual threats to America's economic position.[2] Only limited groups have argued foreign investment, tourism or foreign television have reached such proportions in the United States that they constitute a problem demanding exclusionist solutions or dramatic foreign policy change.[3] Yet all these forms of external penetration *have* reached extensive proportions in many developing countries. Governments cope with them in different ways; among them are decisions to reorient the country's foreign policy, to establish more diversified or balanced economic relationships, to exclude all foreign influences to the maximum extent feasible with economic survival, or to glorify self-sufficiency.

Many abstract academic models of the global system fail to incorporate the inequitable features of contemporary international life. They ignore the problem of non-military threats and the restrictive reactions to processes which are termed interdependence. The literature characterizes our world as a global system, where all sorts of transaction networks crisscross in a jumbled spider's web. In these networks, issues are processed and alliances are constructed between transnational actors. This mechanistic image of the world fails to raise a number of critical questions: in which directions do communications flow? In economic transactions, do benefits distribute equally or proportionally among participants? Who processes global issues - that is, who wields influence, control or authority? Are solutions designed to increase global equality in a variety of goods and values, or do they maintain disparities and dependencies? Do processes support variety or homogeneity? From where do the inputs into the system originate? From the strong and developed, or the weak and underdeveloped? Who commands the capabilities - financial, technical and intellectual - to set up or alter the networks of transactions? Whose values are effectively promoted in the system? Does a system seek stability or homeostasis - often implicitly defined as good? Or, for a system to survive, is radical restructuring of relations necessary? Until recently, statesmen from the industrial countries seldom addressed their thoughts to these problems, unless it was within the context of traditional remedies for underdevelopment, that is , more aid, more trade, more tourism and communication, and more private investment. For a variety of reasons, academics did not raise such questions either until the literature on dependence - despite all its shortcomings - emerged.

Disengagement and foreign policy reorientation have been neglected, finally, because academics have remained largely unconcerned with the phenomenon of nationalism. Somehow, nationalism does not square with the notion that increased interdependence and regional integration are progressive developments or trends. Yet, if anything, the demand for political, economic and cultural autonomy, and exclusion of dominant foreign influences, has grown increasingly strident since the end of World War II. One paradox of our age is that as the world shrinks, as communications grow and as awareness of the outside world penetrates even into remote villages, the desire for autonomy and separateness appears to have become more pronounced. The fear that local cultures and languages will be overwhelmed by outside forces exists among hundreds of groups and nations, from the Quebecois to the Basques, from the Amazon Indians to Ukrainians. To many among these people, integration and interdependence imply cultural dilution and possible extinction.

Describing and explaining foreign policy reorientation and restructuring: a framework

In studying foreign policy change, the dependent variables - what we want to describe and explain - would be indicated by a) significant changes in the patterns of externally directed diplomatic, cultural, commercial and military relations, and b) identification of new policies with regard to foreign agents within the country. Where evidence is available, we would also add to our dependent variables the policy-makers' *intent* to restructure foreign policy, that is, foreign policy reorientation.

The distinction between intent to change policies and actual repatterning is important. It also raises several problems. First, governments' foreign policy rhetoric may *not* change, yet in the realm of actions, repatterning is obvious. This was the case in Burma, where Ne Win's foreign policy pronouncements in the 1960s changed very little in tone and substance from those of the U Nu government of the 1950s. Non-alignment and peace continued to be the main themes. Yet the pattern of externally directed activities changed fundamentally and, even more important, the Ne Win government literally sealed off Burma from the outside world. In such instances, we must rely extensively upon the hard data to describe foreign policy change.

The reverse problem is where policy-makers give strong

94

evidence of *intent* to restructure policy, but for a variety of reasons, fail to bring about degrees or types of change that are distinguishable from the slow, incremental changes observed in the actions and policies of all states. Mexico under the presidency of Echevarria may be one example. Political rhetoric suggested reorientation, but aside from Mexico's pattern of voting in the United Nations and a few symbolic acts designed to identify Mexico as a leading Third World nation, not much change in the pattern of trade, cultural and diplomatic relations resulted.

How much change is necessary to constitute restructuring and/or disengagement? The definition offered earlier provides part of the answer: restructuring occurs when there is change in many geographical and functional sectors simultaneously. If Tanzania establishes diplomatic relations with China, that act in itself is hardly sufficient to indicate reorientation or restructuring. But if in a reasonably short period of time - let us say within three years - Tanzania drastically diversifies its trade partners, establishes restrictive conditions on foreign investment, ceases accepting aid from Great Britain (its former mentor), terminates long-standing military commitments, and generally reduces the foreign presence within the country, there are grounds for arguing that reorientation was intended, and restructuring was achieved. Obviously, some arbitrary judgments on the degrees of change have to be made. It is possible, of course, to establish *a priori* how much change must be achieved along each dimension before a country is categorized as having changed its foreign policy orientation. But for a variety of reasons it is preferable to work inductively, describing changes in intentions and policies for each case, and allowing the reader to make the ultimate decision. One reason for proceeding in this fashion is that not all types of change are comparable across different types of nations. A country such as Canada, seeking to reduce vulnerability and American penetration, may employ policies and actions quite different from those chosen by China in the early 1960s to reduce its dependence upon the Soviet Union. Change, then, may require different policies for different countries.

At least two types of explanations can be used in accounting for the changes in externally directed actions and policies regarding foreign penetration. First, the study can try to provide evidence about decision-makers' perceptions of the external and domestic conditions which give rise to dissatisfaction with one foreign policy orientation and the desire to restructure external contacts. A variety of factors may be involved, including perceptions of military and non-military threats, calculations of costs and advantages of dependence, domestic political factionalism where creation of an external enemy becomes important, prestige (for example, feelings of guilt about appearing to be dependent), ideological commitments of groups, parties or factions, cultural values (for example, suspicion of foreigners), personality characteristics of key policy-makers, and the like.

A second type of explanation seeks to answer the question, 'why did the policy-makers choose a particular *type* of new orientation, as opposed to some other?'[4] But the data do not always provide sufficient clues. Some governments seemingly are more concerned with breaking down old patterns of relations than explicitly defining the goals toward which they are striving. The goals may be vague, or they may vary over time. Bhutan's decision to end isolation in the 1950s was not necessarily predicated on the understanding that the nation should become dependent upon India. Or, even if that calculation was made (but not likely to be admitted publicly), the government probably would argue that dependence is a short-term goal, or a means to creating more diverse foreign contacts later on.

An analytical framework to guide research is represented in Figure 4.2. This framework outlines only the most common explanatory factors. Other variables may be important and in many cases some conditions would not be relevant. Lack of data might prevent establishing linkages in some instances, and in others, only weak associations can be suggested. The importance of historical and cultural variables is notoriously difficult to establish with rigor, but they might be significant in conditioning elite and popular attitudes. Policy-makers' psychological needs and personality characteristics can seldom be established as important elements in explaining decisions and actions, except where a single figure is clearly responsible for policy leadership and/or implementation, and where reasonable evidence suggests that without such an individual, intent and actions would have differed significantly.

Figure 4.2
Accounting for foreign policy restructuring

Independent variables	Intervening variables	Dependent variables
1) External factors		
a) military threats		
b) non-military threats		
c) structure of previous relationship (vulnerabilities, penetration, etc.)	1) Policy-makers' perceptions and calculations	Intent to restructure (orientation)
2) Domestic factors	2) Policy-making process	disengagement policies (if any)
a) internal threats	3) Personality factors	restructuring actions in external environment
b) economic conditions		
c) polit. factionalization	4) Elite attitudes toward external actors	actions toward external penetration (if any)
3) Background historical and cultural factors		
a) attitudes torward foreigners		
b) colonial experience		

Organizing the data

Where available, statements by policy-makers indicate intentions to change foreign policy patterns. Speeches, press conferences, party statements and radio broadcasts serve as the basic sources of information. Where official pronouncements are either misleading or rarely available, studies would have to rely heavily upon hard data and reported government activities. Restructuring of foreign policy is indicated by significant changes in the following types of actions, transactions and or commitments:

1)   numbers of treaties signed (for example, a significant reduction per annum would indicate isolationist tendencies since the world trend is significantly upward);
2)   numbers of states as treaty partners (for example, while maintaining some treaty arrangements with Britain, Tanzania rapidly increased its number of treaties with China, the Soviet Union and East Europe after 1967, indicating a

pattern of diplomatic and commercial diversification and an attempt to reduce the relationship with Great Britain);

3) new commitments of military capabilities abroad, or terminating prior commitments;
4) significant changes in numbers and destination of students sent abroad to study;
5) voting patterns in the General Assembly;
6) direction of foreign trade; degree of trade concentration;
7) absolute size of trade;
8) number and direction of visits abroad by head of state or government;
9) numbers and location of diplomatic missions abroad.

Outward-directed actions and commitments are not the only indicators of foreign policy. Governments also may institute a set of policies which is designed to reduce or increase the amount of foreign penetration, whether official or unofficial. Which foreign governments or non-governmental actors are allowed access to the state, society or economy? What sorts of policy are fashioned to monitor, control or reduce foreign penetration? In the reverse situation, what sorts of restriction are reduced or terminated in order to allow in which sorts of foreign influence? Or, does a government literally terminate the diplomatic, cultural and economic presence of one mentor or friendly state, only to allow in the agents and agencies of a new friend or ally? A typical example would be the expulsion of all American influences and institutions in Cuba after 1961, and their replacement by Soviet technicians, party officials, military advisers, foreign aid personnel, literature and films. The indicators would include the following:

1) expulsion or admission of foreign military personnel, bases and or equipment;
2) expulsion of aliens living in the country; restrictions on new aliens entering the country; lifting such prior restrictions;
3) new restrictions on the size of foreign diplomatic establishments or on the movement of foreign diplomats within the host country; liberalizing such restrictions;
4) closing the country to tourists from certain other countries, or erecting such administrative barriers as effectively to discourage tourism; terminating such restrictions;
5) selective or total censorship on incoming books, periodicals, films, radio and television, or lifting such censorship;
6) restrictions on private investment from abroad, or from particular countries; lifting such restrictions;
7) nationalization or expropriation of alien property or

98

enterprises;
8) severe restrictions on numbers of students or academics coming form specific countries; significant alterations to such restrictions;
9) expulsion of foreign humanitarian, educational or cultural organizations already in the country or serious restrictions on those attempting to gain access; changing such policies;
10) restrictions against import of certain commodities from certain countries, where other than economic reasons are given.

Any of these actions taken separately may, of course, be directed toward ends other than fundamentally changing a government's foreign policy. Yet when a number of such policies and actions are taken seriatim or simultaneously, thus fundamentally altering traditional relationships and/or establishing significant new external relationships, we can use these data to demonstrate foreign policy restructuring.

The use of these and other indicators raises some methodological problems. First, the lists are not exhaustive. Since a country such as Canada, whose economy remains highly integrated with that of the United States, may require substantially different policies to alter commercial patterns than would a former colonial territory whose trade ties to the former metropole are weak and confined to a few commodities, other indicators may be more appropriate. Second, change might be observed in many of the indicators, but not in all of them. Judgment must be used to decide how many indicators must show significant change before we can argue that restructuring is, or has been, occurring. Third, how *much* change must there be across all indicators? Scientific precision might require the researcher to establish benchmarks or gates which must be passed before he could argue that restructuring of foreign policy has taken place. Some might claim, for example, that at least 50 per cent of a nation's trade must be redirected before this sector has achieved change. But such a figure would surely be arbitrary. Given the great volume of American-Canadian trade, a change of 10 per cent could be considered highly significant, whereas a 30 per cent change in Burma's diversified trade pattern would be less noteworthy. And while some indicators are easily quantified, others present more qualitative information. One new military treaty may be more significant than a change of voting patterns in the General Assembly. Fourth, should the indicators be weighted? The example of military commitment versus votes in the General Assembly implies that some sorts of actions are more significant than others. But, the importance of various actions depends upon the entire web of relations within which a country operates. It is difficult, therefore, to specify outside of the context of each case which types of action are more important than others. A nationalization of foreign property in one nation might be primarily of symbolic importance, whereas in another its ramifications could spread to the totality of its foreign relations. For South Korea to establish an embassy in Moscow or Beijing is of greater significance than for Thailand to do so. It would be unwise, therefore, to attach separate weights, *a priori*, to any of the indicators.

Finally, what unit of time should be used to measure significant change? Cuba's disengagement and restructuring occurred within a relatively brief span - less than two years. Tanzania's attempts to diversify external contacts and limit foreign penetration took much longer, even if the intent to reorient was made known over a relatively brief period in Nyerere's presidency. We are less concerned with the methodological problems time may raise than with its substantive and theoretical significance. The theoretical concern is not the 'suddenness' of change, but the intention or fact of fundamental change. Thus, it is only important to distinguish ordinary foreign policy change from the deliberate intent and attempt of some government to recast their role in world politics and economics.

Notes

1. For theoretical formulae to measure dependence and vulnerability, see James Caporaso (1974), 'Methodological Issues in the Measurement of Inequality, Dependence, and Exploitation', in James Kurth and Steven Rosen (eds), *Testing Economic Theories of Imperialism*, Lexington, MA: D.C. Heath (Lexington Books), pp.87-116. For further elaboration see Raymond Duvall (1978), 'Dependence and Dependencia Theory: Notes toward Precision of Concept and Argument', *International Organization*, 32, pp.51-78; and David A. Baldwin (1980), 'Interdependence and Power: a Conceptual Analysis', *International Organization*, 34, pp. 471-506.

2. Maxwell Taylor (1974), 'The Legitimate Claims of National Security', *Foreign Affairs*, 52, pp. 577-94

3. There are regions in the United States where foreign penetration has become a local issue, however. For example, Japanese investment in Hawaii has grown rapidly, causing some local residents to call for controls. The amount of foreign investment and ownership in the United States, particularly in banking and purchase of farmland, has caused some observers to demand restrictions. See, for example, John Congers and Marcus G. Raskin (1979), 'Taking over America', *New York Times*, p. A25.

4. Jeanne Laux, University of Ottawa, proposed the distinction between the two types of explanation.

5. Politics in Command: Foreign Trade as National Security Policy

Many of the contemporary debates among theorists of international relations are cast in terms of the appropriateness of single approaches or theoretical lenses, or conversely, of the inadequacies of competing perspectives. As political scientists, we seem to have developed habits of intellectual exclusiveness, preferring authoritative outcomes - academic knockouts - to synthesis and pluralism.[1] Using dichotomous concepts to view the world may compound the problem.[2] We have heard debates between realism and transnationalism, idealism and realism, behavioralism and traditionalism; and conceptually, between the notions of balance of power and collective security, war and peace, anarchy and authority, conflict and collaboration, and power versus plenty.

It is not clear why academics prefer authoritative outcomes, when we are often taught that one of the distinguishing features of social science scholarship is a healthy respect both for the realities under scrutiny, and the intellectual payoffs from research and theoretical pluralism. Maybe we, like the policy- makers we often criticize, are uncomfortable with conceptual or theoretical grey areas. Yet, the complexities of international life are likely to render any neat, parsimonious account of the structures, processes, and dynamics of the international system suspect. The consequence may be some theoretical confusion. But is this a greater problem than theoretical orthodoxy?

The wavering fortunes of 'realism' indicate the nature of the problem. It has served as the intellectual platform for most theoretical and empirical work on international relations for several centuries, but today it is under serious attack from many quarters. What is revealing in much of the debate is its 'either, or' quality; that is, a theoretical perspective must be entirely correct (and not an 'orrery of errors', as Richard Ashley has termed it) or it must be jettisoned for something else. Many of the ideas formulated as new 'paradigms' of international relations are designed not to supplement realism but to replace it.

Within these broad debates are issues of less theoretical importance, but which nevertheless generate considerable scholarly attention, such as the nature of the nexus between politics and economics, and more specifically, their relationship in the context of a country's foreign policies. Illustrating our penchant for intellectual closure and for employing concepts in dichotomous terms, early discussions of the issue among many nineteenth century liberals tended to analyze it as a choice between 'power' and 'plenty'. More recent discussions have portrayed the dilemma of the policy-maker as a choice between 'guns' and 'butter'. In academia, the textbook literature of international relations of the 1950s and 1960s implicitly or explicitly declared that politics, conceived as the search for security, power, and prestige, was a domain largely separate from economics, or argued that security was the proper sphere of foreign policy, while the maximization of welfare values was the concern of domestic politics.

The rebirth of international political economy as a subfield of international relations has reopened the question, at least in North America. The present conventional wisdom is that governments pursue both security and welfare goals simultaneously and that both are linked in foreign policy actions. But how? Robert Gilpin has suggested that there is a 'reciprocal and dynamic interaction in international relations of the pursuit of wealth and the pursuit of power'. Echoing his views, Robert Keohane argues that there is complementarity between them, that in the long run one cannot have power without wealth and vice versa.[3] That of course is true; but in the short run decisions have to be made and priorities set, because not all states are fortunate enough to enjoy both security and wealth. It is in the states' pursuit (or protection) of wealth and power that we can distinguish distinct sets of values and analyze how governments assess them.

Thus, for analytical purposes, it makes sense to assume distinctions between kinds of value, while recognizing that important connections exist between them, both in the short run and the long run. The question is, then, under what conditions are the values incompatible? Or do governments establish hierarchies of values, implying permanent priorities? Or does it make more sense, as Gilpin has suggested, to treat the realms not as poles but as 'bundles' of values?[4] Governments, in his formulation, do not choose one to the exclusion of the other, nor does one determine the other. They constantly shift priorities to emphasize one or the other. Tradeoffs and 'satisfycing', rather than maximization occur. It is a question of relative preferences.

The problem, then, is to specify both under what conditions the rank orderings will change and how priorities will be established. Is there evidence that governments 'satisfyce', understand tradeoffs, and commonly make formal connections between foreign trade policies and security policies? The cases outlined below suggest that governments seek both power and plenty; but

102

when the two are incompatible, the former predominates, and commercial opportunities have to be managed in such a fashion as to enhance security concerns. This may mean forgoing significant increments to the 'plenty' category. In particular, governments will sacrifice significant or even critical economic opportunities when their independence, autonomy, or national security are at risk.[5]

Before proceeding, the terms 'power' and 'plenty' need some elaboration. The former does not signify only military capabilities, territorial expanse, or prestige. These may be relevant, of course, but we will use the term to mean all those diplomatic arrangements, treaties, commitments, and military deployments that governments enter into or arrange

1)   to shield their territory against immediate threats;
2)   to protect themselves against external pressures, interference, and ultimatums; and/or
3)   to allow them to remain uninvolved in major conflicts and controversies in adjacent areas.

The purposes of power, from this perspective, are admittedly defensive: successful policies will protect autonomy, maximize latitude of choice in policy-making, reduce constraints emanating from abroad, and maintain domestic political legitimacy and authority. Power in this sense is really synonymous with the concept of security. It is the power to survive rather than the power to expand that concerns us. The findings may not be relevant, therefore, to the experiences of countries bent on external conquest - such as Nazi Germany, which deliberately organized foreign trade policy to increase its war-fighting capabilities.

'Plenty' is conceived as economic opportunities available abroad, opportunities that are considered to increase overall wealth within the society. Policy-makers usually define these opportunities as increased access to new markets for trade and investment or, at a minimum, protection for established markets that are threatened with reduction

The title 'Politics in Command' suggests that economic objectives, in the shifting hierarchy of values, are regularly subordinated to security ones. But, as suggested, situational variables will largely determine the relative weights assigned to the values, and we also have to allow for changing preferences over time. Thus, the hypothesis underlying the two case studies is that policy-makers emphasize 'power' when external threats and/or constraints are high or medium; and conversely, that they rank 'plenty' higher only when the external threats and constraints are low. Using a crude and uncalibrated continuum of high, medium, and low threats/constraints, juxtaposed against high, medium, and low economic rewards, we can illustrate schematically the predicted choices in different states of the two variables.

Table 5.1
Probable choices for 'power' versus 'plenty'

Economic Opportunities	Security Threats/Constraints		
	High	Medium	Low
High	Power	Power	Plenty
Medium	Power	Power	Plenty
Low	Power	Power	Unknown

Although this formulation offers fews precise points, it does suggest the probable rankings of the values under different conditions. It demonstrates that under most combinations power concerns will predominate; that is, the values of security, autonomy, and independence are prized more than wealth. The matrix also suggests that the rankings of the values may change over time. Therefore, there can be no authoritative outcome of the debate on power versus plenty. As with so many generalizations, the validity of a proposition rests on a combination of circumstances. In other words, 'it all depends on ... '.

Selecting cases

Analyses of two cases cannot support a hypothesis. But they can be suggestive insofar as they challenge many assertions found in the mercantilist, liberal, and Marxist literatures, assertions that usually claim universal validity and that often deny or ignore the possibility of change. And the cases may provide some empirical clues about the priorities of governments which prove telling.

I have deliberately avoided selecting either the United States or the Soviet Union: the former, because too much of international relations literature uses American experience as a prototype for all states; and the latter because data are lacking, or because most

Western experts provide cut-and-dried answers, namely that all Soviet trade is subordinated to political goals. Moreover, compared to many other kinds of states, the superpowers are relatively self-sufficient and hence may not face the constraints common to 'weak' states. Where both guns and butter are relatively cheap (or where there is no public discussion of the issue, as in the Soviet Union), tradeoffs may not have to be made or politicized, and competition between values may be difficult to discover.

Many lesser countries - particularly those that must define a relationship with a powerful neighbor or hegemon - regularly organize their external trade to make it more consistent with the expectations of one or more large partners. That is, foreign trade becomes just one of several means of validating a particular security relationship. Such 'weak' states enjoy limited foreign policy options, face major constraints, and have few possibilities for resolving their security problems through military means or diplomatic pressures involving various kinds of threats. Trade patterns are skewed to reflect and symbolize the overall security relationship between the states, and attempts to deviate from those patterns - that is, to maximize economic opportunities - frequently lead to diplomatic crises between them.

I am uncertain about the universe of such cases. But certainly it would include most of the East European countries, whose postwar economies have been linked structurally to that of the Soviet Union. Syria has redesigned its economic links to the socialist countries, reflecting its reliance upon the Soviet Union for military and diplomatic support. Nepal and Bhutan forgo certain economic opportunities in order to maintain the trust and support of a local hegemon, India. Prior to its invasion in 1979 by Soviet troops, Afghanistan had to balance its trade in such a manner as to provide evidence that it was genuinely non-aligned; and North Korea's trade patterns have often fluctuated, reflecting its difficult balancing between the Soviet Union and China.

For the purposes of this article, I have selected postwar Japan and Finland, at first glance two incomparable countries. But initial hunches were subsequently borne out by data: both countries demonstrated the compelling nature of external constraints, a clear ranking of values between 'power' and 'plenty', and how those rankings change over time. Japan and Finland in the 1950s and 1960s had unique characteristics, but fundamental similarities also existed. Each illustrates the state's crucial responsibilities, namely directing and managing the foreign trade sector to meet security objectives. And both had to resolve their long-range security problems before they could seriously turn their attention to developing a diversified and wealth-maximizing foreign trade policy.

Japan and the United States: the hegemon's embrace

Notwithstanding widespread Japanese hopes that after a period of reform and tutelage it might be restored to full sovereignty and self-direction, America's security needs circumscribed Japan's role and position in the postwar system. Japan's fate in the 1950s and 1960s was to become part of American strategy toward the communist powers. Japan's external relations were oriented toward the United States and other members of the 'free world'. Although after the peace treaty of 1952, Japan theoretically regained the attributes of sovereignty, in practice the expectations and pressures of the United States continued to constrain the fundamental choices in its external relations. Japanese policy makers were operating essentially within a realm of necessity rather than of choice.

The Occupation effectively isolated Japan from contacts with other countries. Japan had no diplomats abroad, its citizens could not travel, and foreigners were allowed into the country only with the permission of the Occupation authorities. Summarizing the Occupation policies, Robert Ward has suggested that they 'heavily concentrated Japan's national attention, hopes, and fears on America'.[6]

In the trade sector, the postwar reorientation toward the United States was thorough. Prior to World War II, Japan had developed extensive commercial ties with China, Manchuria, and Korea - the latter two being colonies. In the years 1934-36, 24 per cent of Japan's trade was directed to China; it was the fourth largest source of Japanese imports and the largest single market for Japan's exports.[7] Trade with Canada and the United States the same years was also large (22 per cent of exports, 35 per cent of imports), but beyond these two poles, Japan's trade displayed a pattern of considerable diversification.

Under the Occupation, the authorities strictly controlled trade through a licensing system administered by the Supreme Commander for the Allied Powers (SCAP). By the late 1940s, Japan's commercial relations had been heavily reoriented toward the United States, with a corresponding diminution of connections with its traditional trade partners in East Asia. In 1948, for example, 65 per cent of Japan's imports came from the United States - many of them at prices substantially higher than would have been paid to traditional sources - and almost 26 per cent of its exports went to North America. Australia became Japan's second largest customer. Trade with mainland China existed, and in fact grew slightly during the Occupation years, but by 1950 had reached only the annual sum of about $60 million, a minuscule fraction of Japan's total trade.[8]

In 1950, Japan was allowed to re-establish diplomatic representations abroad. Trade with China, though slight, was beginning to redevelop, and despite extensive American economic subsidies to Japan, many Japanese intellectuals and business circles looked forward to the day when commercial relations with mainland China would assume their former importance. While not aspiring to Japan's predominance in Asia during the 1930s, many Japanese considered an autonomous diplomacy a distinct possibility after the conclusion of peace treaties and the end of the Occupation.

The Korean War and especially the Chinese intervention rendered the normalization of Japanese-Chinese relations impossible. The United States imposed a total embargo on Communist China and compelled Japan to join. In July 1952 NATO organized a special China Committee as part of the Coordinating Committee (COCOM) to regulate the sale of strategic goods to communist countries. Japan joined the committee and accepted strict regulations on exports to China.

The major outlines of Japan's foreign policy were embedded in the multilateral peace treaty and the security treaty with the United States. The history of the negotiations of these treaties indicates how the United States intended to use Japan as the major Asian bastion against mainland China. In 1950 President Truman appointed John Foster Dulles to work out the details of the peace treaty. Dulles's approach to the project assumed that Japan should become a loyal member of the Western bloc, linked militarily to the United States but encouraged to forge commercial relations with a variety of countries in the 'free world'. To Dulles, 'Japan should ... set an example to the rest of Asia by thriving in the free world, thus contributing to a general will to resist communism'.[9] Dulles's thoughts were echoed by Douglas MacArthur who, only six months after having stated that Japan would become the Switzerland of Asia (implying neutrality), proclaimed that Japanese-Chinese trade was inconceivable.

[Under communism], deterioration proceeds until ... with the incentive completely lost, the human energy and individual initiative in production, give way to indolence and despair. In such an unhealthy climate industry and commerce cannot thrive and realism warns that the potentialities of trade with any people under the strictures of a collectivist system must be discounted accordingly. For the time being, therefore, and for some time to come, Japan must look elsewhere [than China] for the sources of her needed imports and the markets for her manufactures.[10]

When approached on the outlines of a peace treaty, the British took the position that Japan should decide for itself when and how to re-establish diplomatic relations with mainland China. Facing considerable pressure in the Senate Foreign Relations Committee, however, Dulles assured its members that Japan would conclude a peace treaty only with the Republic of China (ROC), and would do so shortly after the multilateral peace treaty was signed.

The Japanese, however, never began discussions with the ROC. Fifty-six members of the American Senate thereupon threatened to block approval of the peace treaty as well as the security treaty, should Japan move to sign a separate peace with mainland China. To placate the rising concern in the United States, Premier Shigeru Yoshida eventually established a commercial office in Taipei, but he also indicated that Japan would consider sympathetically any Communist Chinese offer to open a similar office in Tokyo.[11]

Dulles and several senators traveled to Tokyo in December 1951 to warn Yoshida that Senate approval of the treaties would be jeopardized if Japan did not give some concrete indication that its China policy would be consistent with that of the United States. The outcome of the demarche was the famous Yoshida letter to Dulles, dated 24 December 1951, in which the Japanese premier referred to the establishment of trade relations and a commercial office in Taiwan, and indicated a readiness to conclude a separate peace treaty with the Nationalist government. Formal diplomatic relations would follow. Yoshida concluded by giving assurances that Japan had no intention of concluding a bilateral peace treaty with Communist China. Although the letter contained no binding obligations, it established the framework for Japanese trade and diplomacy for the next decade. The basic tradeoff was an American commitment to ensure Japan's security - thereby obviating the need for Japanese rearmament - in exchange for Japanese independence and conformity with American foreign policy, particularly as it related to the communist countries.

Dulles was realistic enough to understand that Japan could not structure its trade totally with the United States. Thus, in subsequent years he constantly reiterated the need for Japan to diversify, particularly into Southeast Asia. And in the mid-1950s the United States provided, against European opposition, the necessary support for Japan's entry into the Generalized Agreement on Tariffs and Trade (the GATT). Japan's trade with Nationalist China, though hardly a substitute for the hoped-for robust mainland market, grew substantially after the peace treaty and the establishment of diplomatic relations.

Decisions in Tokyo

The main outlines of Japan's external relations were thus manufactured in Washington, not Tokyo. It is difficult to say how seriously other options were considered, but there is little evidence that high government officials ever regarded as viable a policy of genuine autonomy. American expectations and pressures were compelling. Most observers agree, however, that Japan gave up potential economic rewards - at least in the long run - by forsaking the commercial relationship with mainland China.

Even during the Occupation, important groups had urged the Japanese government to create a formal framework for the conduct of trade with China. This implied a peace treaty and diplomatic relations. For some, the issue was potential economic gains. For others, a pro-Chinese policy would symbolize Japan's autonomy, which, they thought, was impossible as long as trade ties were skewed toward the United States. Illustrative of the many pressures placed on the government was a 1950 resolution in the Upper House of the Diet, passed by a large majority:

> Before the war about 65 per cent of our trade was with Asia, and most of that with China. These facts are particularly significant in light of the steadily diminishing U.S. economic aid. Business and trading circles and the Japanese people urgently desire the renewal of direct trade relations with China in order to relieve the stagnation in trade and commerce... Japan absolutely cannot exist unless trade is promoted. The government should leave aside ideological and political differences and look at the purely economic problems, exchange economic missions with the new China, restore trade with her immediately, and set forth a bold course of action.[12]

Although by no means all Japanese political factions and bureaucratic elements held such views, they were not untypical among a large segment of the population.[13] At the highest level, Prime Minister Yoshida authored his famous letter to Dulles, but it reflected his surrender to necessity, not his personal preferences, which appreciated the long-standing ties between Asia's two main nations. Although he did not share the opposition's expectations of lavish economic gains through trade with China, he had long-range visions of an autonomous Asia, with Japanese-Chinese collaboration as the centerpiece.[14]

By 1951-52 Japan had accepted the position of a client to the United States. It benefited in numerous ways from this type of association (including preferential entrance to the American market), but no Japanese politician could simply ignore the perceived potentialities that lay with mainland China. Concerns of 'power' - fulfilling the role of a faithful ally, meeting American expectations on relations with communist countries, and obtaining low-cost military protection - prevailed over the economic potentialities in a Chinese market. External constraints were high, as were potential economic rewards through trade with China. Throughout the 1950s and 1960s the official preference ordering was clearly on the side of 'power', but unofficially there were numerous attempts to reconcile the competing values.

Escaping the hegemon: separating trade from politics

The story of Japan's commercial connections with Communist China in the 1950s and 1960s is long, convoluted, and the subject of several detailed studies.[15] Its lengthy history does not bear recapitulation, but it is important to point out that the development of Japanese-Chinese relations did not follow a straight line leading inexorably to the establishment of full diplomatic and commercial relations.

After the termination of the Korean War, Japan's trade with China grew, but not in a steady upward line. Aside from US and Nationalist Chinese views on the matter, the mainland Communists' attitudes and actions circumscribed commercial possibilities. The main Chinese principle was that trade is a political weapon. The ups and downs of bilateral trade reflected deviations in Chinese policies as much as domestic Japanese or American concerns. For a period in the 1950s the Chinese attached uncompromising political conditions to any trade agreements, and for about four years, starting in 1958, trade between the two countries evaporated to a mere $23 million in 1959 and 1960, rising slowly to $84.5 million in 1962.[16] This sum was an insignificant proportion of Japan's total trade.

The overall Japanese strategy for the first two decades after the end of the Occupation was to separate politics from economics (*seikei bunri*). This was of course impossible, as political implications surrounded all Japanese-Communist Chinese contacts. The Japanese, starting with the Yoshida prime ministership, followed a two-track policy. On the one hand, they maintained strong ties with the United States and Nationalist China. This meant support of the security treaty and its renewal, diplomatic recognition of the Republic of China, official trade relations with the latter, and support for most American anti-Communist Chinese diplomatic initiatives, including the annual votes in the United Nations against seating the Communists. On the other hand, the Japanese gave subtle and sometimes open

110

support for various private cultural, political, and economic missions to the mainland, and accepted an official Chinese trade mission to Tokyo in the spring of 1955. Negotiations between Japanese trading companies and manufacturers led to the opening of the China Fair in Tokyo and Osaka in the same year, and the Japan Fair in China in 1956. The Chinese, always mindful of the political opportunities in organizing trade with Japan, agreed to two channels of commercial relations: 'friendship trade' and 'memorandum trade'. The former was trade with Japanese firms deemed politically acceptable to Peking (those not involved in trade with Taiwan or South Korea), while the latter amounted to semi-official, long-range barter trade agreements. The Japanese government officially played no role in these arrangements, but it was in fact an important facilitator.

Over the years, the role of the government increased so that the slogan of separating economics from politics became virtually meaningless. But this development was not smooth. Throughout the 1950s Japanese governments had refused to guarantee long-term credits for plant exports, but in 1963 the Export-Import Bank provided a $22 million credit to the Kurashiki Rayon Company for construction of a plant in Communist China. The deal led to an uproar in Taiwan, resulting in the rupture of diplomatic relations, and expressions of great concern in Washington, whose spokesmen in the State Department let it be known that Japan's allowance of the deferred payment method to China 'amounted to a form of foreign aid to the enemy'.[17] Subsequent loans were denied, but as the Chinese began to relax their less than subtle use of trade for political purposes, including interference in Japanese domestic politics, the levels of trade began to grow at an impressive pace. They reached more than half a billion dollars by 1967. But despite the proliferation of Japanese-Chinese contacts, the trade never neared prewar proportions. By 1968 Japan's exports to China were less than one half of those to Latin America and remained substantially below the value of the commerce with Taiwan.[18]

The varying fortunes of Japanese-Chinese commercial relations reflected not only China's policy shifts but also changing constellations of public, political, and bureaucratic support in Japan. Japanese public opinion polls from the early 1950s to the establishment of formal diplomatic relations with China in 1972 indicated strong grass-roots support for the normalization of relations with Communist China. Important business firms, particularly those from the Kansai region in central Honshu, vigorously lobbied politicians for the establishment of diplomatic relations. The Socialist and Communist parties consistently attacked the postwar governments for their seemingly craven support of American policies. Firms such as Mitsubishi, however, opposed increased ties with the mainland, in part because of the large stakes they had in the commercial nexus with Taiwan. There was also bureaucratic pulling and tugging, with the most pervasive cleavage between the Ministry of Trade and Industry - sympathetic to expanded links with mainland China - and the Foreign Ministry, which was more sensitive to the maintenance of the American connection. Finally, variations in the policy also reflected the priorities of the various postwar prime ministers. On the one hand, the leadership of Ichiro Hatoyama (mid-1950s) and Hayato Ikeda (early 1960s) led to the development of contacts with the Chinese; Nobusuke Kishi (late 1950s), on the other hand, was the least enthusiastic and actually vetoed the establishment of a resident Chinese trade mission in Tokyo. His official visit to Taiwan angered Peking, and after the famous Nagasaki flag incident, in which some Japanese tore down a Chinese flag at a trade fair, commercial relations between the two countries plummeted and were not restored until the early 1960s.

That decade saw fairly steady movement toward official relations, as the Japanese government became increasingly involved in 'private' trade arrangements. But it was the Kissinger and Nixon trips to China which made possible the last few steps toward the goal of establishing official diplomatic relations. The Nixon 'shock' was significant not only because the United States had failed to consult Japan on the new American policy on China but also because, until the early 1970s, the American government had consistently warned Japan against developing more elaborate ties with mainland China. Suddenly, the Americans were doing exactly what they had counseled the Japanese not to do. It remains, then, to describe the hegemon's responses to the various Japanese moves to 'escape' from the client status in which, many thought, important economic gains were being forsaken in order to please the Americans.

American responses to the escape strategy

The official American policy was stated in the multilateral Treaty of Peace: Japan was free to trade with whomever it saw fit. This view was occasionally reiterated, but in fact the United States let it be known repeatedly that it opposed the development of contacts between Japan and Communist China, whether private or official. In the more or less regular economic consultations between American and Japanese officials following the conclusion of the peace treaty, for example, the American side emphasized the importance of maintaining a 'high level of controls' over trade with China.[19] Dulles often mentioned his hostility to China and the necessity of isolating it from the international community.

Throughout the 1950s American embassy officials cautioned the Japanese against any official Japanese-Chinese relations and did not always hide their displeasure about the flourishing private intercourse.[20] In 1958, when the Nationalist government in Taiwan suspended all commercial relations with Japan in retaliation against the latter's 'deals' with the mainland (establishment of an official Chinese trade mission in Tokyo, for example), American officials visited Taipei and Tokyo, condemned the Peking regime, and advised the Japanese to be very cautious in dealing with the Chinese Communists.[21] Japanese assurances that trade was a private matter - the doctrine of separating economics from politics - hardly assuaged either Taipei or Washington.

In the 1960s, however, American pressures for conformity to the general policy of ostracizing Peking began to subside, or at least they were expressed less frequently and perhaps more privately. Edwin O. Reischauer, then ambassador to Tokyo, could concede that in the 1950s Japan's close association with the United States impeded the development of contacts with mainland China; but he argued that in the decade of the 1960s 'American control of Japanese foreign policy exists only in the minds of those who assume it; it is a feeling rather than a fact'.[22]

Whatever the case, the volume of Japanese-Chinese trade did not grow dramatically, as many had expected. Moreover, during the late 1960s, relations between the two countries stagnated due to China's self-imposed isolation during the Great Proletarian Cultural Revolution. Yet, it is significant that there was no *official* change in Japan's postwar policy toward Peking until after the Kissinger and Nixon visits to China. Japan could 'escape' only so far. In 1972 Japan's commercial policies toward mainland China were highly infused with national security considerations, defined as the necessity to remain a loyal ally of the United States.

The policy of separating politics from economics was, however, a successful fiction that made it possible for Japan to adhere to a close partnership with the United States and Nationalist China, while simultaneously promoting a variety of contacts with mainland China. Welfare objectives encroached on security requirements and the two-track policy provided an outlet for some domestic pressures. In general, the mix of security and economic considerations was weighted toward the former. Nevertheless, the case does illustrate the changing nature of the nexus between economics and politics.

Reconciling welfare and security goals: Finland's neutrality requirements

Like Japan, Finland was a defeated nation in 1945. It was spared a military occupation, but under the terms of the Paris Peace Treaty (1947) and the overview of the Allied Control Commission - always headed by a Soviet official - Finland's early postwar foreign policy, domestic politics, and military planning were highly circumscribed. Limited to an armed force of less than 40,000 men, security and the maintenance of independence had to be achieved by diplomatic means alone. Leading Finnish politicians had come to realize that the only possible means of maintaining independence was to develop friendly relations with the Soviet Union, to create trust in those relations, and to avoid involvement in the conflicts of the great powers.

As a grand duchy in the czarist empire, Finland until World War I traded extensively within the empire; up to 30 per cent of its exports and 27 per cent of its imports were with its eastern neighbor. In the interwar period, there was virtually no commercial connection between Helsinki and Moscow.[23] After the wars, then, a new structure governing Soviet-Finnish relations had to be fashioned.

This was done largely through the 1948 Treaty of Friendship, Cooperation, and Mutual Assistance, which helped meet Soviet security requirements but also acknowledged Finland's desire to remain outside of great power conflicts. In the commercial sector, the Finns successfully avoided Soviet initiatives to create joint Soviet-Finnish companies, modeled on the Soviet practice with Eastern Europe,[24] but the $300 million (1937 dollars) in reparations which Finland had to pay to the Soviet Union constituted an important impetus for developing trade relations between the two countries. These reparations were made up largely of machines, metal goods, and ships, all relatively new industries in Finland. In 1947 an agreement between the two countries also extended most-favored-nation status to Soviet goods entering Finland. Thus, by the early 1950s Finland's eastern connection accounted for between 15 and 20 per cent of the country's imports and exports. Compared to the interwar period, this amounted to a major restructuring of Finland's trade relations. The critical issue, however, was how to reconcile Finland's need to maintain access to Western markets, where important trade developments were occurring almost monthly, with the suspicion the Soviets held against all Western schemes of economic cooperation and integration. If the Soviets acknowledged Finland's right to remain outside great power conflicts, how could Finland participate in Western economic plans that the Russians saw as intimately connected with NATO?

In the hegemon's shadow: the prerequisites of neutrality

Through the 1948 Treaty of Friendship, Cooperation, and Mutual Assistance, the Soviet Union more or less resolved a traditional security problem in Northwest Europe: under the terms of the treaty - which differs significantly from the bilateral alliances Stalin made with the East European states - Soviet-Finnish military collaboration is required in the event of a German or allied attack on the Soviet Union *through Finnish territory*. But such collaboration can be undertaken only with the consent of the Finns. The two countries achieved further understanding during the 1961 'note crisis' - when the Soviets invoked the treaty in response to West German military undertakings in the Baltic - as the Finns successfully argued that even consultations under the treaty can taken place only if both parties agree there is an emerging threat to Soviet interests. In brief, the terms of the treaty are to become operational only with Finnish consent.

Soviet observers did not judge the reliability of Finland solely through the provisions of the 1948 treaty, however. The treaty provides only a general context for developing relations of reasonable trust. The overall view of Finland was embedded also in the Soviets' general perceptions of developments in Western Europe. Among these was a concern with the variety of plans and programs for economic collaboration and integration in Europe and Scandinavia. The Russians have seen these as political, mostly anti-Soviet, and linked to NATO. Hence, every move made by Finland to protect or expand its economic interests and its traditional markets in England, the Continent, and Scandinavia created considerable concern in Moscow. Russian observers typically viewed these situations in zero-sum terms: diplomatic moves that made Finland more economically involved with the West were deemed to cause a diminution in Soviet-Finnish ties. In some instances, as we will see, the Soviets even considered Finnish efforts to safeguard or increase access to Western markets as essentially anti-Soviet.[25]

The Soviets were concerned about the immediate economic stakes that could be lost were Finland's commercial ties to the West to lead to a diminution of commercial relations with the socialist countries. By the 1970s the Soviet Union had a very substantial economic stake in Finland. For example, in 1972 Finland ranked fourth among the Soviet Union's capitalist trade partners, behind Japan, West Germany, and the United States, but ahead of France, England and Italy.[26] In addition, the Soviets

115

found in Finland major markets for oil exports, nuclear plants, military equipment, and some large special purchases such as locomotives. In general, Soviet-Finnish commercial relations developed in volume and balanced composition far faster than similar Soviet ties with other Western countries. This was the case until the 1970s when, under detente, East-West trade boomed and Finland's comparative position as a major Soviet market and source of machinery declined somewhat.[27]

Although the Soviets have sought to protect this economic stake, they have never viewed it solely from a commercial perspective. To Soviet observers, the overall trade, scientific, and technical collaboration with the Finns is politically symbolic, a barometer of the overall character of the Soviet-Finnish relationship.[28] When the proportion of Finnish-Soviet trade has declined compared to Finland's increased trade share with the European Economic Community (EEC) and the European Free Trade Association (EFTA), the Soviets have been quick to point out that the overall distribution of Finnish imports and exports is becoming unbalanced and hence a matter of concern in Moscow. Less subtly, the Soviets have cut off trade relations and impending commercial negotiations several times in the postwar period as a means of pressuring the Finns to conform more strictly to the Soviet interpretation of Finnish neutrality. Although each of the postwar crises in Soviet-Finnish relations - in 1948-49, 1958 (the 'night frost'), and 1961 (the 'note crisis') - had a complex etiology, Raimo Väyrynen suggests that perhaps it was not mere coincidence that prior to each of the three applications of Soviet economic sanctions against Finland, the latter's trade with the socialist states had declined, whereas with the West it had increased proportionately.[29]

Under these circumstances, the Finns found themselves in the 1940s and 1950s substantially constrained in their foreign economic relations. Virtually no move toward the West could be launched without considering its potential effect on the predominant Soviet-Finnish security relationship. To the extent that there is any pattern in postwar Finnish foreign policy, including commercial policy, it has been to forgo those ties with the West that cause the most consternation in Moscow, while taking steps to bolster Soviet confidence. As that confidence has increased and as Soviet-Finnish commercial relations have deepened, the constraints have relaxed. The strategy has been called the 'Paasikivi-Kekkonen line', recognizing the two postwar Finnish presidents who instilled in the Finnish population and the various political parties the view that Finland's continued independence and security depend ultimately upon Soviet trust and that, therefore, commercial undertakings would have to be

116

fashioned in the context of this primary foreign-policy goal. When necessary, welfare goals would have to be subordinated to security goals - and in the 1940s and 1950s this was usually the case.

The overall thrust of diversifying contacts and the credibility of Finnish neutrality have been dependent upon maintaining good relations with Moscow. As President Urho Kekkonen stated in a speech in 1958, 'The more confident relations we have with the East, the better the opportunities for strengthening ties with [other] countries'.[30]

For the first three decades of postwar Soviet-Finnish relations, then, external commercial policy was subordinated to foreign policy to the extent that no association or commitments could be made to the West, no matter how commercially advantageous to Finland, without at least tacit Soviet agreement. Finnish diplomacy thus had this single overriding purpose: to convince the Russians that Finland's attempts to extend and protect economic and other ties with the West were not anti-Soviet. In many cases, as we will see, the Finns succeeded, but only by fashioning innovative associative agreements with the Scandinavian and continental countries and by balancing every new entry to the West with some corresponding new association with the East. This is not to suggest that policy developed along a straight line, moving consistently from virtual client status in the 1940s and 1950s to a position of considerable freedom by the 1970s. Intermixed with expanding contacts with the West have been self-denials, procrastination, and occasional buckling under to Soviet threats and virtual vetoes. But overall, the Finns have succeeded in achieving what no military force could: they have bolstered, balanced, and sometimes beguiled the Soviets - and sometimes Western governments - to the point where today commercial relationships are determined largely by economic rather than security considerations.

Subordinating welfare goals to security requirements, 1948-55

Harto Hakovirta has chronicled the postwar Soviet-Finnish relationship, analyzing Russian responses to Finnish initiatives toward the West and the various ways Finnish government officials weighed external expectations and constraints ('power' considerations) against economic opportunities in the West.[31] In sixteen cases, ranging from the invitation extended to join the Marshall Plan to Finland's association with the EEC in 1972, the Soviets initially opposed all but three of the initiatives. In two of the three exceptions, the Soviet position, though not entirely

117

negative, was nevertheless reserved. In each other instance, the opposition was more or less explicit, usually on the grounds already mentioned: that Finnish membership in various Western or Scandinavian economic integration or collaboration schemes is inconsistent with neutrality.[32]

The Marshall Plan

Like all countries in Europe, including the Soviet Union, Finland was invited to attend a conference in Paris to establish the modalities for joining and administering the Marshall Plan. The Soviets branded the program an American initiative to create European 'slaves', and after consulting Moscow, all the East European countries declined to attend. In Helsinki political parties and business groups strongly supported Finnish participation, because at this time the Finns were desperately short of capital necessary for postwar economic reconstruction. There was, in brief, a demonstrated set of economic needs that could be met through the Marshall Plan.

The Soviet vice-chairman of the Allied Control Commission in the Finnish capital apparently informed the Finnish prime minister that the Soviet Union expected Finland to turn down the invitation to attend the Paris conference. The government's decision, after much soul-searching, was to reject the invitation on the grounds that because the Marshall Plan had become a subject of great power controversy, and because Finland wanted to remain outside great power conflicts, it would not be possible to participate in it.[33] Sympathizing with its plight in this instance, the United States after 1948 made significant loans to Finland. These went, however, to the woodworking industry and superstructural projects, not to engineering companies that were exporting to the Soviet Union.[34]

The Nordic Council

Negotiations to organize the Nordic Council had begun in 1953. The Scandinavian countries, recognizing Finland's particular situation, were generally sympathetic to its cautious approach to the enterprise. In the early stages of discussion, the Soviets had remained mute, but Hakovirta suggests that the Soviet Union likely let it be known through diplomatic channels that Finnish membership in the council would be inconsistent with good Soviet-Finnish relations.[35] In December 1953 Finnish negotiators announced that Finland could not join the Nordic Council presently but would review the decision at an appropriate future time. President Juho Paasikivi's judgement was critical. Given the

118

background of the Korean War and the general high state of international tension in the early 1950s, he concluded that it was in Finland's best interests - security interests, that is - not to take risks. Although the economic stakes of abstention were not perhaps as significant as in the Marshall Plan case, there was considerable support for Finnish participation among the non-Communist political parties and the public in general. The official Soviet position is unknown in this case, but it is significant that in 1955, as the Finns kept the issue of joining on the political agenda, the Soviet government newspaper *Izvestia* stated that Finnish membership in the council would be against the interests of peace and would involve Finland in America's aggressive anti-Soviet policies.[36]

In the context of a fundamental change in Soviet foreign policy toward the West later in 1955, as manifested in the Austrian treaty, the Soviet Union's return of the Porkkala peninsula to Finland, and the major compromise with the United States whereby a number of states, including Finland, were able to join the United Nations, the Soviet position on the Nordic Council altered as well. Soviet objections to the organization waned, and when Kekkonen, then the Finnish prime minister, met with Nikita Khrushchev in September 1955, the latter raised no objections to Finland's proposed membership in the council. The Finnish government thereupon applied for membership, but the prime minister declared that Finland's representatives would not participate in any council discussions that entered the military realm or involved policies relating to conflicts between great powers. This was to become a familiar recipe for Finnish involvement in Western collaborative projects: participation in economic, scientific, technical and cultural enterprises, but withdrawal from any or all discussions or plans that might impinge upon the Soviet Union's security concerns.

Reconciling welfare goals and security needs: the balancing strategy

Despite the Soviet Union's about-face on the question of the Nordic Council, it continued to oppose Finnish participation in various schemes for a Nordic customs union and an extended free trade area. The objections raised in the years 1956-59 were traditional political ones: Finnish participation in such schemes is inconsistent with its neutrality policy, and these economic associations are inextricably linked to NATO. From the Finnish perspective, these discussions were not entirely critical, as Finland's main export markets were not located in the

Scandinavian countries. A cautious attitude toward economic association did not, therefore, involve compromising extensive commercial opportunities. The creation of EFTA raised much more serious issues.

FINEFTA

The creation of the 'Outer Seven' presented a serious dilemma for Finnish policy-makers. The challenge was to gain the rights of participation in a trading group that represented a market of 100 million consumers, more than one-half of whom were in England, Finland's largest single export market, while not appearing to alter significantly the direction of foreign policy, that is, to reduce ties to the East. Part of the solution was fashioned by a complicated institutional formula whereby Finland became only an associate member of the organization in which certain decisions were made by a special EFTA-Finnish Council. The final formula was a special free trade association of the Outer Seven plus Finland, which operated under the special FINEFTA treaty.

Soviet reaction to the Finnish-EFTA negotiations were initially hostile, but significantly, it did not emphasize the political dimensions of the problem. Most Soviet commentaries did not try to establish a link between EFTA and NATO. When the Soviet foreign trade minister and Vice-Premier Anastas Mikoyan visited Helsinki in the autumn of 1959, they emphasized only that any Finland-EFTA arrangement should not be made at the expense of Soviet-Finnish trade relations.[37] The Finnish strategy, in addition to offering verbal assurances that a Finland-EFTA agreement was designed solely to guarantee continued Finnish access to European markets, was to begin simultaneous trade negotiations with the Soviets. The resolution of the problem took more than one year. But in September 1960, when Khrushchev paid a visit to Helsinki on the occasion of President Kekkonen's sixtieth birthday, a communique announced that the Soviet Union appreciated Finland's desire to maintain a competitive position in Western trade and that the two countries would explore ways and means of ensuring that Finnish-Soviet trade would develop as well. The Finns signed agreements with the Soviet Union extending most-favored-nation treatment - that is, allowing Soviet access to Finnish markets on terms similar to those extended to members of the EFTA - and concluded a special customs agreement less than one week after the signing of the FINEFTA agreement.

The successful resolution of the problem was of great significance to Finnish foreign policy. It demonstrated, among other things, that the Soviets were able to decouple Western economic projects from the military realm and that, therefore, they could concede that special trade arrangements with European trade blocs did not compromise Finland's neutrality provided, however, that Finland could offer reasonable economic compensation.

The problem was not resolved permanently, however. Shortly after the FINEFTA agreement, Britain, the keystone of the Outer Seven, began negotiating the terms of entry into the EEC. Once again, Finland was faced with the possible loss of a major market. The Soviets undoubtedly see EFTA and the EEC in very different lights. Austria, Switzerland, Sweden and Finland, members of the EFTA, were neutral, whereas all the members of the EEC were members of NATO. The strategy of balancing worked for Finland's association with the Outer Seven. What would be the case where economic-military links were much more apparent, as in the EEC?

Finland and the EEC

Finland's negotiations with the EEC ended successfully in 1972. The major concern of access to markets was resolved favorably, and the agreement referred to Finland's previous treaty obligations, which of course would include the 1948 treaty with the Soviet Union. Although the agreement was initialed in 1972, it was not signed until October 1973, more than one year after the other EFTA members had made their own arrangements with the EEC. The reason was that during the interval, the Finns were busily engaged in commercial negotiations with the socialist countries - another application of the balancing strategy.

That Finland's association with the EEC was dependent upon maintaining and expanding contacts with the East was made clear in President Kekkonen's speech of November 1972. It nicely summarizes the symbolic importance of trade and the predominance of political considerations underlying all of Finland's commercial contacts abroad:

Neither the EEC treaty presently under consideration... nor any other commercial arrangement which we make in the West can, against our own interests, force us on a road which would lead to the weakening of the preconditions for economic coopera-tion in the East. That is something we can take care of. As my own opinion, I would like to put forward that if the customs treaty with the EEC were concluded, and if it were later found out that the treaty would prevent Finnish-Soviet trade from increasing, as it should keep on doing, Finland must resort to her right to give notice of discontinuance [with the EEC] within three months as stipulated by the treaty.[38]

Three month withdrawal or abrogation clauses are not often found in major international treaties. That it was included in the Finland-EEC free trade treaty suggests the critical sensitivity of the Finns toward any possibility that the treaty would work against the interests of Finnish-Soviet commercial relations.

The Soviets had not been enthusiastic about Finland's association with the EEC. The Russian view that the EEC is essentially a political creation could very well have led to a Soviet veto against Finnish association on the grounds that the 1948 security treaty precludes either party from participating in a coalition directed against the other. The other tack would have been to object on the grounds that Finland's neutrality is not consistent with even associate membership in the major Western trade bloc. The Russians did not, however, invoke the treaty, nor did they launch an anti-Finnish propaganda campaign. The reasons for the relatively low-keyed Soviet opposition included a series of high-level Finnish reassurances about the compatibility of EEC-Finnish free trade with expanding commercial relations toward the socialist countries, several high-level meetings (including the critical sessions between Leonid Brezhnev and Kekkonen in Zavidovo in August 1972) and perhaps most important, the continuation of the balancing strategy.

While Finland was negotiating with the EEC, it began negotiations - the first of their kind between a capitalist economy and the socialist group - to join with the Council for Mutual Economic Assistance (CMEA) in a special relationship. Although not a customs or trade agreement, the Finland-CMEA treaty of May 1973 established a joint commission that conducts research and gathers information on trade, technical, and scientific collaboration between all CMEA members, Yugoslavia and Finland.[39] In the autumn of 1973, Finland also began bilateral discussions with the East European countries aimed at reducing obstacles to trade (the KEVSOS agreements) and at offering the socialist countries access to Finnish markets on virtually the same terms as those offered to the EEC countries. These agreements did not go unnoticed in Moscow. Moreover, although the growth of Soviet-Finnish trade in the 1960s was not as dynamic as some might have wished, in general throughout the decade the institutionalization of Soviet-Finnish trade (through five year and one year agreements overseen by a high level commission) had developed well. In addition, there were numerous joint industrial projects and special Finnish purchases of Soviet goods and services that had prominent political overtures.

At least two instances of special purchases involving political factors in decision-making should be mentioned. The first was the Finnish government's reversal of a preliminary decision to award a contract to a British firm to build a nuclear generating plant in southern Finland: the contract was ultimately signed with a Soviet agency. Although Finland received significant economic benefits from the reversal - subcontracting and the use of this large contract to offset a Soviet-Finnish trade imbalance - many observers outside the government were convinced that the decision had been motivated primarily by a need to create a better balance between Soviet and Western trade.[40] Similarly, the Finnish state railways placed a large order for Soviet-built electric locomotives that, most agree, could easily have been built by Finnish firms.[41] And, finally, it should be noted that in the purchase of military equipment for the Finnish armed forces, the government has pursued a policy of diversification and balance; fighter aircraft, for example, have been purchased from England, Sweden, France, and the Soviet Union.[42]

From necessity to freedom: neutrality validated

Many Westerners, and particularly those who improperly impute to Finland a quasi-satellite status under the term 'Finlandization', view the general pattern of Finnish-Soviet commercial relations as a result of Russian pressures: the Finns are compelled to augment their trade relations in the East, regardless of costs or gains; the potential economic gains of further integration with the West are forsaken for the politically necessary but economically poor commercial nexus with the socialist states.[43]

In the first two postwar decades, Finland's latitude of choice was seriously circumscribed. The pursuit of economic gains through foreign trade and association with Western economic projects could be realized only with Soviet consent; and that consent had to be earned through a variety of means, including the 1948 treaty, the encouragement of greater trade ties with the Soviet Union, special purchases, and constant diplomatic efforts to reduce Soviet suspicions of Finnish intentions. Where there were conflicts, welfare goals had to be forsaken or postponed for the more compelling concerns of national security.

The need to create credibility for Finnish neutrality - not only in the socialist states but in some Western states as well - required balancing and constant efforts to reassure *both* sides that arrangements with the other were not at anyone else's expense. Both the socialist and some Western governments had viewed Finland's situation in essentially zero-sum terms. The thrust of Finnish diplomacy has been to dispel this view. Hence, it is largely off the mark to suggest that today Finnish trade with the socialist states involves no welfare gains. The facts of the case are that a large part of Finland's metal industry was created and is sustained by exports to the East (about 50 per cent of total metal exports). Several hundred thousand jobs rely directly on these exports, in a labor market of about two million. Finnish engineering firms have profited extensively from turn-key and other projects in the Soviet Union. And in areas of high unemployment, as in eastern Finland, the building of manufacturing plants in Soviet Karelia by Finnish workers has helped alleviate the problem.[44] Moreover, under the special institutional arrangements for CMEA-Finnish trade, Finnish firms are offered virtually guaranteed markets at predictable prices. In the 1970s and even today numerous Finnish firms are fighting to obtain even larger sales to the Soviet Union. Guaranteed markets over a minimum five year period offer a cushion against variable trade opportunities in the West, which during the past decade has been plagued by serious fluctuations and recession.[45]

Overall, the Finns have achieved their major goals: association with the EEC, long-term arrangements with the Soviet Union that bring considerable economic rewards, and an impetus to develop relations with the rest of Eastern Europe on terms similar to those obtained through the EEC. The trade pattern is not entirely balanced between geographic sources and destinations, but trade with socialist countries, which accounts for about 20 per cent of Finland's total foreign trade, appears to be politically satisfactory. There are problems in the composition of trade. Finnish imports of Soviet oil are offset by Finnish exports of manufactured goods, while the proportion of Soviet manufactured exports is generally declining. But these have become essentially economic problems, largely devoid of great political symbolism. Perhaps most significant, the Soviets have not pressed the Finns for further joint institutionalization or integration of their economies. In brief, through a variety of treaties, undertakings, understandings, and 'rules of the game', Finnish governments have managed to create a structure of economic relationships which maximizes welfare goals but which is also consistent with national security needs. Except for some tinkering and fine tuning, Finnish officials are generally pleased with this structure, which now makes it possible to base decisions primarily on economic considerations. Political concerns continue to underlie some undertakings, but the successful implementation of neutrality has taken foreign trade policy-making from the realm of necessity to one of relative freedom.

The Finnish case illustrates the fluctuating relationship between the values of 'power' and 'plenty'. In the early postwar years the

Soviet-Finnish relationship had not been carefully defined, and few 'rules of the game' had developed. In these circumstances, Soviet constraints on Finnish foreign policy, including external trade, were compelling, with the consequence that the Finnish government on numerous occasions had to forgo significant economic opportunities in the West to meet Soviet objections and expectations. Over the years, however, the relationship became more stable, trust developed (not without ups and downs, however), and through the balancing mechanism, the Finns were able to offset deepening economic involvement in the West with favorable compensations toward the East. As the concerns of military security and political autonomy became less problematic, the Finns could more vigorously pursue opportunities with the West, to the point where economic and security considerations today have become largely uncoupled. Within certain parameters worked out slowly over years of careful diplomacy, trade decisions are currently made with economic calculations clearly in the forefront.

Observations

No single model of the nexus between economics and politics is sufficiently rich to account for the very different circumstances of all countries. Nor will static models do. The connection between economics and politics cannot be essentially the same in the United States and Fiji, or Japan and Bhutan. All countries have welfare and security goals, yet the manner in which they pursue them varies across time and over different issues. For some states the diplomacy of security and the diplomacy of foreign trade have few links; that is, the criteria and values used in decision-making on various issues within the two realms tend to be exclusive and seldom intrude on each other. For others, in contrast, trade and security concerns may be so inextricably woven together that it is impossible to tell where the one ends and the other begins. For these countries, all trade has important diplomatic connotations. Foreign trade policy must be organized to be consistent with national security requirements, even if considerable economic losses or forsaken opportunities result. Contextual characteristics largely determine the nexus.

Many countries face such highly restrictive, almost compelling security situations in which various forms of mercantilism - defined as the subordination of welfare goals to diplomatic and security considerations - are adopted as a means of national survival. Trade is structured to maximize national security, independence, and autonomy. State and private economic interests are intertwined, as in the Marxist view of political economy, but the cause-effect relationships run in directions contrary to those in dependency theory: the state is not the handmaiden of class interests; rather, class interests are mobilized, constrained, and directed in order to meet state objectives that are critical to the maintenance of independence and military security. In other words, the survival or autonomy of the political community is a more fundamental value than economic maximization. Structural constraints for such states are compelling, though not in the way portrayed in the Marxist literature. The critical issue is national independence and security, not exploitation, and thus class interests are basically irrelevant.

The primacy of security concerns for such states does not always go unchallenged. A variety of domestic groups understand that although diplomatic necessities require less than optimum economic decisions, favorable trade and investment opportunities abroad cannot go begging. Strong forces within the society demand some sort of 'escape' from the pattern of trade that the state has fashioned for its security and diplomatic purposes. The two case studies presented here illustrate the *changing* relationship between economics and politics, and show how external constraints can under proper circumstances be reduced or circumvented in order to provide more latitude of choice and to give greater weight to welfare goals. Astute diplomacy can eventually reduce the determinative reasons for strict mercantilism and enhance the opportunities for creating a better balance between 'power and plenty'.

It came perhaps as a surprise to a number of American international relations scholars in the 1970s that issues of trade, resources, debts, financing and loans could become issues of 'high policy'. Symptomatic of the shift in focus in international studies was the publication of the article by Richard Cooper entitled 'Trade Policy Is Foreign Policy', as if this were some new insight.[46] As the cases of Finland and Japan illustrate, the combination would be a mere truism to policy-makers and academics in many other countries.

The two cases do not warrant any overarching generalizations about the nexus between politics and economics in international relations. It will vary from country to country, depending more on geographical and strategic conditions than on any structure in the Marxist sense. However, the cases do support the contention of some that when there is a conflict between sets of values, the choice will be on the side of security. As Gilpin has put it, 'noble [foreign policy] goals will be lost unless one makes provision for one's security in the power struggle among social groups',[47] and Kenneth Waltz, underlining the separateness of the economic and political realms, argues that in a self-help system, 'considerations of security subordinate economic gains to political interest'.[48] There is, after all, a hierarchy of values; the pursuit of wealth through external contacts can only be consistent with security requirements - which means that often wealth is not optimized.

The cases also show, however, that the connection changes over time. Although Finland and Japan in the era under discussion had contrasting positions in the international system - one was a neutral bordering a superpower, the other a distant ally of the other superpower - both countries faced a similar problem, namely having to restructure patterns of foreign trade to accommodate the expectations and security requirements of a superpower. The discussion suggests that economic opportunities had to be subordinated or forsaken until, through diplomacy, the two states could build up trust, both by overcoming the attitudinal legacies of former battlefield enemies and by establishing parameters of foreign policy roles and orientations acceptable to the superpowers. The Japanese shaped their diplomacy and trade to be consistent with the role of a faithful ally; this strategy precluded extensive ties with a major opponent of the United States, Communist China. The Finns had to work out over a period of years exactly what forms of behavior were consistent with the role of a neutral. In the early postwar years of the Soviet-Finnish relationship, trust was lacking in Moscow and hence the Russians interpreted Finnish neutrality as requiring the absence of any links with Western economic organizations. As the Finns demonstrated that the protection or expansion of trade arrangements with the West would not be at the expense of Soviet security or commercial interests, Moscow found increasingly acceptable Finland's interpretation of 'balanced' neutrality. Both cases suggest, then, that security considerations predominate in the hierarchy of values when national roles are ambiguous and diversely interpreted, when trust is lacking, and when reputations have not been established. As the nature of the relationships becomes more fixed, the latitude for choice expands, and the security and commercial realms tend to become separated. Neither is subordinated to the other, and the states in question can have the best of both worlds, power *and* plenty. Even though international tensions increased in the 1980s to levels often found in the 1950s, neither Japan nor Finland had to revert to the policies of that decade. The particular characteristics of bilateral relations - especially trust, reputation, and role behavior - seem to be more important in explaining the changing value hierarchy than broad contextual features, such as detente or declining polarity.

Notes

1. Some of the flavor of the debate is indicated by the vigorous attack on 'neorealism' offered by Richard K. Ashley (1984), 'The Poverty of Neorealism', *International Organization*, 38, Spring, pp. 225-86.
2. The problem is raised in R. B. J. Walker (1985), 'Realism, Change and International Political Theory', paper presented at the annual meeting of the Canadian Political Science Association, Montreal, 1-3 June.
3. Robert Gilpin (1975), *U.S. Power and the Multinational Corporation*, New York: Basic, p.43; Robert O. Keohane (1984), *After Hegemony*, Princeton: Princeton University Press, pp. 21-2.
4. Robert Gilpin (1981), *War and Change in World Politics*, Cambridge: Cambridge University Press, pp. 19-20.
5. I do not pose the problem in terms of economic costs directly associated with pursuing 'power' policies, since any foreign policy action involves economic costs. Recent studies that substantiate the 'primacy of politics' argument fail to distinguish between normal economic costs of such policies and costs conceived as forsaken economic opportunities. See, for example, Jorge I. Dominguez and Juan Lindau (1984), 'The Primacy of Politics: Comparing the Foreign Policies of Cuba and Mexico', *International Political Science Review*, 5, 1, pp. 75-101.
6. Robert E. Ward (1966), 'The Legacy of the Occupation', in American Assembly, *The United States and Japan*, Englewood Cliffs, NJ: Prentice-Hall, p. 34.
7. Figures are from Chai-Jin Lee (1976), *Japan Faces China: Political and Economic Relations in the Postwar Era*, Baltimore: Johns Hopkins University Press, chap. 4.
8. Figures are from Ward, 'The Legacy of the Occupation', pp. 42-3; Lee, *Japan Faces China*, p. 144.
9. Quoted in Frederick S. Dunn (1963), *Peace-Making and the Settlement with Japan*, Princeton: Princeton University Press, p. 99.
10. *New York Times*, 2 September 1949.
11. John R. Maeno (1973), 'Postwar Japanese Policy toward Communist China, 1952-1972: Japan's Changing International Relations and the New Political Culture', Ph.D diss., University of Wisconsin, pp. 30-2.
12. Quoted in *ibid.*, p. 38.
13. Cf. Shogo Yamaguchi (1953), 'Economic Difficulties Facing Japan', in Edwin O. Reischauer et al., *Japan and America Today*, Stanford: Stanford University Press, p. 116.
14. Maeno, 'Postwar Japanese Policy', p. 24.
15. In English, Lee's study, *Japan Faces China*, is the most definitive.
16. *Ibid.*, p. 144.
17. *Ibid.*, p. 145.
18. For comparative figures, see the annual publication of the Tsuneta Yano Memorial Society, *Nippon 1961: A Survey of Japan*, Tokyo: Kokusei-Sha, yearly.
19. Peter Ping-Chii Cheng (1964), 'A Study of John Foster Dulles' Diplomatic Strategy in the Far East', Ph.D diss., Southern Illinois University, p. 44.

20. For examples, see Maeno, 'Postwar Japanese Policy', p. 44.
21. *Ibid.*, p. 56.
22. Quoted in Elaine Burnell (ed.) (1970), *Asian Dilemma: United States, Japan, and China*, Rutland, Vt.: Charles E. Tuttle, pp. 72-3.
23. Fred Singleton (1981), 'The Myth of "Finlandization"', *International Affairs*, 57, Spring, p. 275.
24. George Maude (1976), *The Finnish Dilemma*, London: Oxford University Press, p. 104.
25. Harto Hakovirta (1976), *Puolueettomuus ja Integraatiopolitiikka*, Acta Universitatis Tamperensis, ser. A. vol. 78, Tampere: Tampere University, pp. 132-33.
26. Hannu T. Linnainmaa (1975), 'Finland's Cooperation with CMEA-Member Countries and the Agreement between Finland and the CMEA', *Co-Existence*, 12, p. 5.
27. Harto Hakovirta and Pasi Patokallio (1975), 'East-West Economic Cooperation: Is There a Finnish Model?', *Conflict and Cooperation*, 10, pp. 33-50.
28. Osmo Apunen (1977), *Paasikiven-Kekkosen Linja*, Helsinki: Tammi, p. 309. A general discussion of the political foundations of Soviet-Finnish trade is in Raimo Väyrynen (1975), 'Talous ja politiikka suomen ja neuvostoliiton suhteissa vuosina 1945-1970', in Harto Hakovirta and Väyrynen (eds), *Suomen Ulkopolitiikka*, Jyväskylä: Gaudeamus, pp. 315-74.
29. Raimo Väyrynen (1972), *Conflicts in Finnish-Soviet Relations: Three Comparative Case Studies*, Acta Universitatis Tamperensis, ser. A, vol. 47, Tampere: Tampere University, p.322. Also, Väyrynen, 'Talous ja politiika suomen', pp. 364-70.
30. Hakovirta, *Puolueettomuus ja Integraatiopolitiikka*, p. 187.
31. *Ibid.*
32. The outcomes of the cases are summarized in Hakovirta, *Puolueettomuus ja Integraatiopolitiikka*, p. 304. Much of the discussion about the Finnish cases comes from this valuable study. A few other details are found in Apunen, *Paasikiven-Kekkosen Linja*.
33. Hakovirta, *Puolueettomuus ja Integraatiopolitiikka*, pp. 146-50; Apunen, *Paasikiven-Kekkosen Linja*, pp. 41-2.
34. Raimo Väyrynen (1977), 'Finland's Role in Western Policy since the Second World War', *Cooperation and Conflict*, 12, pp. 92-4.
35. Hakovirta, *Puolueettomuus ja Integraatiopolitiikka*, p. 156.
36. *Ibid.*, p. 159.
37. *Ibid.*, p. 205.
38. Harto Hakovirta (1975), *Suomettuminen*, Jyväskylä: Gumerus, quoted on p. 145.
39. Details in Linainmaa, 'Finland's Cooperation with CMEA-Member Countries', p. 5-12.
40. Interview, officials in Finland's Ministry of Foreign Affairs, 17 June 1983; also Paavo Kähkölä (1971), *Suomen Idänkauppa*, Helsinki:Otava, pp. 69-78.
41. *Ibid.*, pp. 75-83.
42. Vilho Harle (1979), 'Convergent vs. Conflicting Interests in Processes of Armament Requisition: A Case Study of Two Finnish Decisions on the Procurement of Military Aircraft', *Conflict and Cooperation*, 14, pp. 21-33.

Considerations other than balance are of course involved in such purchases.

43. A discussion of the Soviet pressure model is in Paavo Laitinen (1975), 'Suomen Kansainväliset Taloudelliset Suhteet Vuosina 1956-1975', in Keijo Korhonen (ed.), *Urho Kekkonen: Rauhanpolitiikka*, Helsinki: Otava, p. 189.
44. Ari Salminen (1983), 'Tapaustutkimus Talouden Politiikan ja Hallinon Keskenäisistä Kytkennöistä: Suomen Idankauppan Suuryritykset', ser. A, Mimeo, Helsinki University, Political Science Department Studies, p. 9.
45. Interviews, officials in Finland's Ministry of Foreign Affairs and Ministry of Foreign Trade, 17-18 June 1983.
46. Richard N. Cooper (1972-73), 'Trade Policy is Foreign Policy', *Foreign Policy*, 9, Winter, pp. 18-36.
47. Robert Gilpin (1984), 'The Richness of the Tradition of Political Realism', *International Organization*, 38, Spring, p. 291.
48. Kenneth Waltz (1979), *Theory of International Politics*, Reading, MA: Addison-Wesley, p. 107.

6. Revolution in the Revolution: World Views and Foreign Policy Change in the Soviet Union

We are seeing a revolutionary transformation of the intellectual bases of Soviet foreign policy - how the Soviet leaders see the outside world, and how they define Russia's roles, tasks, commitments, and responsibilities in the international system. I will be less concerned with dissecting the meaning of specific policies than with outlining changes in the perceptions of Soviet leaders and the role of ideology in foreign policy formulation. This essay is thus an examination of ideas rather than of actions, although I wish to demonstrate some connections between them.

The problem of perceptions, images, 'operational codes' and, in general, of the intellectual bases of foreign policy-making inevitably raises that old and insoluble issue of the nexus between Marxist-Leninist ideology and Soviet foreign policy. The positions range from those who argue that ideological principles are virtually determinative of all actions, to those that suggest that since the early years following the Bolshevik revolution, the Soviet Union has been impelled primarily by considerations typical of all great powers, namely expanding power, prestige, and security. When there is a conflict between ideological imperatives and strategic opportunities and necessities, the latter will always prevail.

I cannot provide further arguments to the debate, but I would argue that the problem has usually been posed in simplistic, dichotomous terms. Ideological principles can be used in many ways: as guides to action, as plans for long-range goals, as philosophies of history, as perceptual lenses through which complex events in the world are assessed, sorted out, and generalized, and as justifications for actions taken. They are not immutable, seldom determinative, and rarely even commanding. But they are nevertheless important. They constitute the intellectual milieu of policy-making, providing a host of functions, such as categorizing types of regime, helping to define historical eras and their 'correlations of forces', identifying the sources of adversaries' foreign policy behavior, and outlining preferred futures, including the tasks and responsibilities of the Soviet Union in working towards those futures.

Though many dismissed the great Sino-Soviet ideological debates in the 1960s as little more than smokescreens for hegemonical pretensions,[1] it is hard to believe that the polemics dealing with such standard Marxist-Leninist issues as the nature of revolutions, the organization of the world revolutionary movement, the implications for socialism of the development of nuclear weapons, the nature of imperialism, and the like, were just window-dressing. My estimation is that the ideological issues between China and the Soviet Union - indeed throughout the world communist movement - were highly significant. Certainly they masked power rivalries between Beijing and Moscow, but one can make the case that the more mundane issues of territory, trade, and sharing nuclear technology would not have been sufficient to cause the total break between the two communist giants. The ideological issues were a necessary, and perhaps sufficient, source of the split, and thus were highly significant in explaining the behavior of both parties. As western pragmatists, it is often difficult for us to understand how 'true believers' see the world, and how ideological principles function in generating ideological conflict. We only have to remember that 340 years ago, the delegates to the conferences of Münster and Osnabrück representing the forces of Protestantism and Catholicism following the Thirty Years War, refused to talk to each other. The peace delegations had to meet in two separate cities, using horseback riders to dispatch communications between them. By the end of the seventeenth century, religious issues had almost disappeared as a source of international conflict, but for more than a century they had generated some of the longest and most brutal wars seen until the twentieth century. That the participants in the Thirty Years War also fought for more conventional 'reasons of state' does not diminish the fact that religious differences played a fundamental role in the genesis of the conflict, and in the intellectual bases of policy-makers in the early seventeenth century.

What we have seen during the Gorbachev period is the rapid growth of pragmatism in policy-making, and the systematic alteration, and in some cases, jettisoning, of traditional ideological components of foreign policy. Though there is room for debate about the sources of these changes, I will argue that they arise primarily from the realization that past policies have led to dead ends, and that unless the Soviet Union undertakes critical reforms both at home and abroad, primarily to take advantage of the new international division of labor, the Soviet Union will emerge as a second or third rate power early in the twenty-first century.

This essay will examine four major ideological tenets or beliefs that have underlain, without fundamental change, Soviet foreign policy since 1917. In all four areas Gorbachev and his colleagues have made substantial revisions, sometimes explicitly, sometimes implicitly, resulting in a different way of analyzing foreign policy problems and changes in the international system. Although there were minor changes in some of them in previous years, particularly under Khrushchev's leadership,[2] the record indicates a rather sturdy imperviousness in Soviet intellectual habits. The four areas are:

1) the role of conflict in history;
2) the nature of the capitalist world;
3) the roles and tasks of the Soviet Union as the bastion of the world revolution; and
4) the Soviet Union as the builder of a socialist world order.

There are other important sets of ideas (for example, the concept of 'correlation of forces') but I believe the four examined here are most significant because they constitute the Soviet leaders' self-definition, their views of Russia's historical tasks, their conceptions of the obligations of revolutionary leadership, and the nature of the opponents in international affairs. None of these areas determines specific policies, but they constitute the intellectual background for all policy-making; and they have remained remarkably constant throughout Soviet history.

Change in Soviet foreign policy

The problematic connection between world views and policy actions is illustrated by significant shifts in foreign policy, without accompanying alterations of doctrinal position. But it can be argued that those shifts were tactical, the inevitable adaptations to events and trends in the international environment, particularly to developments that the Soviet Union could not by itself control. In many cases, the shifts in policy were the result of necessity rather than choice. We note here some of those significant changes in policy; in each case there was no fundamental alteration of the four doctrinal areas discussed here.

The first shift of note was the Soviet adjustment to the failure of world revolution after 1917. We can recall Trotsky's famous comment to the effect that the new Soviet foreign ministry would issue a few revolutionary proclamations and then shut up shop. The Russians learned by the early 1920s that their expectation of world revolution had been premature, and for the Soviet regime to survive in a world of capitalist encirclement, it would be necessary to enter into the traditional games of international politics. In the 1920s, the Soviet Union established diplomatic relations with Germany (Rapallo), England, Japan, its immediate neighbors, and many other countries. Diplomatic 'representatives' were replaced by ambassadors and ministers, and external revolutionary activities mostly went underground. In 1934, the Soviet Union joined the League of Nations, signifying that if it could not immediately create a new world socialist system, it would have to operate in the present one, even dominated as it was by the great imperialist states.

Stalin's pact with Hitler in 1939 proved that the Soviet Union could operate as a cynical great power as well as anyone else. This dramatic change in policy cost the Soviet Union dearly in terms of the defection of millions of party adherents and sympathizers throughout the world. Yet even such a notable change in foreign policy orientation did not lead to a redefinition of the major ideological principles that relate to international affairs. For example, the notion of the implacable hostility of imperialism did not change; only the cast of characters altered.

Through the war and early postwar years, the pantheon of Soviet ideological principles remained basically intact, although there were shifts in definitions of the world situation. During his years of collaboration with Nazi Germany and the Western allies, Stalin never proclaimed that the fundamental nature of imperialism had changed, that the Soviet Union no longer had an internationalist, fraternal duty toward revolutionary movements, that the forces of historical change had altered, or that a world of socialist states was no longer a long-range goal of political activity. Many in the West believed, or hoped, that the common struggle against Nazism had reformed the Soviet Union, had shed it of its commitment to Marxist-Leninist principles and views of world history. There was the expectation as revealed in many post-Yalta declarations and treaties that the Soviet Union, having led the forces against Hitler, would now become just another major power, recognizing its special responsibilities for the maintenance of international peace and security, acting in collaboration with the other great powers, as in the manner of the nineteenth century Concert of Europe.

But it was clear to most as early as 1947 that the Soviet Union was not just another great power. True, it was not the sole instigator of the diplomatic syndrome we have come to call the Cold War. The West made many mistakes as well and even without stretching the realities too far, we can at least understand some of the Soviet fears of the era. The Soviet Union had significant security problems, and often in the West, its attempts to deal with them were taken as evidence of a plan to conquer the world.

The vast shifts in Soviet diplomacy between the early 1930s and the postwar period were not accompanied by intellectual and doctrinal changes. The prewar, war, and postwar experiences were in a sense imposed on the Soviet Union, and it responded mostly out of necessity. Nothing in that experience suggested that the main tenets of Marxism-Leninism, as they applied to international relations, were incorrect. Opportunities for revolutionary activity were seriously curtailed, and the first priority of Soviet diplomacy (as Lenin would also have conceded) was to provide for the security of the Soviet Union, the homeland of the first socialist revolution. But once the Nazi threat had been eliminated, the Soviet Union reverted to its revolutionary tasks and to the project of building a community of socialist states. Zhdanov's famous speech in 1947 re-established the primacy of world revolution in Soviet thinking about international affairs, discipline was reimposed over the world's communist parties, and all the old prognostications about the crises of capitalism, the inevitability of conflict between socialism and capitalism, and the rapacious nature of imperialism became standard fare for ideological pronouncements, party gatherings, and in the Soviet media. There was little in Soviet diplomacy to indicate that Stalin and his successors saw great power collaboration as the cornerstone of postwar peace and stability. Indeed, conflict served many Soviet foreign and domestic purposes; the idea of peace in the Soviet lexicon meant something very different from typical Western conceptions: peace was a situation in which active struggle for the revolutionary cause could be stepped up.

Khrushchev introduced significant ideological innovations during his tenure, but none of them touched upon the four themes discussed here. The doctrine of war inevitability had been used and abused more or less to suit the convenience of Stalin. Khrushchev was bending to technological realities in arguing that peaceful coexistence was the logical consequence of possessing weapons of mass destruction. In a pitch to obtain support for Western communist parties, he argued that the path to socialism could be a peaceful one. And after his trip to the United States in 1959, he even allowed that President Eisenhower was a man of peace - suggesting that there were at least some key figures among the imperialists that were not committed to unleashing a war against socialism. For these ideological innovations, he was roundly condemned by the Chinese, who retained much of the Stalinist demonology. But despite Khrushchev's symptoms of pragmatism, he did not change qualitatively many of the basic views of socialist doctrines as they relate to foreign policy and international relations. During the 1960s, ideological pronounce-ments on the character and sources of imperialism, the role of conflict in historical change, the long-range goals of Soviet foreign policy, and the Soviet Union's internationalist duties sounded familiar to statements in the 1920s.

Let us now examine in more detail the four themes that have remained largely constant throughout Soviet history, and note how they have been altered in recent years. To make comparisons, we employ references to speeches, commentaries, and interviews, to diplomatic initiatives, and most importantly, to non-events. Changing foreign policy can be measured not only by what has happened, but also by what did not happen.

The role of conflict in history

One of the intellectual roots of the Cold War syndrome lies in fundamentally inconsistent views about the nature of conflict in international relations. Nineteenth century liberal thought which has had great impact on the foreign policies of many European countries and the United States, proposed that the normal state of relations between societies is peaceful. There is a natural harmony between societies. It is best indicated by the great growth of trade and communications during the nineteenth and twentieth centuries, by the development of various forms of international collaboration and cooperation, and by the spread of liberal political and social institutions. In the West, conflict in international politics has usually been explained as the consequence of various forms of autocracy and militarism, as the result of poor communications and misunderstanding, or as the external manifestation of hostile ideologies, particularly those of fascism and communism. From Woodrow Wilson to Ronald Reagan, explanatory statements about the sources of international conflict have emphasized these institutional and ideological determinants. Sprinkled throughout myriads of speeches, news conferences, and political pronouncements are arguments to the effect that if the Marxist-Leninists disarmed themselves ideologically, or if authoritarian and totalitarian regimes gave way to democracies, harmony would be the rule rather than the exception in international relations. Westerners commonly regard conflict as a form of *deviant* behavior.

Marxist thought about conflict is almost exactly the opposite. Rather than a deviation from the norm of social intercourse, conflict is an inherent condition of all relationships between different kinds of social formations, international ones being no exception. Conflict is the motor of history, the source of human and social progress. Soviet foreign policy constantly contends with conflict not just because the interests of the great powers

136

may clash, but more importantly, because socialism, a higher form of economic organization, and its leaders *must* confront the forces of reaction, representing the narrow class interests of the bourgeoisie. Diplomatic conflict is a positive indicator that the two antagonistic forms of socioeconomic organization are performing the historical roles assigned to them in scientific Marxist-Leninist thought. There can be no solution to the problem of conflict until the world is organized along the lines of a single socialist division of labor. The 'golden age' will then have arrived, as there will be no more class warfare and contradictions within societies, and therefore no cause for conflict between societies. International conflict will become a deviant form of behavior only when there is, on a global scale, no more exploitation of man by man. In Marxist thinking, there is only a potential harmony between societies. In the meantime, the persistence of conflict between socialism and imperialism indicates that the world is developing according to the laws of Marxism. The internationalist duty of the Soviet Union is to continue giving history a nudge, to maintain the ardor of the revolutionary parties, to confront the forces of imperialism and reaction, and never to give way to bourgeois pacifist thinking, which is based on the notion of world harmony achieved through the *convergence* of antagonistic social systems. Soviet pronouncements have always spoken of the victory of socialism, not of convergences of ideologies and social systems.

This view of history has had several significant consequences on the conduct of Soviet foreign relations. The most important is the assumption that on every issue there are only two sides, one that is correct and progressive - consistent with the requirements of historical development - and the other that is wrong, reactionary, and contrary to the forces of progress. One of the reasons that Soviet leaders have almost never conceded errors in foreign policy results from this philosophical stance. There may be tactical mistakes, but usually these are accounted for by various forms of ideological deviation (Stalin), by 'adventurism' (Khrushchev), or by excessive concentration of decision-making authority (Stalin and Brezhnev). There has never been a statement to the effect that Marxist-Leninist principles are themselves the cause of errors. A type of moralism has imbued Soviet policy statements for decades. And when one is convinced that one's positions are correct, progressive, and principled, diplomatic compromises may be more difficult to achieve.

Gorbachev may not have initiated the idea that the Soviet Union's opponents have legitimate interests - some of Nikita Khrushchev's comments, and the 1972 Soviet-American agreement on the principles governing their relations imply it - but in introducing the concepts of 'balanced interests' and 'mutual security'[3] he has explicitly acknowledged that even imperialist states may have core interests that transcend the narrower concerns of the capitalist class, interests that have some legitimacy from the point of view of a system of states, of independent political orders whose motivations and security concerns are more fundamental than those of a single class.

When one concedes that international relationships are more complex than a morality play between the forces of good (and progress) and the forces of evil (and reaction), the room for compromise and flexibility increases. When one also acknowledges one's *own* errors, this further implies that international conflict may result not from the playing out of historical processes, but from the clash of national interests, and from faulty decision-making.

The notion of international politics as the adjustment of national interests, rather than as a historical process involving fundamentally different and antagonistic class interests, does not concede an underlying harmony between societies. A world of clashing interests can be a Hobbesian one as well as a liberal one, a world where the search for power and predominance is ubiquitous. But it vastly reduces the scope for moralism and thus allows more flexibility in diplomacy. Moreover, the Soviet Union in a world of 'balancing interests' becomes just one among many national actors, perhaps unique in some of its domestic arrangements, as well as in its size and economic potential. But it no longer occupies a special place in a historical process, with attending special responsibilities and commitments to encourage the world revolutionary process and to build a glorious new commonwealth of socialist states on the ashes of the capitalist world system. The policies of opponents, finally, are no longer seen as rooted in historical roles determined by class interests, but are inspired by the ordinary national concerns of security, economic welfare, prestige, and status. Location, level of economic development, the international perspectives of political elites *and* class interests account for national interests. If international politics is constituted primarily of the adjustment of national interests, there is also the possibility of *converging* interests - not just tactical arrangements, but long-term commonalities that can lead to collaboration and cooperation. In brief, Gorbachev's views of international politics suggest, at least by implication, that conflict is not an inevitable and progressive element of international relationships, but that it is, on the contrary, a potentially lethal phenomenon, a type of deviant behavior, but one that can be controlled for the benefit of all. In his own words, 'Security... can only be mutual, and, if we take

138

international relations as a whole, it can only be universal. The highest wisdom is not to be concerned exclusively for oneself, especially when this is to the detriment of the other side. It is necessary that everyone feel equally secure....[4] In the same speech, he proclaimed that global problems 'that affect all mankind' cannot be solved 'through the efforts of a single state or group of states. What is needed here is cooperation on a worldwide scale...' These are not the vocabularies and concepts of Marxism-Leninism. Security and problem-solving through world cooperation have little to do with traditional Soviet visions of world historical processes.

The nature of the capitalist world

Since the birth of the first socialist state, it has been a fundamental tenet of all Soviet leaders that the leading capitalist states are implacably hostile to the Soviet Union. The Allied interventions in Russia from 1918 to 1921 provided evidence in support of the proposition, as did certain Western policies after 1945: the unification of the Allied occupation zones of Germany, the creation of West Germany, the organization of NATO, numerous American, French, and British interventions against national liberation movements, and the like. The imperialists could be more or less aggressive, depending upon various factors in the international environment, but no Soviet spokesman since Trotsky and Lenin - some of Khrushchev's 'deviations' aside - has argued that the imperialists could change their essential characteristics or fail to play their historical roles.

During the Brezhnev years it became an article of faith that less belligerent policies by the leading imperialist states could be explained by the growth of Soviet military power. That vast military arsenal that the Soviets developed through the 1970s, Brezhnev suggested, was a mighty contribution to world peace. It was the factor that instilled caution and prudence among the leading statesmen of the capitalist states. Brezhnev adopted a classical 'peace through strength' diplomacy, noting that no fundamental change had taken place among the imperialists; they would revert to their predatory ways if the Soviet Union relaxed its vigilance. Detente was the fruit of nuclear weapons and Soviet military strength, not a change of heart among the leaders of the capitalist world. A particularly favorable correlation of forces made peace and detente possible, not an alteration in the nature of imperialism.

Gorbachev and his colleagues have had to face a serious intellectual dilemma. While Soviet military strength has continued to grow, the American arms buildup during the Reagan presidency and the threats implied by the development of new weapons systems, combined with Soviet diplomatic reverses in various areas of the world, have forced a change in the rather optimistic evaluation of the international situation that characterized the Brezhnev years. All the economic and military indicators suggest that imperialism has been growing stronger, and that there has been a relative decline in the Soviet Union's international position. Yet, Gorbachev has stated that during such a transition, imperialism has *not* been growing more aggressive.[5] Quite the contrary. In agreeing to accept various Western arms control proposals, Soviet diplomacy has implied that there may be an inherent reasonableness in Western policies despite the relative growth of Western power. One can deal with the West not so much out of necessity, but out of a genuine concern for creating a more stable international order. Gorbachev's attitudes and policies imply that imperialism may indeed have changed its fundamental characteristics, and not just because of Soviet policies.

Such a view would be a most serious deviation from classical Soviet pronouncements about, and analyses of, the opponent. It is inconsistent with many of the fundamentals of Marxist-Leninist thinking about international affairs, and it at least creates the possibility that the West can no longer be blamed for the sacrifices that ordinary Soviet citizens have endured since the Bolshevik revolution. In seeking a wide range of agreements with the imperialists, the current Soviet leadership has implicitly acknowledged that the imperialist states may not be implacably hostile, and that various arrangements between the powers may enhance the cause of peace and security - regardless of Soviet military strength. Gorbachev has even hinted that the West has legitimate reasons to fear Soviet military strength and deployments, and Yevgeny Primakov, Director of the Institute of World Economy and International Relations, has allowed that the West may be less of a threat to the USSR than had hitherto been assumed.[6]

The Soviet Union and world revolution

On numerous occasions Lenin declared that it was an obligation for the Soviet Union to intervene politically and militarily to assist the world's struggling proletariat. Subsequent statements have been more permissive, but until Gorbachev, the internationalist revolutionary obligation remained a cornerstone of Soviet self-perceptions and external activities. Even when speaking of the necessities of peaceful coexistence, party and government leaders constantly uttered the refrain of the Soviet Union's fraternal and internationalist duties. These derived from ideological premises and from Marxist-Leninist definitions of legitimate forms of political activity and their views of world historical processes. This is not to argue that such international duties to promote, support, and sustain the struggles of the world's proletariat overrode considerations of Russian national interests - they have traditionally abandoned clients and sympathizers abroad when it served their interests. But no Soviet leader failed during his incumbency to profess belief in Russia's international revolutionary role, and most committed substantial resources to fulfilling those fraternal and internationalist responsibilities.

Even during the height of detente, the commitment did not falter. It could be accommodated under the idea of a clear distinction between inter-state relations and inter-party relations. The 1972 agreement on the basic principles of relations between the United States and the Soviet Union foundered over this distinction. To the Americans, the agreement constituted a Soviet commitment to avoid interventions and military forays around the world. The Russians, in contrast, argued that the principles governing the conduct of mutual super-power relations applied only bilaterally, and only in the relations between governments. The Soviet Union would refrain from challenging American security interests (the United States would practice similar self-restraint), it would do nothing to exacerbate Cold War conflicts, and it would undertake to avoid all forms of behavior that could lead to escalation and nuclear war. Such an explicit commitment to create a regime of peaceful coexistence between Washington and Moscow did not mean, however, that the Soviet leaders had redefined their self-image as a special agent of the world revolutionary process. Nowhere in the agreement did the Russians renounce their internationalist duties; indeed, in subsequent speeches, they went out of their way to reaffirm Soviet commitments to the world revolutionary process. Involvements in Yemen, Angola, and Ethiopia provided concrete evidence of the continuation of traditional revolutionary policies. Those involvements could not be explained on grounds other than ideological imperatives. The Soviet Union had no traditional interests in those areas, and the slight strategic benefits they might have derived from them were hardly adequate compensation for the extensive costs they involved. Soviet policies in the Third World in the 1970s largely matched ideological pronouncements dealing with questions of the world revolutionary process and the Soviet Union's role therein.

Much of that has changed in the last few years. In particular, we note non-events and their significance. In the first place, the

Sino-Soviet relationship has become devoid of ideological content. The agenda for the normalization of relations between the two socialist states has been constituted of traditional-type diplomatic and territorial problems. None of the great ideological issues, over which so much ink, and a little blood, flowed in the 1960s, is mentioned in the numerous *demarches* taken by the Russians to mend fences. Soviet commentaries on Chinese economic heresies have been muted, and the struggle to see who would lead the world communist movement no longer makes headlines. If the Soviet leaders continue to see themselves as the bastion of the revolution, they are not proclaiming it loudly, and most of their diplomatic actions contradict such a role.

A second non-event was the non-intervention (military) of the Soviet Union in the years of unrest in Poland.[7] The Solidarity movement represented as much a threat to ideological orthodoxy as did the reforms of the 1968 Prague spring. By acknowledging the legitimacy of at least the economic parts of the Solidarity program, the Polish and Russian party authorities more or less implied that the 'legitimate' working class parties do not have a monopoly on truth and wisdom. Gorbachev has stated this in reference to the situation of the CPSU when discussing the necessity of reforms at home, but the genesis of this innovation may well have been in the shipyards of Gdansk.

The declining importance of the Soviet perceptions of the 'bastion of the revolution' role is indicated by several other recent developments. The domestic political reforms and rearrangements of high office announced at the extraordinary conference of the CPSU in June 1988 suggest a downplaying of inter-party relations and an upgrading of government-to-government relations. The largely symbolic presidential function is to be transformed into an effective locus of power. Although this may be reminiscent of Stalin's concerns about status equality at international meetings, it is likely that Gorbachev has more serious purposes in mind. From the perspective of international relations, the important point is that all post-Stalin leaders were primarily party leaders, indicating the need to maintain the pre-eminence of this office when dealing with other communist parties. No doubt under the proposed reforms the First Secretary of the CPSU will also be the President of the Soviet Union, but ultimately, the President's office may develop into (and be seen as) the source of real authority in the Soviet Union. The Soviet Union will then be identified even more strongly as another *state* in a community of states, with a corresponding diminution of its identity as a revolutionary internationalist party with global tasks intended to promote world revolution.

Finally, recent Soviet policy maneuvers have indicated an

increasingly arm's-length approach to client states and foreign communist parties. Moscow is currently on the defensive among its traditional Middle East allies for taking steps to establish diplomatic relations with Israel, and for promoting the idea of an international conference to deal with the Palestine issue. It has encouraged clients in regional conflicts (Vietnam and Angola) to seek peaceful solutions to their problems, using threats to cut off sources of supply if the clients did not adhere to the new Soviet priorities on the broader international arena. Apparently, performing one's internationalist duty, as conceived originally by Lenin and his successors, will no longer command such great priority if it conflicts with other concerns. Here is another realm where the ideological component of foreign policy is being not only downgraded, but systematically altered and perhaps eventually jettisoned.

The Soviet Union as the builder of a socialist community of states

Since its birth in 1917, leaders of the CPSU have repeatedly proclaimed their commitment to the long-range goal of helping to build a community of socialist states and, ultimately, a united world socialist economy. The vision of a new type of international system - although rarely spelled out in much detail - has never failed to inspire Soviet rhetoric, and sometimes policy as well. The significance of transcending the system of bourgeois-led states that emerged in the seventeenth and eighteenth centuries lies not just in creating a supposedly more just and peaceful world order, but also in eliminating the essential sources of international conflict. Soviet leaders and ideologues never conceived of disarmament, detente, and peaceful coexistence as ends in themselves, but as strategies that would reduce the risks of uncontrollable wars, allowing the world revolutionary process to build strength and eventually to sweep away bourgeois-dominated states, imperialism, colonialism, and neocolonialism.

Throughout its history, the Soviet Union has been at best only a cautious operator within a hostile environment of capitalist states, and often a state that is committed to destroying the system's norms, institutions, and 'rules of the game'. There has been only limited Soviet participation in international organizations and in many less-formalized international regimes. Soviet diplomacy in international institutions has often been propagandistic and expedient, less often committed to constructive problem-solving and conflict resolution. While the Soviet Union joined the League of Nations in 1934 and was a co-founder of the successor organization, most of its policy pronouncements, ideological battle calls, and numerous actions indicated that it had not internalized many of the purposes and norms of those organizations. At home and abroad, the Soviet Union maintained that there are two orders of international law, one socialist, egalitarian, and progressive, the other bourgeois, reactionary, and exploitative. The wave of the future as far as international institutions and law is concerned, is epitomized in the fraternal relations between socialist countries, and in organizations such as the CMEA.

Soviet behavior in global institutions substantiated this bifurcated image of world order. In the United Nations, the Soviet Union often paralysed the organization in its conflict-resolving tasks, and even in the era of detente, the Soviets continued to wield vetoes (now joined by the other great powers), refused to help fund peace-keeping operations, and employed the Secretariat for espionage tasks. While often posing as the champion of the Third World, the Soviet Union frequently undercut efforts by non-aligned countries to bring about the end of armed conflicts - Kampuchea being the most notable example. The Soviet Union regarded with skepticism, and usually condemned, efforts at regional collaboration, arguing that they were surrogates of American policy, and anti-Soviet. We might also mention the Soviet record for joining many intergovernmental and non-governmental international organizations; it has been weak. Often, they have preferred to organize their own institutions, or to subvert existing ones to turn them into instruments in the campaign against imperialism.

It has been fashionable among some theorists of international relations to characterize the world as a 'society of states' implying that there are strong elements of order and stability, exemplified in international organizations, international law, international regimes, and numerous 'rules of the game'. A cursory and unsystematic review of Soviet attitudes toward such institutions and rules indicates their strong adherence to some traditional norms that provide them with security - sovereignty, non-interference, legal equality, and diplomatic immunities - while insisting that such rules can be brushed aside in the interests of building socialism and defending the commonwealth of socialist states. The Brezhnev doctrine is one example. Unwillingness to employ international institutions and processes for conflict resolution when their own interests were involved, it another. The Soviet Union has never submitted a case to the International Court of Justice and until 1988, it never allowed the United Nations to probe into its foreign policy conduct or into the affairs of its clients. Its consistently negative stance towards stringent means of

144

verifying arms control agreements suggests lack of interest in this issue and an almost obsessive reliance on arms buildups as a mode of providing security. The record of Soviet negativism and obstructionism toward the society of states and its institutions is long and dreary.

Meanwhile, Soviet leaders have never hidden their hopes that the system would ultimately be transcended. Their commitments to the society of states have at best appeared temporary, half-hearted, and dilatory, and at worst positively hostile and destructive. Nowhere in Soviet actions or rhetoric did we see develop a well-articulated notion of international responsibility. True, Brezhnev and Khrushchev often spoke of the responsibilities of the United States and the Soviet Union to save mankind from the horrors of nuclear war, but at the level of action they accomplished very little: the ABM treaty, SALT I and II. In terms of the risks involved, this is not very much. This comment is not meant to imply that the West has always conscientiously developed and used international institutions. The early years of the Reagan presidency were punctuated by unilateralism, withdrawal of support for international organizations, propagandistic approaches to arms control, and the introduction of destabilizing weapons systems. But these were seen ultimately as strategies to improve and strengthen the bases of an acceptable international order, and not as techniques for transcending it. The Soviet Union in contrast, has given the appearance of being in the system, but not really for it. The long-term goal of building a socialist commonwealth of states, with its own institutions, norms, and processes, has appeared more important.

One of the most fundamental transformations of recent Soviet thinking about international relations concerns views of this society of states. Through numerous statements, writings, and recent actions, Gorbachev and his colleagues seem finally to have come to terms with the fact that the world socialist utopia is not on the horizon. The purpose of policy is to maximize gains and limit losses *within* the present system, and not to destroy or transcend that system. At the heart of this recognition is the idea that the security of the United States and the Soviet Union are interconnected. Moreover, Gorbachev has even enunciated a notion of international responsibility, the idea that as a great power, the Soviet Union has, as is written in the Charter of the United Nations, a particular responsibility to contribute to the lessening of tensions, and to gear its diplomacy towards norms such as those of the United Nations.

Proposals have been dramatic in scope and conception. In his address to the General Assembly in September 1987, for example, Edvard Shevardnadze stated that the Soviet Union would like to see a world in which peace is secured by the United Nations. During the same month, Gorbachev, among other proposals, urged the International Court of Justice to expand its jurisdiction, an idea that would have appeared preposterous to any of his predecessors. There is a significance to the Soviet pullout from Afghanistan that goes beyond the military abandonment of a fraternal party. It is the first time in history that the Soviet Union has been a party to a United Nations mediation effort. Although it was used as an avenue for retreat, the acceptance of UN intermediaries to help terminate an unsuccessful military effort is unique for the Soviet Union (and, it might be added, it has never so been used by the United States). Beyond this symbolic event, the Soviet government has announced that it will now pay its share for United Nations peace-keeping efforts, it will allow Soviet citizens to become real international civil servants, and it proposed a collective effort, much as envisaged by the founders of the United Nations, to maintain the freedom of navigation in the Persian Gulf.

The fundamental change in Soviet attitudes toward world order (and thereby an implicit downplaying of older conceptions of world revolution and a commonwealth of socialist states as its end result) is well summarized in an interview given by a Soviet Deputy Foreign Minister, Vladimir Petrovsky, to Flora Lewis of *The New York Times*. He claimed that the Soviet Union

...now wants a new system for comprehensive security. We need a stable structure for international affairs, and we see the United Nations as a major way of achieving it. We have a different way of seeing the world since 1985. We see that interdependence matters; we no longer have a simple picture. We are working very hard to overcome this enemy image which was created on both sides... You can't export revolution or counterrevolution. [Our approach] is to create external conditions for people to settle issues themselves, to remove foreign interference. We want to take the superpowers out of crisis situations.[8]

The reader will note that these words have much more in common with the thoughts of Dag Hammarskjold than they do with the opinions and world views of Lenin, Stalin, Khrushchev, or Brezhnev. If we are to take them seriously, they indicate a critical shift in Soviet attitudes toward the society of states, toward the world community. This is not the statement of a revolutionary, of a spokesman for the long tradition of praising progress towards the transcendence of the bourgeois-led states system. Stability, order, interdependence, and conflict avoidance replace world revolutionary processes, the supposed progress toward a global socialist utopia, and the inherent right and obligation of the Soviet Union to intervene politically and militarily to help with its birthpangs. The statement even contains the implication - sometimes alluded to by Khrushchev but not developed since - that the traditional animosity between the United States and the Soviet Union lies in faulty images, not in the objective character of class relations, the intentions of rapacious imperialists, or the inevitability of conflict in the world historical process.

Explanations

Explanations for the changes in Soviet thinking about the nature of world politics, revolution, and Russian roles, functions, and tasks within the international system necessarily focus on the personality of Mikhail Gorbachev. He, of course, deserves much of the credit, but it would be erroneous to think that he has promoted 'new thinking' about the world as an act of international charity. Aside from his intellectual qualities, the rise of a new generation of leaders, many with substantial experience abroad (Yakovlev, Dobrynin, Shaknazarov), and the need to have a pause from heavy international involvement in order to clean up the house at home, the attitudinal shifts can be largely accounted for by the failure of previous Soviet policies, and by the increasingly obvious discrepancies between traditional Marxist-Leninist-based analyses of the world, and the realities. Only a gerontocracy steeped in apathy could afford to ignore what is happening in the outside world, could reissue standard cant about the great strides of the world revolutionary forces and the impending collapse of capitalism, and could dream about a utopia of a world socialist society, as if that were on the visible horizon. There are too many facts in the world that speak for themselves, and none from Moscow's perspective is more apparent than the relative decline of the Soviet Union and its consequent loss of international influence, including influence over the programs and personalities of communist parties throughout the world.

It should be adequately clear from a variety of indicators that the Soviet Union's military power has not translated into political influence. The bases of power in international relations are increasingly scientific, technical, informational, and commercial. Leadership in these domains will not only determine economic opportunities and serve as the basis of international prestige, but will increasingly provide powerful levers of diplomatic influence, in some instances buttressing or replacing military forms of coercion. But in these areas, the Soviet Union - comparatively speaking - is fading fast, and an extension of current trends would render it a second- or third-rate power by the early twenty-first century. Already Japan, with less than one-half of Russia's population, has matched the GNP of the Soviet Union. The dynamic Asian-Pacific Basin constitutes an area of tremendous vitality and commercial opportunity. Japan, Korea, Taiwan, and Singapore, most of them poor, developing nations just a generation ago, today outstrip or approach the Soviet Union in per capita income. Others are not too far behind; they will probably pass the Soviet Union by the early twenty-first century, given a continuation of present growth rates. The record of the Soviet Union, along with its main non-European allies and clients - Yemen, Angola, Ethiopia, Cuba, and Vietnam - is by comparison dismal. Of the fraternal socialist countries of East Europe, only the GDR made progress almost comparable to that of some major industrial nations. In its foreign trade, the Soviet Union resembles a middle-level developing nation. Even though it has a highly industrialized economy, it exports mostly raw materials and semi-finished goods; only 15.5 per cent is composed of machinery and equipment. In the areas of data gathering, processing, and dissemination, it remains in an infant stage.

These and many other realities have not escaped the notice of Soviet analysts. One prominent Soviet commentator, Alexander Bovin, declared in July 1987 that '... if the socialist countries do not rise to a new level, if capitalism, not socialism, manages to ride the new wave of the scientific and technical revolution, then the worldwide balance of power could change in favor of capitalism'.[9] Even more pessimistically, he conceded that the Soviet Union has not successfully served as a model for other nations. All the optimistic prognostications of the Brezhnev years have proven illusory, and for the Soviet Union the long-range outlook is bleak.

The habit of making commercial decisions on political criteria has cost the Soviet Union dearly, particularly in terms of lost opportunities. When commercial and political values have clashed, the USSR has traditionally opted for the latter (e.g., Soviet hostility to the EC, ASEAN, and the like). That is changing now, as indicated by recent Soviet overtures to several ASEAN countries, and by serious efforts to become involved even in regional non-governmental organizations such as the Pacific Economic Cooperation Council. These and many other *demarches* to patch up diplomatic relations indicate a shift in priorities: economics will now come to dominate political decision-making, not the other way around. A commitment to traditional ideological principles and slogans, where various forms of international and regional collaboration are rejected on the grounds that they serve the interests of the capitalists, or that they are anti-Soviet, will just speed up the relative decline of the Soviet Union.

The Soviet foreign minister has stated that common sense has to replace 'scientific' (meaning Marxist-Leninist) analysis: 'We are people of ideas, but their power should not be put above considerations of common sense. Otherwise, in being completely subordinate to them, you lose many things, among them the ability to improve the economic conditions of your own country, and, in that manner, to increase the degree of its political influence in the world'.[10] This statement nicely summarizes the reasons for recent shifts in the intellectual and doctrinal bases of Soviet foreign policy. There is little doubt that the bolder leaders of the Gorbachev group are convinced that the present domestic and international problems of the Soviet Union have derived from too heavy reliance on 'scientific analysis' in the past. In their estimation, adherence to the standard shibboleths and world views will leave the Soviet Union far behind the new power centers of the world.

Political rhetoric and old habits of thinking do not die out overnight. There is no reason to believe that the 'new thinking', much less its promoters, have become institutionalized in the Soviet political culture. Moreover, there is much further to go; the habits of foreign policy analysis which we take for granted in the West, have not yet permeated the Soviet establishment. There have been a few criticisms of foreign policy, but as yet the 'new thinking' comes from the top and, as in past years, is simply transmitted without critical analysis by those below. What has been on the whole a welcome set of changes in Soviet attitudes and diplomatic actions during the past few years presumably can become undone if widespread benefits do not derive from it. But whatever the forms opposition may take, no new set of leaders can afford to ignore what is happening in the real world unless they are committed to the proposition that the Soviet Union must and should become a second- or third-rate power, to be bypassed by dynamic new power centers in the world, including China, within the next two decades. Ideological slogans, traditional views of Soviet roles in the world, and full commitment to 'scientific analysis' will not provide successful guidelines for avoiding this fate. The Chinese came to this realization more than a decade ago. The Russians are late, but on the whole the new sense of realism may help salvage the situation. It remains to be seen for what purposes a revitalized Soviet Union is committed. Long-range goals could be more-or-less benign, leading the USSR to operate constructively in an interdependent world, or under particular circumstances, they could once again become highly aggressive.

The turn toward pragmatism in the intellectual foundations of foreign policy has no predetermined consequences. But on the whole, the dramatic shifts in world views and attitudes toward the international system are to be welcomed. It may be premature to observe an epidemic of peace, but the significant transformation in Soviet thinking about international relations and about the Soviet roles and tasks therein are at least one ingredient that provides grounds for optimism about the future.

Notes

1. For example, Edward Crankshaw (1963), *The New Cold War: Moscow vs Peking*, Baltimore: Penguin Books.
2. For an excellent and balanced account of shifting Soviet perspectives on international relations, with particular emphasis on Khrushchev's ideological innovations, see Paul Marantz (1988), *From Lenin to Gorbachev: Changing Soviet Perspectives on East-West Relations*, Ottawa: Canadian Institute for International Peace and Security, Occasional Paper #4.
3. For a discussion of these concepts, see Stephen Sestanovich (1988), 'Gorbachev's Foreign Policy: A Diplomacy of Decline', *Problems of Communism*, Jan-Feb, p. 6.
4 Quoted in Marantz, From Lenin to Gorbachev, p.63.
5. For further analysis, see Sestanovich, "Gorbachev's Foreign Policy', p. 5.
6. Christian Science Monitor, 16 July 1987.
7. The Soviet Union was on the verge of intervention in December 1980 and during the spring of 1981. Warsaw Pact maneuvers on Poland's frontiers, reminiscent of similar forms of coercive signalling during the Prague Spring, at least implied the possibility of intervention. The imposition of martial law by General Jaruzelski, Russian educated and trained, accomplished Soviet objectives. Western threats no doubt inhibited Soviet policy-makers, but the fact remains that despite the great doctrinal heresies implied by Solidarity activities, the Soviet Union acted more cautiously than in previous analogous situations.
8. The New York Times, 6 July 1988, p. A23.
9. A. Bovin (1987), 'Restructuring and the Fate of Socialism', *Izvestiia*, 11 July, 1987, in *Current Digest of the Soviet Press*, 39, 29, 12 August, 1987, p. 6. Bovin goes on to suggest that such a shift would increase the aggressiveness of the imperialists. This is a Brezhnevian rather than Gorbachevian prognosis.
10. Sestanovich, 'Gorbachev's Foreign Policy', p. 5.

Part II

Change in the Study of International Politics

7. Retreat from Utopia: International Relations Theory, 1945-1970

A theorist of international relations, if asked by a young student what he taught, would undoubtedly grope unsuccessfully for the catch-all term that might capture the essence of the work in which he and his pupils were interested. In a graduate international relations seminar they might review other people's data to 'see what emerges'; read Frank M. Russell, F. H. Hinsley, or Kenneth Waltz to learn what great thinkers in the past have said about the enduring problems of peace and war; or they might devote the semester to attempting to operationalize one traditional, but troublesome, concept such as power or crisis. Though it is clear that our professor does not teach diplomatic history or current affairs, his title - theorist of international relations - does little to clarify his major intellectual concerns.

The beginning graduate student, possibly even the undergraduate, soon appreciates that what goes under the name of 'theory' in the field includes a variety of intellectual activities. The literature with some type of theoretical content is voluminous; even that small portion that theorizes about theory is substantial enough to warrant the status of a subfield. No longer is it possible for one person to know intimately all the work that has a theoretical content. Defining concepts, linking variables, proposing and testing hypotheses of different levels of generality, studying such questions as decision-making processes in crisis situations, or examining the ethics of using herbicides in war - all of these and many other areas would qualify as theory. It would be presumptuous, therefore, to assess briefly the vast body of literature appearing over the past quarter century which could be classified as theory.

My main concern is to analyze the unifying characteristics, assumptions, and rise and decline of what might be called 'grand theory', contained in those monumental works which have sought to formulate an original approach to the field, and which have had as their objective the description and explanation of the characteristics of state action and interaction, or of the structure, functioning, and change of international systems. The utopia the authors of these works have sought is a general theory of international politics. The essential names include Hans J. Morgenthau (1948), Richard Snyder and his associates (1963),

Quincy Wright (1955), A. F. K. Organski (1958), Morton Kaplan (1957), John W. Burton (1965), and Raymond Aron (1966). Charles A. McClelland (1966), Karl Deutsch (1963), Andrew Scott (1967), Johan Galtung (1964, 1967) Herbert J. Spiro (1966), and Richard Rosecrance (1963), major developers of the systems approach, would also belong to this group, though their focus has been more on how to look at international phenomena rather than on explaining and describing the essential characteristics of state behavior or of the international system.[1]

The works of these theorists are well known. They have been subjected to ample praise and criticism, and compared, favorably and unfavorably, to each other. But in these assessments, the uniqueness and novelty of each work has been emphasized. What may have escaped out attention - no doubt because of the dust raised in the behavioral versus classical controversy - are some essential similarities in the diverse 'grand theories'. What were these scholars attempting to do? What were the critical questions - comprising the core of the field - that needed to be explored? What assumptions regarding the nature of theory and the world of international politics did they make? The answers to these questions reveal some striking likenesses in the general approaches of these scholars.[2]

The prewar study of international relations was dominated by description of diplomatic minutiae, perpetuation of the balance of power and world government models, and praise of the trinity of self-determination, collective security, and disarmament. Extensive generalization appeared in theories of power balancing and world government; but aside from a few stirrings among geopoliticians and power monists there were few attempts to create theory in terms of defining the central questions of the field and making causal statements and generalizations, verified by empirical, rather than anecdotal, means. In *Politics among Nations* (1948) Hans Morgenthau broke from tradition and set the tone for most of the 'grand' theoretical activity in the field for the next two decades. An assumption of Morgenthau's classic text, spelled out explicitly in later writings, is that the purpose of international relations theory is to bring order and meaning into a mass of unconnected material, and 'to reduce the facts of experience to mere specific instances of general propositions'.[3] Whatever may be said of the substance of Morgenthau's theory, his innovating contributions were:

1) explicitly to show the value of generalization;
2) to emphasize that interstate relations, in their essence, display patterns of behavior and recurrence;
3) to define the core of the subject as the sources of state

154

behavior (the search for power); and
4)   to explore the causes of war and conditions of peace in the international system.

There is, however, one new element of 'grand theory' which has developed subsequent to Morgenthau's innovations. The systems outlook has alerted us, among other things, to conceptual distinctions that have had important consequences on the division of labor in the field. Whereas Morgenthau did not clearly distinguish action theories (foreign policy) from interaction theories (international systems), the division has now become firmly established. To supplement the more traditional inquiry on the sources of state behavior, scholars today are equally concerned with questions such as: what is an international system? Is it a set of attributes (as Wright proposed), established power relationships, patterns of interaction, or social, psychological, cultural, economic, and technological 'distances' between states? What are its 'motions'? How and why does it move from one state to another? How are these patterns or attributes distributed in subsystems? Do the main actors shift in different issue areas? Some of these questions concern change from one system 'state' to another; they suggest dynamic analysis. Morgenthau's world was essentially static - or at least movement was in only two directions, the struggle for power and the struggle for peace, the attempt to upset the balance of power and the attempt to redress the balance. These were eternal processes; issues, differences in national attributes, subsystems, and 'distances' between states had little to do with change whereas now they are recognized as critical. Simple pressure models are no longer deemed adequate.

The list of independent variables, outlined in both the 'grand theories' and less ambitious works, which help account for shifts in foreign policy and changes in international systems, is extensive. In Snyder's work, for example, the factors which must be taken into account in explaining a single decision are numerous, ranging from broad social values to the policy-maker's memories and spheres of competence; but to Morgenthau foreign policy was a function only of the never-ceasing search for power and the distribution of power in the international system at any given time. At the system level the 'grand theories' also provide an extensive list of possible explanations of change from one type to another. To Rosecrance the major variables explaining these shifts are the relations between actor disturbances and 'regulator' capacity, and the degree of internal instability in the major actors. To Kaplan both domestic and external variables are also noted. Empirical work at a lower level of generality has explored more

155

carefully the connection between national attributes and major system-changing actions such as war (Rummel, 1968, 187-214). Others have investigated the same question using system attributes, such as alliances, as the independent variable (Singer and Small, 1968, 247-86). The division of the field into foreign policy and systems perspectives has thus opened up many new areas of investigation and has brought increasing awareness of the broad range of possible influences on both foreign policy and the functioning and change of international systems.

Even with the new systems perspective and all that it promises for the future development of the field, however, the underlying conception of the world has remained essentially the same among 'grand theorists'. For them, the main actors are nation-states and the interactions identified and measured are between national societies and/or governments. While the 'great power' or 'Cold War' world images, so common in the 1950s, are often recognized today as inadequate, certainly no 'Copernican revolution', proposed in 1959 by Stanley Hoffmann[4] has occurred in the way in which the world is portrayed in systems and foreign policy theories. Quincy Wright (1955), James Rosenau (1969, chaps 1 & 3), Herbert Spiro (1966), Johan Galtung (1967), and John Burton (1968) have portrayed the world, respectively, as fields of national attributes, as issue areas in which all sorts of government and non-governmental actors are involved, as a developing community in which issues are processed, as social change processes, and as networks of transactions. These conceptions certainly are attuned to the growth of multinational corporations, 'penetrated' states, integrating economic communities, issue areas dealt with mainly by non-governmental actors, and international interest groups and voluntary associations. Yet the demise of the territorial state, predicted and explained by Herz in 1957, has decidedly not occurred in the minds of most writers on international politics.[5] The collectivity of independent decision-making centres, assumed by Morgenthau (as well as Rousseau), continues in 'grand theories' as the context in which the critical questions of the field are explored.

I do not make these remarks as criticisms. Adherence to the classical conception of a system comprised of independent nation-states is undoubtedly appropriate for theories of international politics, since the questions of war and peace are still decided in most instances by national governments. However, theories of international relations, which would seek to describe and explain all types of 'world' relationships, might profitably employ units of analysis other than states, governments, or foreign policies.[6]

The procedural focus on pattern and recurrence and the substantive concentration on the sources of state behavior in a world setting of sovereign, independent states, are not the only similarities uniting the 'grand theorists' of the past quarter century. An important epistemological assumption of the group has been that the diverse data of the field, the sources of state behavior, and the international patterns and recurrences could be integrated, explained, or described in a single theory, model, approach, or framework. Both Morgenthau and Easton made pleas for the development of a general theory of politics, and subsequent 'grand theorists' heeded the call willingly. Their contributions have been (in most cases) inclusive, offering organizing devices for the entire field, not only portions of it. They have commonly assumed that they could bring together the essential, if not all, the animals of world politics into one theoretical ark, usually without asking whether such an enterprise could succeed, or even if it was worthwhile. Many have taken the limited theories of natural scientists as their model while presenting their work as comprehensive. (Apparently it did not occur to them that there is no general theory of physics or biology.) Why, then, should they have devoted their talents and energies to the construction of such inclusive theoretical devices? I would argue that 'grand theory' in international politics represents an effort to bring precision and order to the current affairs reporting and crude theorizing typical of the field prior to Morgenthau, and an attempt to broaden the field to include phenomena other than institutions, events, and law. It also results from an optimistic expression of faith (Morgenthau and Aron excepted) in the view that all knowledge in the field could be unified by coupling theory with scientific method.

The major theoretical works of Morgenthau, Easton, Snyder and his associates, Wright, Liska, Kaplan, Organski, Burton, and Aron contain innumerable insights, many broadening new perspectives, and useful concepts which today form part of the accepted vocabulary and assumptions of the field. For a variety of reasons they remain important creative works. A few have made bold conceptualizations of international phenomena. Others have increased our historical and geographical perspectives, offered useful typologies, or explored links between concepts. These are adequate grounds for us to express the hope that scholars will continue working at a broad level of abstraction. But no framework or theory which has aspired to acceptance as *the* approach to the field, has in McClelland's words, laid 'down intellectual policy for the field'.[7] None has yet spawned the empirical work required to give it validity. None has met other requirements of a general theory, such as comprehensiveness, coherence, and self-correction.[8] None has been able to claim status either as *the* form or approach to a general theory or as an important step towards general theory.

It is a paradox that Easton's plea for rigorous empiricism, which accompanied his demand for general theory, should be at least one major factor in the declining appeal of broad, all-encompassing works. If few 'grand theorists' have openly questioned the intellectual gains or losses involved in seeking the utopia of a general theory, empirical work since the 1950s - the areas of 'payoff' it would seem - have suggested somewhat different functions for theory than those proposed by Morgenthau and his successors. The major preoccupations of many theorists have been to explore specific problems, to form hypotheses or generalizations explaining limited ranges of phenomena, and, particularly, to obtain data to test those hypotheses.

The role of theory in the field has changed in the past decade. While much attention remains devoted to the sources of state behavior and the structure and functioning of international systems, it seems scholars are concerning themselves increasingly with what James Rosenau has called 'pre-theory', attempting to discover relationships between operationalized and carefully delineated variables, distinguish necessary and sufficient conditions, and establish classification systems for specific international phenomena or processes. Operating within limited frameworks, paradigms, or hypotheses, scholars roam around collecting data (or employing data collected by others, made available through data banks), manipulating them to see what statistical relationships emerge, defining indicators, and writing up the results of their endeavors. Contemporary theory, in short, guides research into specific phenomena, problems, or processes, and avoids explanations at a high level of generality.

This is not to concede that the field remains distressingly weak in theory, as Ransom has suggested.[9] McClelland has noted that 'islands of theory' seem to be developing to explain these limited phenomena, problems, or processes.[10] The question of 'spillover' in international integration, though not once and for all confirmed or refuted, is one example. Studies have demonstrated that whatever the necessary and sufficient conditions for successful economic and/or political integration, cooperation or unification in the technical sectors does not necessarily carry over into the diplomatic or defence sectors, or vice versa. The area of public attitudes, opinion formation and change, perceptions, stereotypes, and the impact of events or foreign experience on values and opinions - in brief, the area which links the average citizen to the international system - is progressing well. Foreign policy analysis is no longer descriptive of single nations, deterministic, or monistic. While major empirical work remains to be done and some classification of foreign policy outputs is badly needed,

158

Rosenau's contributions, adding to the theoretical works of Snyder, Modelski, and Frankel, have alerted us to the necessity of comparing nations and looking for multi-factor explanations of external behavior, combining internal and external variables, in different issue areas and in different domestic and external circumstances. A number of analyses of concepts such as power, threat, credibility, integration, subsystem, and the like, have appeared, often accompanied by illustrative or explanatory data. 'Mapping' operations of the attributes of states and societies, proposed by Wright have appeared in the work of Russett, Banks and Textor, Rummel, Tanter, the Feierabends, and others. Rosenau and Scott have developed the concepts of issue area and the 'penetrated state'. While all this work may not contribute to a general theory of international politics, it can hardly be said that theoretical progress in the field is lacking or that theory remains distressingly weak. It is alive and strong, but not at the 'grand' level.

Serious theoretical problems, do, however, persist, even in research on limited phenomena or processes. Perhaps one of the major issues yet to be faced by the contemporary theorist of international politics is the limitations of quantitative studies. Data collection and the development of indicators (many of which represent concepts, but not facts) may become so much a preoccupation in the field that unique events having system-changing consequences are averaged out in the pool of typical behaviors or statistical trends. There is a problem concerning what can and cannot be measured meaningfully and related to central questions in the field. Indicators such as per capita income, percentage of Catholics in a population, common intergovern-mental association membership, or suicides, literacy, and alcoholism rates may reveal something about nations and their foreign policies, but geographic location, ideologies, historical experiences, and traditional enemies are, in my opinion, more important explanations of externally directed conduct. Yet these 'soft' factors are often omitted in analyses because they cannot be easily measured or quantified. Many contemporary studies also have conspicuously little to say about human purpose. Stanley Hoffmann's 1959 criticism of Morgenthau is as applicable to the field today as it was when written '... the consideration of men's values, beliefs, and emotions, of these purposes and ideas, is indispensable'.[11] Personalities, aberrant events, or historical accidents must not be forgotten under a mountain of numerical indicators and attributes.

Moreover, we do not yet possess an agreed-upon definition of foreign policy. Whether used as a dependent variable in 'nation-as-actor' studies, or as one independent variable in systems studies, it is assumed that the content of foreign policy is self-evident. Is foreign policy the objectives and interests of states, as in the classical sense of 'national interest'? Is it the actions and rules, or the anticipated future state of affairs in the external environment that Snyder and his associates discuss? Is it the 'principles' such as the Hallstein, Monroe, or Stimson doctrines that guide actions in certain circumstances? Is it the commitments that are made and maintained through treaties, and which prescribe appropriate behavior and decisions on a day-to-day basis? Could it be the continuing roles and functions that some governments perform in the system or in a subsystem? Or is it just the actions and decisions that are taken or made on a daily basis in a bureaucratic organization? Some sorting out, classification, and definition are needed here if an 'island of theory' is to grow in the foreign policy field. In the period under review, studies have employed broad, undifferentiated terms such as image, interest, action, security, or power, or they have concentrated on single decisions, usually in crisis situations. Aggregates of actions by governments for a specified period of time might serve as indicators of foreign policy, but it remains to be demonstrated that the sum of threats, warnings, reprisals, protests, and various forms of cooperative behavior over, let us say, a five year period, would adequately express the key concerns of policy-makers which may involve problem-solving strategies, objectives, rules, commitments, and interests. Careful work on the concept of foreign policy is also required if some synthesis between system-oriented and state-oriented studies is to emerge. Though these orientations provide different intellectual perspectives, there is no reason why foreign policy cannot denote roughly the same phenomenon in both approaches.

Paul H. Nitze once wrote that 'A general theory of international relations which does not provide an adequate framework for the analysis of restraints upon the free exercise of national power...would appear to be insufficient and not closely enough related to the real world of international politics and the questions with which statesmen do in fact wrestle'.[12] One of the major characteristics of the 'grand theories' is that they have divorced law from politics. Kaplan's 'rules' referred to behavior necessary to maintain types of international systems; there is no discussion, in his 1957 volume, of the conservative effects of law. Likewise, most other studies in the 'grand theory category' have dealt with law, if at all, only as some obscure outside force that had little impact in decision-making situations. Only recently have scholars begun to explore the *functions* of law in foreign policy, particularly in crisis situations.[13] Studies comparing legal restraints across types of states and situations or issue areas

160

(looking at the role of law only in crisis situations undoubtedly distorts the issue) are still needed, as are the analytical models which would guide research in this area.

In the past only a few of the 'grand theorists' had much to say about law and ethics in foreign policy. Even fewer have unashamedly arrived at evaluative statements based on their descriptions and explanations. Morgenthau stated explicitly that a theory of the field should provide standards against which the conduct of foreign policy could be judged. Raymond Aron, in *Peace and War*, did not distinguish precisely between descriptive or causal statements, and evaluative propositions. His advocacy of prudence as a guide to policy-making and rejection of 'realism' and 'idealism' derive to an extent from his preceding descriptions and characterizations of the essential processes of international politics.

Morgenthau and Aron, are, however, exceptions to the generalization that, at the 'grand' level, normative components of theory and policy prescriptions have been ignored. Explanations are not difficult to put forth. Causal theory, empiricism, and the development of rigorous methodologies have been the dominating preoccupations of the field since the mid-1950s. Empirical theorists have by no means monopolized insight into the essential questions facing international relations scholars. The best works of Inis Claude Jr., Stanley Hoffmann, Hans Morgenthau, and Kenneth Waltz, to name a few, demonstrate the continuing vigor and reward of more traditional modes of analysis. Yet, the 'research frontiers' of the field have been populated during the past few years primarily by the scientific 'grand theorists', empirical explorers, and methodologists. The contributions of these scholars have been overwhelming as well as promising (anyone reading the standard literature of the field produced thirty years ago will surely admit that great progress has occurred), yet it is unfortunate that in the commitment to rigor, many of the developers of the field have condemned others, like Morgenthau, for not observing the most elementary requirements of scientific method, the separation of fact from value. While fact and value might not always mix well, assessing the normative implications or assumptions of an approach, framework for analysis, or concept need not be inconsistent with scientific detachment.

This is not the place to review the battle over this question, but we should note that most 'grand theories' or approaches have emphasized *processes*, while slighting issues. This is one reason why analyses of the value implications of various conceptual schemes have been so rare. Systems change or collapse because 'essential rules' are violated, supports are insufficient, or because disruptions overcome the systems' capacity to deal with them. We

161

are exhorted to study decision-making procedures, equilibrium processes, the 'power-transition', systems' regulatory processes, and adaptive behavior. (The very notion of process implies regularity, movement, and order that may not exist in reality.) But with only a few exceptions, the issues - the stuff of politics - are not discussed. The units of analysis in 'grand theories' and works at lower levels of generality may also explain this characteristic. When we look at a single decision (or, more likely, how that decision was made), single actions, or even aggregates of actions, we lose sight of the more fundamental foreign policy patterns which are occurring in the long run. The notions of imperialism, neocolonialism, isolation, autarky, spheres of influence, and revolutionary change may be traditional and difficult to deal with systematically, but that is not sufficient reason to pass over them lightly. These phenomena form the diplomatic characteristics of an age. Without acknowledging them, we lose a perspective that would provide more meaning to processes such as decision-making in a foreign office or trade fluctuations in an international system.

There is evidence that the scientific formalism, which prompted most 'grand theorists' to avoid the normative implications of their approaches to a general theory of international politics, will face challenges by younger scholars. This is not to say that scientific method will be thrown out in favor of ideologically oriented polemics. The best works emanating from the peace research movement, as well as some other theoretically oriented research, indicate that scientific method can be employed to explore essentially policy-oriented problems. However, we can at least expect that serious examination of the hidden normative assumptions of 'grand theory' and of theoretical activity concerning more limited problems in the field will begin to appear.[14]

Studies in the period 1945-70 offer many new and important ideas in the development of international politics theory, of which the purposes and assumptions of Morgenthau and the analytic perspectives of the systems approach are only the most dramatic. But the uniqueness of the 'behavioral revolution' and the original contributions of each work of 'grand theory' should not prevent us from acknowledging the common characteristics of theoretical activity in the field. Since Morgenthau, the essential questions to be explored, the emphasis on recurrence and generalization, the assumption of all-encompassing theory, and the underlying model of a world of independent nation-states have remained, for the most part, unaltered.

Aside from the new approaches, greater rigor, and insights offered by the 'grand theorists', the most important trend in the field has been the increasing emphasis on research in selected areas, problems, and processes. This work has been done quite independently of any contribution to a general theory of international politics. Studies with a narrow theoretical focus contribute greatly to our fund of empirical knowledge. Yet, broader speculation, even if not fully rigorous by contemporary standards, has inestimably enriched our insights and helped us to see our field much more broadly and imaginatively than ever before. If there is a retreat from attempting to reach the utopia of a general theory of international politics, let us hope it will not lead to a total abandonment of the effort.

Notes

1. The reader can obtain the references for the major works discussed here in the bibliography appended to Chapter 8 in this volume.
2. Major differences between the approaches must be acknowledged as well. For example, the deductive theorizing of Kaplan contrasts with the inductive work of Rosecrance; the 'value free' systems approach obviously differs from Morgenthau's concerns with normative problems. These and other differences have been discussed and debated adequately in the literature of the field.
3. Also see Morgenthau, H. (1962), *The Decline of Democratic Politics*, Chicago: University of Chicago Press, p. 72.
4. S. Hoffmann (1959), 'International Relations: the Long Road to Theory', *World Politics*, 11, pp. 346-77.
5. Herz reassesses his thesis in (1969), 'The Territorial State Revisited: Reflections on the Future of the Nation-State' in James N. Rosenau (ed.), *International Politics and Foreign Policy: A Reader in Research and Theory*, rev. edition, New York: Free Press.
6. For a forceful critique of the classical international relations model see George Modelski (1970), 'The Promise of Geocentric Politics', *World Politics*, 22, pp. 615-35.
7. C. McClelland (1960), 'The Function of Theory in International Relations', *Journal of Conflict Resolution*, 4, p. 305.
8. These and other requirements are outlined in an essay by Quincy Wright (1964), 'Development of a General Theory of International Relations' in Horace V. Harrison (ed.), *The Role of Theory in International Relations*, Princeton: Van Nostrand, pp. 15-44.
9. Ransom lists the following requirements of theory as lacking presently in the field: 'a distinct subject matter; agreed-on abstractions and models; concepts uniquely adapted to the analysis of international behavior; specialized vocabulary with precise definitions, standardized analytical methods allowing retesting or replication of initial analyses; or a central system of cataloging, evaluating, and communicating the state of research and its results'. It is debatable whether these weaknesses exist throughout the field. In terms of developing a general theory the criticism is apt. In areas such as

game theory and integration studies the comments would seem inappropriate. Many of these criticisms could also be directed toward biologists.

10. C. McClelland (1966), *Theory and the International System*, New York: Macmillan, p. 96.
11. S. Hoffmann (1959), 'International Relations: The Long Road to Theory', *World Politics*, 11, p. 366.
12. Paul H. Nitze (1959), 'Necessary and Sufficient Elements of a General Theory of International Relations' in W.T.R. Fox (ed.), *Theoretical Aspects of International Relations*, Notre Dame: University of Notre Dame Press.
13. For example, Lawrence Scheinman and David Wilkinson (1968), *International Law and Political Crisis*, Boston: Little Brown; Louis Henkin (1968), *How Nations Behave: Law and Foreign Policy*, New York: Praeger.
14. One example is the criticism of game theory and systems analysis in Philip Green (1966), *Deadly Logic: The Theory of Nuclear Deterrence*, Columbus: Ohio State University Press.

8. Along the Road to International Theory

A retrospective on the development of international theory over the past quarter-century will emphasize elements of continuity and change, vigorous debates about both the appropriate subject and methodologies for research and a substantial advancement and cumulation of knowledge. As we would expect in any field that inevitably reflects innovations in social sciences, as well as the day-to-day changes and longer trends in international life, false starts, disappointments, intellectual faddism and parochialism are also evident. Overall, however, one cannot fail to be impressed. A graduate course in international theory in the late 1950s would have in its reading list a selection quite deep historically and philosophically, going back to Hobbes, Rousseau, and Kant, but theoretically rather narrow in its range of problems and perspectives. The prevailing wisdom would be concisely summarized in the great works by E.H. Carr, Hans Morgenthau, Georg Schwarzenberger and a few others. The year's readings would be organized within a single paradigm (unless Kant were emphasized) or intellectual tradition, describing and explaining the behavior of states within a states system or 'society of states'.

Today, it would be impossible to organize a similar course for one or two semesters and call it comprehensive. The outpouring of literature, much of it of high quality, has been so profuse in the intervening quarter-century that today we would be justified in claiming a special status for international theory as the core of international relations studies. For it is the debates and developments at the theoretical level that have inspired most of the innovative empirical work appearing in recent years. But unlike the 1950s, contemporary work takes place within a context of serious theoretical fragmentation and competing paradigms. Questions about the structure and processes of the states system no longer command singular attention. Competing theoretical formulations, such as dependency theory and global society models, have to be described and evaluated as well.

This essay has three main purposes. First, it will outline briefly and non-exhaustively the main streams of theoretical activity, linking major contributions and innovations to classical antecedents. Second, the discussion will illustrate how recent debates have challenged the intellectual consensus that bound major streams of thought into a single paradigm. Finally, the later pages will offer some evaluations of the contemporary debates. Before proceeding, however, we must have some idea of the terrain we are covering. What, in brief, is 'international theory'?

The domain of discussion

International theory is that part of the study of international relations which offers descriptive and explanatory statements about patterns, regularities, and change in the structural properties and processes of international systems and their major component units. It is concerned with classes of events (typical behavior or trends), not with specific occurrences. Rousseau sought to explain why, in a probabilistic sense, war is an inevitable consequence of a world fragmented into separate political communities. He was not concerned with the War of the Austrian Succession, or the 'Seven Years' War, but with war in general. He clearly delineated his problem area (the dependent variable) and, with insight that few have matched, specified a range of causal variables. His analysis, like most of those considered below, was designed to transcend time, location, event and personality. Similarly, F.H. Hinsley has recently proposed that the development of nuclear weapons has fundamentally changed one of the primary characteristics of all previous international systems, namely the frequent recourse to armed force by the major powers against each other.[1] Today we may be observing the transformation of this significant property of the states system. While Hinsley's observation - and let us hope it is not only accurate but also prophetic - is bound by time, it transcends location, event and personality. Though not presented in a formally rigorous fashion, it nevertheless has the form of most general social scientific propositions: a change in variable or property x produces a major (new) consequence in the pattern of behavior y. But the format of the statement is not the critical question. It is, rather, the scope of the proposition: theorists seek to discover relationships and causes of change in them for classes of events, not for particulars. Hence, we will omit from discussion the myriad special studies and monographs dealing with current affairs and the foreign policies of individual states.

Optimism and pessimism: prelude to the great methodological debate

The graduate student beginning a seminar in international theory in 1959 would learn initially that theoretical approaches to international politics developed coincidentally with the formation of the European states system. (Thucydides has made a comeback as a major international thinker only in the past decade or so.) Recurring warfare between the sovereign principalities of the seventeenth and eighteenth century European *Respublica Christiana* had caused so much consternation among sensitive philosophers that it led them to seek formal explanations for the phenomenon as well as approaches for overcoming the problem. International theory has always had as its core a normative concern with the causes of war and the conditions of peace, security and international order. While their plans for peace differed considerably, Grotius, Hobbes, Saint-Pierre, Kant and others shared this substantive focus, a common *problematique*. The student would also learn that in the twentieth century up to the Second World War, most systematic thinkers about international relations rejected the pessimism of Hobbes and Rousseau and adopted the intellectual stance of Bentham and numerous nineteenth century liberals who preached that wars were caused by despotic governments, mercantilism and such artifacts of dynastic regimes as secret diplomacy and treaties, militarism and elite insecurity. The way to peace was through the development of people-to-people contacts - what today we call transnational institutions. Even the slaughter of the World War I did not shake the faith of the optimist liberals (personified by Woodrow Wilson) who viewed the catastrophe as an aberration, an accident, or as the final death throes of the old order. Few regarded the war as just another and inevitable eruption of a states system which had not yet developed sufficient steering, balancing or crisis managing capabilities to keep conflicts muted to levels short of total war.

The rise of the great dictators and the resulting carnage of World War II dealt a severe blow to the optimist theorists of international relations. The pessimism of Hobbes and Rousseau, expressed in their insistence that war is a recurring feature of the states system and in their denial of any significant restraining or ordering elements except for deterrence and balance of power, reappears in the 1940s works of Carr, Morgenthau, Schwarzenberger and others. Power politics is now the name of the diplomatic game, and the purpose of the study of international relations is not to develop more peace plans or to argue how the world should run, but to understand the structure, recurring processes and dynamics of the states system. This school earned the title of 'realists'.

The realist onslaught against the liberal-optimistic tradition did not go unanswered. The intellectual descendants of Bentham and Wilson argued that idealism - the practical application of specified liberal beliefs in the conduct of foreign policy - was the ultimate realism. The 'realism' versus 'idealism' debate of the early 1950s was in part a replay of the intellectual contest between Rousseau and Bentham; but it was more than a question of political faiths. It reflected, also, a profound controversy about the appropriate intellectual stance toward the study of international politics. Morgenthau and many others of the realist school argued that the object of study is to search for and reveal the hidden similarities, patterns of behavior, recurrence and the significant changes in the structure and processes of the international system. While Morgenthau in particular said a great deal about the principles upon which to found a successful foreign policy, his lasting intellectual contribution was to the *scientific* study of international politics - a paradox, because he rejected much of the research which explicitly adheres to social scientific methodologies. For their part, the idealists were less concerned with observing, recording and testing general propositions than with elaborating the necessary conditions for peace and order, *regardless* of the 'realities'.

Our student would conclude that by 1959 the realists had clearly won the debate. Although textbooks used in this period were marked by elements of parochialism, unsystematic inquiry, sloppy methodology and a fascination with current affairs, most theorists agreed that the ultimate form of the field should follow the model established by Morgenthau. Indeed, it could be argued that Morgenthau's work was a necessary prelude to the great methodological revolution that was to sweep the field in the late 1950s and throughout the 1960s.

The great schism: competing roads to knowledge in international theory

In the 1950s the debates about 'behavioralism' in the study of international politics were just beginning. Most instructors would have been uncertain whether abstract, formal metaphors such as field theory (Quincy Wright) or systems theory (Morton Kaplan) would add much to knowledge or pave the way for meaningful research agendas, but none could ignore completely the innovations that were being added to the intellectual menu of the field. The revolutionaries made numerous claims for their new

168

scientific perspectives. First, there are important insights and methodologies to be gained from a familiarity with cognate disciplines such as psychology, anthropology, sociology and systems analysis. Quincy Wright's monumental *Study of International Relations* (1955), for example, demonstrated how a discipline of international relations could be organized around field theory, an approach to sociological analysis developed by Kurt Lewin. Second, proponents of behavioralism celebrated the intellectual rewards of using analytical constructs that are not derived inductively, but are the products of creative imagination, designed to meet the requirements of logical consistency and the capability of generating hypotheses that can be tested in the 'real world'. Model-building exercises were often debunked by those who did not understand that Hobbes, Rousseau and many of the other classical figures also built models, although in a less explicit or formal manner. Third, the innovators insisted that research be based on systematic and replicable procedures. They faulted the 'traditionalists' for grounding knowledge on selected historical examples, general impressions and judgments which could not be tested for validity. Finally - and disregarding Karl Popper's warnings about the fundamental differences between the practice of science in the natural and social domains - the most zealous of the behavioralists claimed that adherence to rigorous, laboratory-like procedures would eventually result in an intellectual nirvana comprised of general 'laws' of behavior and an overall theory of international politics with full explanatory and predictive capabilities. What, exactly, would be explained or predicted in such a manner was much less clear.

Such views were hardly likely to go unchallenged. The claims were too extensive even to many of the moderate enthusiasts for new approaches and methodologies. Many objected on grounds ranging from the inelegant writing style of scientific researchers and the proliferation of jargon and gobbledygook, to more fundamental concerns: there are significant differences between data and facts; the object of inquiry is not to 'discover' a reality that has remained mysteriously hidden during all the years that scholars and philosophers have contemplated the continuing problems of international life, but to push forward our knowledge about insights and debates emanating from the classical figures in the field; much of what we want to know about international relations - the really important questions - cannot be learned solely through formal measurement techniques. Qualitative judgments are as important as quantitative 'data'; and the model of science promoted by the behavioralists is too strict - it is not even applied in many of the 'hard' sciences.

There were zealots, too, on the side of the traditionalists, those who rejected any systematic approach to the field. To them, even Morgenthau's work was of little value, because in his search for patterns and regularity, he challenged the view that all politics are contingent and that generalizations not solidly rooted in a given historical and geographic context are meaningless.

The cleavage between the two sides was great, and the debates often were bitter. The two traditions largely went their own ways: neither took the trouble to remain familiar with the other's work. In the past decade or so, however, signs of interfaith communication have appeared. Some of the scientific persuasion have come to recognize that the classical figures in the field offer important hypotheses to be researched; that there are formidable limitations to the scientific method, both in terms of exploring crucial questions and the availability of data; that a 'grand theory' of international politics is an enterprise with no expected payoff; and that contextual and historical features are important. Likewise, many of the defenders of ideographic-philosophical approaches have become familiar with the major research agendas of the behavioralists and have collaborated in some joint research projects. There is as yet no robust movement of oecumenism or formal synthesis, but there are signs of greater tolerance and mutual acknowledgment. The great debates of the 1950s and 1960s have not been settled in the sense that an authoritative outcome has issued. Instead, methodological pluralism reigns today, probably to the benefit of knowledge. Moreover, on the critical substantive issues - what we should study - there is a continuing consensus among the methodological schools. The classical *problematique* of the cause of war and conditions of peace, security, order and the exercise of power continues to serve as the animating concern of all research. In this sense, Rousseau and Rummel, Bentham and Deutsch, and Bull and Lasswell have much in common.

Streams of theoretical development [2]

A contemporary student, unlike his 1959 predecessor, would face a bewildering array of topics and approaches to international theory, research claiming intellectual legitimacy and many commanding not only ambitious research programmes but extensive funding as well. The subjects on a syllabus might range from questions of world order (how much is there, what are its prerequisites, and how do we get more?), the sources of stability and change in international systems, the growth and consequences of the world capitalist system, to the dynamics of bargaining in crisis situations as illuminated by game matrices entitled 'chicken'

170

or 'prisoner's dilemma'.

To make sense, and to bring some organic unity to the seminar, the instructor might use the traditional levels-of-analysis distinctions as organizing devices. The main streams of theoretical activity and empirical research would thus fall under headings of 1) international systems; 2) regional and sectoral subsystems; 3) the relationship between foreign policy and national attributes; and 4) the influence of personality, role and information on foreign policy decision-making. In addition, the syllabus might include a section crossing the various levels, with a focus on power and bargaining. We will list a few of the major contributions within each of these categories.

International systems

The temporary eclipse of the West European states and Japan as major international actors as a result of World War II alerted writers to the possibility that a bifurcated system of power might display behavioral characteristics quite different from those existing in a system characterized by a more dispersed power distribution. Richard Rosecrance, Morton Kaplan, and George Modelski wrote influential monographs and articles outlining the different kinds of historic and hypothetical international systems. The purpose of these exercises was to delineate the criteria that can be used to distinguish types of systems (taxonomic work), to speculate on the conditions that result in stability or turbulence in the systems, and to locate processes that cause them to transform into different kinds of systems.

The relationship between system type and the incidence of war, a question deriving directly from the classical *problematique*, has animated an important agenda of thought and research. The results to date provide no firm conclusions, but some results, when embedded in contextual features, are intriguing even if they offer no distinct patterns. Theoretical works by Karl Deutsch and David Singer, Kenneth Waltz and A.F.K. Organski have delineated the arena in which much of the empirical research has taken place.

Even though this section of the course can provide only a small sample of system-level studies, the student would be required to read *in toto* one of the modern masterworks that examines the elements of order, stability and continuity in a political universe characterized by an absence of overarching authority. Hedley Bull's *The Anarchical Society* is the most notable exposition on the Grotian concept that a society of states contains many bonds that bring stability and order that would not be found in a mere collection of sovereignties. At the most theoretical level, the student would also read Kenneth Waltz's *Theory of International Politics* for a spirited argument that, as in a free market economic system, the essential characteristics of the system itself provide the best avenue for understanding the typical behavior of its component units. Waltz's book has engendered a considerable debate, but it is essential for understanding what international theory is all about.

Subsystems

In 1959, a veritable subfield, termed 'integration theory', was just beginning to develop. It produced extensive literature and robust debates; yet, in the mid-1970s one of its prime contributors and originators, Ernst Haas, pronounced that no further work of value could be anticipated. Yet, the student can still read the major works profitably, not only for their substantive findings, but also to learn about the opportunities and limitations of the use of scientific method in political analysis. Integration theory also demonstrates the critical link between normative concerns - in this case paths to peace - and empirical research. From the beginning, the theoretical fascination with the experiment which became the European Community (EC) stemmed from its character as an exercise in 'community-building'. For some, of course, the idea of political unification was intriguing in its own right, but for most researchers, the worth of the enterprise came from its novel approach to peace. Europe, the scene of centuries of fratricidal warfare, was now creating a genuine 'zone of peace' through construction of federal or supranational institutions and economic integration. To the extent that the members of the EC maintained formal sovereignty, however, one of the fundamental tenets of the classical tradition was being challenged. To Rousseau and his successors, the logical consequence of a system of political fragmentation into separate sovereignties is the 'state of war'. Nothing can overcome it. But now, the EC experiment demonstrates that one can have one's diplomatic cake and eat it too: nations can maintain their sovereignty in some domains, while integrating in others, and yet construct an area of perpetual peace among the constituent units. Deutsch's classic, *Political Community and the North Atlantic Area*, suggested that there could even be 'pluralistic security communities', areas in which states maintain full sovereignty in all domains, but face virtually no likelihood of mutual war. Canada and the United States, Scandinavia and Australia-New Zealand constitute modern examples. The realist tradition never allowed or accounted for

172

such phenomena.

The work in integration theory thus resurrected the nineteenth century liberal view about the importance of transnational relations in creating world (or in this case, regional) order. Most of the integration theorists emphasized the importance of social interactions - trade, communications, tourism and the like - as necessary conditions for political amalgamation or the evolution of pluralistic security communities. In the European context, at least during the 1950s and 1960s, it seemed that the predictions of Bentham and his successors were to be borne out: let people, goods and ideals flow unhindered across national borders and governments will learn that there is a natural harmony between societies, not inevitable antipathy as Rousseau would have it.

But integration theory was bedeviled by some critical problems. For example, many versions were cast in universal terms, suggesting that integration was a more-or-less inevitable outcome of growth in transnational relations, no matter what the locale. In the quest for generality, the formulations tended to overlook the features that were unique to Europe and other areas, including the critical element of political will. On the whole, they failed to acknowledge nationalism, which seemed to be growing throughout the world, but was perhaps at a nadir in postwar Europe. There were also lengthy debates about definitions and methodology: is integration a process or an end-state? How do you measure degrees of integration? Which comes first, growth in social transactions or political decision to integrate? What are the key dependent and independent variables?

The fate of integration theory illustrates one of the pitfalls of modern academic work in international relations: the need to respond to current developments. While the integration literature contained numerous problems, Haas and others sounded its death knell not so much because a theoretical dead end had been reached, but because *newer* phenomena were appearing on the diplomatic horizon. Integration was out, and suddenly 'interdependence' and 'international regimes' were in. Now the United States as a key actor could be included, and new problems generated by the economic hard times of the 1970s and 1980s could be explored. New fields for theoretical innovation (a must for career advancement in North America) could be mined. Meanwhile, studies on the EC have been left primarily to those whose concerns are more descriptive and policy-oriented than theoretical. But the student may conclude that this stream of research has just gone underground. The last word about pluralistic security communities, about the relationship between transnational activities, economic community-building and peace surely has not been pronounced. There are many theoretical

173

puzzles left to ponder, not the least of which is the incompatibility between the 'realist' model of international politics and the EC experience. Was integration theory a victim of fad or, as some would have it, of theoretical deficiency? Or was it because the seeming harmony of the EC in the 1950s and 1960s declined in the face of economic recession? The problem of integration within the context of scarcity surely merits extensive research in future.

National attributes and foreign policy

While system characteristics can account for the enduring problems of international politics such as the security dilemma and war, they are less successful in explaining variations and major orientations of the component units' foreign policies. For example, Rousseau in his famous parable of the stag hunt (he developed a rational choice model) could demonstrate why war is an inevitable outcome of a world divided into sovereignties, but he could not (and perhaps did not wish to) explain variations in the incidence of war, why some states are seemingly more 'war prone' than others, or why some states cope with their security problems through alliance-building strategies, while others choose neutrality or isolation, or seek regional or global hegemony. Nor can most system-level analyses render satisfactory accounts of foreign policy change except those associated with power balancing.

To explore such questions, theorists have focussed on the internal attributes of states. The optimistic liberals account for war, aggrandizement and hegemony seeking by elite insecurities and the whimsical proclivities of autocratic regimes. In contrast, in democracies where public opinion serves as a restraint on governments, and where the public is assumed to be interested in personal welfare goals rather than in national prestige or foreign territories, more pacific policies will prevail. To Marxists the main outlines of foreign policy derive from types of economic systems. In the highest stage of capitalism - imperialism - governments as the handmaidens of economic interests are compelled to follow expansionist policies, to carve out colonial empires, and to strive for monopolistic positions for access to raw materials and investment opportunities. The inevitable consequence of such lateral expansion is war between capitalist states. Socialist states are inherently pacific, however, because their economic systems are burdened by no contradictions and because their governments, which are genuinely representative of the masses, seek only their welfare. Like the liberals, the Marxist theories of international politics assume that there is an underlying

174

harmony of interest between the peoples (or at least between the proletariats) of all nations.

An extensive literature, based on aggregate data, comparative case studies, and historical development, has examined such competing explanations of the sources of foreign policy behavior. The student, after reading major works by Raymond Tanter, Jonathan Wilkenfeld, Rudolph Rummel, and Robert C. North and Nazli Choucri, would find that the conclusions are sometimes contradictory and that often statistical relationships are weak. As a body of knowledge, however, they do establish that many of the propositions coming from the classical literature do not hold up well when confronted with systematic evidence.[3] In a work that is destined to become a classic of comparative historical research, Charles Reynolds in his *Modes of Imperialism* shows both the relevance and shortcomings of single-factor explanations of foreign policy behavior.

In this stream of literature, students will readily observe the habit of cumulation that is a characteristic of the 'aura of science', and they may even observe a few rare cases of replication. But they will also confront some of the limitations of quantitative techniques. Measures of cooperation and conflict, both domestic and external, are relatively easy to construct even with presently available data. But *other* forms of foreign policy, such as the various methods of coping with security dilemmas, must rely on more traditional forms of inquiry. With the exception of Reynolds' volume, not many others are yet available.

Explaining foreign policy: personality and political variables

Although assumptions about human nature underlie most of the classical works in international theory, few of the masters explored the relationship systematically. Hobbes and Rousseau, whose constructs of diplomatic life are based on explicit statements of political personality, nevertheless failed to account for variation. Hobbes's statesmen are prudent creatures, always poised, like gladiators, ready for combat, but sufficiently rational to avoid such combat when the costs would outweigh gains. Morgenthau's political man ceaselessly seeks power, either to defend or to extend his domain of control. The logic of the international system forces statesmen, whether saints, sinners, or just plain bullies, to behave within strict limits defined in terms of the national interest.

Modern researchers have not accepted such reductionist analyses. They have produced an extensive literature based on assumptions of relatively free choice in foreign policy-making:

175

how policy choices are influenced by individual pathological and perceptual constructs, operational codes and belief systems, bureaucratic procedures, communications flows, pressures for conformity, or elements of 'group think'. Richard Snyder, Alexander George, Michael Brecher, Ole Holsti, Robert Jervis, Graham Allison and Irving Janis, among others, have produced works of enduring value. In them, the student will again observe the process of intellectual cumulation, the constant effort to introduce more precise research methodologies, to correct one-dimensional or determinist portrayals, and to test the accuracy of assumptions about cognition, choice sequences, and world images.

This body of work is based on a normative concern with war and crisis avoidance. Its roots in the classical tradition are obvious, if not always spelled out explicitly. But in its assumption of choice - individuals do matter, and their behavior can vary greatly - it challenges some of the other views of international politics which explain foreign policy characteristics and variation by system or national attributes. The problem here is in the differing scope of explanation. Most of the work dealing with choice examines single decisions - usually crisis decisions - whereas the other levels of analysis direct research toward the enduring, the typical and the patterned behavior over time. Because of the difference in scope, there is little possibility of synthesis. The streams of research go their own ways, creating understanding, but at different levels of generality. From the policy perspective, however, the research that examines individual and bureaucratic variables is critical. The other levels have little policy relevance (one can hardly counsel a government to change the regime or level of industrialization if it wants to become less war prone). But if the assumptions guiding the psychological literature are correct - namely that war and crises can be avoided if 'rational' decision-making procedures are employed, if policy-makers can suppress their personal psychological needs, and if communications between adversaries are clear and open - then research can show how governments can at least minimize the possibility of going to war as a result of miscalculation, misperception, or other personal foibles.

Power and bargaining

Power is the concept *par excellence* of international theory. Within a system of anarchy, most of the early theorists argued or assumed, outcomes of conflict are largely determined by the power capabilities governments mobilize in pursuit of their

176

objectives. Power potential can be measured by indicators such as population, size of armed forces, level of technology, availability of raw materials and the like. But the lack of a strong correlation between capabilities and outcomes observed in diplomatic-military life (the many cases of the weak prevailing over the strong, for example) inspired researchers in the 1960s and 1970s to delve systematically into the intricacies of power (or influence) in action. They discovered that bargaining is indeed a complex question, that outcomes may be influenced by a variety of factors, only one of which is available capabilities. Thomas Schelling, Robert Jervis, Alexander George and Richard Smoke, Glenn Snyder and Paul Diesing, and Coral Bell have produced seminal works in this area, identifying both coarse and subtle techniques of diplomatic exchange involving signals, deception, credibility of commitments, flexibility, argumentation and occasionally coercive diplomacy as crucial in explaining any outcome.

Most of these works have been embedded in the context of crisis situations, however. It is useful to explore the anatomy and physiology of power, and to show how our understanding can be increased by borrowing from the theory of games, but how about power and influence in non-crisis situations? Or, how do power and influence operate in a system increasingly characterized by interdependence, where vulnerabilities and sensitivities are augmented even for the 'great powers'? Can even great powers play the power game in issue areas such as trade, technology transfer and the law of the sea, when to do so would harm their interests more than those of many lesser states?

To ponder such questions, the student will have to rely extensively on Robert Keohane and Joseph Nye's *Power and Interdependence*, a work published only in 1977, but already one that would be on most international theorists' list of all-time best sellers. It demonstrates how technology and economic changes underlying the contemporary international system have changed diplomatic processes, power and influence. The book is a convincing demonstration of the intellectual gains made by combining theory with focussed comparative studies. It also presents a challenge to the models of power elaborated in earlier works by Morgenthau, Schwarzenberger and their successors.

Power and Interdependence is a good indicator of current displeasure with the 'old' models of international politics, personified in Morgenthau's elaboration of the power politics tradition. In the last decade, important voices have claimed not only that we need new research areas, but that entirely new paradigms, more consistent with current realities and recent socio-economic-technological changes, must be developed to guide research. The current debates are indeed fundamental; at stake is an intellectual tradition that dates back to the seventeenth century and a vast body of literature that constitutes our present storehouse of knowledge and hypotheses about international theory. In the last section of his course, our student must evaluate two particular noteworthy challengers to the classic tradition, dependency theory and models of the global society.

Dependency theory

Conspicuous by their absence in the list of thinkers who have contributed to the classical tradition in international theory are Marx and Lenin. While they had many things to say about international relations, until recently their works have been - perhaps properly - bypassed. But with the increasing concern over the roles and problems unique to the developing countries today, Marxist analytical categories and world views, emphasizing class actors, the fundamental importance of modes of production, the constant play of the dialectical processes of history, the constructive role of conflict and the economic underpinnings of political and diplomatic processes, have not only become fashionable, but also have fundamentally brought into question the continued paramountcy of the classical states system paradigm as the foundation of international theory.

Dependency theory, which has already spawned conflicting schools of thought on the problem of 'centre-periphery' relations, began as an intellectual revolt against the conventional liberal wisdom regarding the development process. A number of Latin American officials and academics during the 1960s challenged the orthodox view that development can be accelerated through a variety of standard mechanisms including foreign aid, foreign investment, export-led growth and domestic reforms. Western economists and sociologists typically regarded the 'barriers' to development as essentially indigenous - government corruption and ineptitude and such typical cultural patterns as the extended family, religious practices, work attitudes, inequitable land ownership patterns, the social and political influence of the church and the like. The Latin Americans argued instead that the barriers are located essentially in the structure and processes of the global capitalist system where terms of trade consistently favor the industrial countries, where the economies of the former colonial territories have been organized to suit the needs of the centres of world capitalism, and where further incorporation into that system through the promotion of foreign aid and private investment only compounds the mechanisms of exploitation. Their image of the world is one wherein the centre and periphery perform fundamentally different economic functions, the latter serving the interests of the former. Thus, international economics in the context of a global capitalist system are inherently zero-sum; exchange relationships are characterized by winners and losers.

A brief sketch of dependency theory can hardly do justice to the elaborate set of propositions embedded in the theory or to the important epistemological and methodological positions around which several schools of thought have organized. Despite its many problems, it offers a view of the world and its dynamics which has generated considerable intellectual sympathy and even enthusiasm in North American international relations circles, even thought it bears the most direct relevance to the areas of comparative politics and development theory. Some of its major propositions have been tested empirically - for example, the relationship between the degree of economic involvement of states in the world capitalist system and their comparative growth rates. (Contradictory findings tend to be explained by the methodology or statistical base used, and sometimes by the authors' value predilections. In most cases, the dependency hypothesis does not hold up.) This has caused a further intellectual debate, because most of the original developers of dependency theory heartily reject both the positivist methodology and studies which use states rather than class formations and exchange as units of analysis.

Dependency theory contains a fundamentally different *problematique* from the classical paradigm - no less than the causes of exploitation and the conditions of international or global equality. World images, units of analysis, and essential actors also differ.[4] The pedagogical question the student has to ponder is whether dependency theory can be synthesized with the body of knowledge we now call international theory, whether it should assume a pre-eminent theoretical platform for future analysis, or whether it should be relegated to the peripheries of our theoretical concerns.

No matter what one's ultimate conclusion, the theorist must confront three facts about dependency theory:

1) with all its scholarly warts, it has addressed a problem in international politics - the position of the developing countries - which has been systematically ignored in the Eurocentric traditional literature;
2) it has helped give rise to the field of international political economy which looms increasingly conspicuous in international relations curricula and academic journals today; and
3) it has - finally - displayed how some aspects of the Marxist tradition relate to the study of international relations.

Dependency theory thus appears to be more than a passing fad. It should have staying power, despite all its problems, because the normative concerns it raises are no less compelling to many than the traditional focus on the causes of war and the conditions of peace, security and international order. The problem of equality has been prominent in all modern political thought; it is only natural that it would ultimately find its way into international relations theory as well.

The world as a global society

The second challenge to the classical tradition comes from those who want to replace the underlying image of the states system and its dynamics as the guiding paradigm in international relations inquiry with a model of a global society in which the game of world politics is played by numerous types of essential actors - multinational corporations, terrorist groups, international revolutionary associations, international bureaucracies and numerous kinds of transnational voluntary associations. The world is defined in terms of a *global interest* which is distinct from, and often contradictory to, the separate interests pursued by states.

Modelers of a global society emphasize four discontinuities between traditional international theory and modern realities:

1) there are numerous - and critically important - non-state actors which a) create a number of the 'global' problems, b) help set the international agenda and c) vitally affect outcomes of diplomatic bargaining;
2) the old theoretical separation between domestic and foreign policies has completely broken down, as the interpenetration of societies continues to grow apace;
3) the portrayal of power politics in Hobbesian zero-sum terms is inconsistent with the substantial amount of collaborative behavior in the world - even between governments; and
4) the depletion of resources, worsening ecological balance, malnutrition, global pollution and the like will increasingly force governments to recognize that pursuit of short-run national advantages will only bring catastrophe to all in the long run.

Moreover, the game of power politics will undermine the essential supports of the modern state, among which are the provision of welfare goals, and not just international prestige and grandeur. While traditional international theory was normatively concerned with questions of war, peace and order, the unashamedly didactic purpose of those who develop global society models is to enhance among statesmen and publics an appreciation of the dwindling 'global commons', to promote the will to create international managerial capabilities and to bring about changes in life-styles so that there will be a balance between economic activities and technological innovation on the one hand, and the world's dwindling resources on the other. In brief, the theorists of world society aim to change our intellectual furniture, to wean us away from accepting the logic and philosophy of the states system. The ultimate vision is a world in which nation-states, having become obsolete in numerous policy realms, are replaced by some form of global policy-making that is guided solely by the universal interest.

Evaluation

More than two decades ago, Stanley Hoffmann wrote that the road to international theory would be long. It is probably endless if we use the term theory in the singular. The intellectual experience of the last three hundred years indicates that there can be no single theory of international politics that will comprehensively describe and explain the crucial normative and empirical dimensions of diplomatic life. All of the 'grand theorists' from Rousseau to Morgenthau and Raymond Aron have shed light on critical structures, processes and causal sources of war and peace, in some cases revealing significant essences. But they have all fallen short in one way or another. The major works can be faulted with one or more of the following shortcomings: one-sided world images; essential propositions which cannot be disconfirmed or verified; critical issues ignored or downplayed; failure to account for significant trends or patterns - usually the collaborative aspects of international politics; static rather than dynamic models; and unexamined assumptions. The complexities of international life and the changes induced by technological, demographic, economic, military and political developments will always render suspect any theoretical construct posing as *the* theory of international relations.

But recognizing that a theory of international politics is a chimera is not to claim that theoretical approaches to the subject are inherently deficient. Looking over the achievements of the past quarter-century, one cannot help but be impressed with progress. In my view, the main function of theoretical activity, in addition to showing parsimoniously how the world of diplomacy 'works', is to generate research. Both classical and contemporary theoretical efforts have eminently performed this task. The works cited in the previous pages, along with many others, have been stimulated by the hypotheses, insights and proposed relationships that abound in the classical and modern 'grand theories'. Theories of lesser scope - crisis decision-making, integration, alliances, bargaining and the nature of power and influence in non-security issue areas - are also impressive. While the latter owe less to the classical figures as immediate intellectual antecedents (although integration theory is rooted in nineteenth century liberal thought), they will serve as building blocks in future theoretical work. Although I cannot propose precise measures or indices of progress, an overall impression is that the development of theoretical approaches to international politics since the late 1950s has been noteworthy; our storehouse of knowledge has increased significantly in a number of areas, and almost annually a major theoretical work appears that offers new insights, challenges established orthodoxies, or demonstrates the continuing relevance of older formulations.

Areas of contention remain, of course. The consequences of a balance or imbalance of power - an area of vigorous debate in the eighteenth century - still generate research. Interdependence - assumed by many to be a development leading to more peaceful relations - has recently led others to ponder Rousseau's view that propinquity, commercial relations and transnational contacts are really sources of conflict. The Grotian tradition, as elucidated by Bull and others, enumerates multiple sources of order; but the forces of disorder, turmoil, instability, and in some cases, chaos, continue to make their mark on the daily headlines. We still have not resolved such critical theoretical questions as deciding the criteria to use in distinguishing types of international systems, identifying major sources of system change, measuring the extent to which technological innovations change behavior, assessing the relative importance of non-state actors and the like. The list is long enough to suggest that all the roads to theories are sufficiently long to provide work for generations to come.

Despite these continuing problems, the recent history of our enterprise shows important signs of maturation. The early diatribes, whether realism versus idealism or traditionalism versus behavioralism, have largely and blessedly receded into the past, with the accumulated experience of research and teaching demonstrating how the extremists on both sides made overly ambitious claims. Work has proceeded, with those seeking to establish a methodological orthodoxy properly rebuffed. The current theoretical debates, briefly summarized above, are more important than their methodological predecessors because they concern critical normative and substantive problems. The approaches that contend today do not debate *how* to study the important questions, but *what* to study, how to view the world and how to organize future research agendas. While allowing for a certain amount of faddism and innovation for the sake of innovation, we have entered an era of theoretical debate that promises to be robust and, one hopes, rewarding.

It is doubtful that the long road to theory will ever end, because the problematical consequences of technological and economic changes will render any firm causal or correlational statements suspect. But while traveling along the road, we have shed many of the intellectual habits that made significant progress difficult: reductionist hypotheses, methodological naivete, single-factor explanations, no attempts to cumulate knowledge, failure to examine assumptions and many others. The general level of work is today much higher than previously, although the incisiveness - the ability to reveal essences - of a Rousseau, Hoffmann, or Bull is not often approximated. The road is widening - if not straightening - which means that our knowledge and understanding of life at the international level is increasing; collaboration between theoretical and empirical work has become the rule rather than the exception and increasing numbers of scholars are being attracted to that exciting realm that joins philosophical speculation and argument with the study of war and peace.

Notes

1. *The Fall and Rise of the Modern International System*, The Arthur Yencken Memorial Lecture, 1980, Canberra: Department of International Relations, Australian National University, Canberra Studies, in World Affairs, no 4, 1981.
2. This list of streams is by no means exhaustive. Some areas of the literature, such as those dealing with regional subsystems, arms races, or formal Marxist theories of foreign policy, have been omitted for reasons of space.
3. Variations in the use of force are mostly accounted for by a power continuum. The major powers are much more 'war prone' than lesser powers, although the distinction is less dramatic in the postwar period compared to the interwar period. Variations in conflict behavior - defined as the issuance of threats, denunciations and other verbal forms, combined with reprisals and interventions - are not significantly accounted for by power differentials. The literature describing these associations is extensive. For summaries, see Michael D. Sullivan (1976), *International Relations: Theories and Evidence*, Englewood Cliffs NJ: Prentice-Hall, chaps 4, 5; and K. J. Holsti (1983), *International Politics: A Framework for Analysis*, 5th ed., Englewood Cliffs NJ: Prentice-Hall, chaps 12, 15. A recent examination proposes that 'libertarian' regimes are significantly less war prone than authoritarian

regimes, thus confirming the nineteenth century liberal hypothesis. See R. J. Rummel (1983), 'Libertarianism and International Violence', *Journal of Conflict Resolution*, 27, pp. 27-72.

4.   I have examined in more detail some of the critical incompatibilities between dependency theory and the classical tradition as well as models of global society in (1985), *The Dividing Discipline: Hegemony and Diversity in International Thought*, London: Allen & Unwin.

An Introductory Bibliography of International Theory

Allison, Graham (1972), *Essence of Decision: Explaining the Cuban Missile Crisis*, Boston: Little, Brown.

Aron, Raymond (1966), *Peace and War: A Theory of International Relations*, Richard Howard and Annette Baker Fox, trans, Garden City, New York: Doubleday.

Bell, Coral (1962), *Negotiating from Strength*, London: Chatto and Windus.

Brecher, Michael (1972), *The Foreign Policy System of Israel: Setting, Images, Process*, New Haven CT: Yale University Press.

Bull, Hedley (1977), *The Anarchical Society: A Study of Order in World Politics*, London: Macmillan.

Burns, Arthur Lee (1968), *Of Powers and Their Politics: A Critique of Theoretical Approaches*, Englewood Cliffs, NJ: Prentice-Hall.

Burton, John W. (1968), *Systems, States, Diplomacy and Rules*, Cambridge: Cambridge University Press.

Butterfield, Herbert and Martin Wight (eds), (1966), *Diplomatic Investigations: Essays in the Theory of International Politics*, London: George Allen and Unwin.

Buzan, Barry (1983), *People, States, and Fear: The National Security Problem in International Relations*, London: Wheatsheaf Books.

Carr, E.H. (1939), *The Twenty Years' Crisis, 1919-1939: An Introduction to the Study of International Relations*, London: Macmillan.

Claude, Inis L. Jr. (1962), *Power and International Relations*, New York: Random House.

Deutsch, Karl W. et al. (1957), *Political Community and the North Atlantic Area: International Organization in the Light of Historical Experience*, Princeton: Princeton University Press.

Deutsch, Karl W. and J. David Singer (1964), 'Multipolar Power Systems and International Stability', *World Politics*, 16, April, pp.

390-406.

Falk, Richard (1971), *This Endangered Planet: Prospects and Proposals for Human Survival*, 1st ed., New York: Random House.

Galtung, Johan (1967), 'On The Future of the International System', *Journal of Peace Research*, 4, pp. 307-27.

Galtung, Johan (1971), 'A Structural Theory of Imperialism', *Journal of Peace Research*, 8, pp. 81-117.

George, Alexander L. (1969), 'The "Operational Code": A Neglected Approach to the Study of Political Leaders and Decision-Making', *International Studies Quarterly*, 13, June, pp. 190-222.

George, Alexander L. and Richard Smoke (1974), *Deterrence in American Foreign Policy: Theory and Practice*, New York: Columbia University Press.

Gilpin, Robert (1981), *War and Change in World Politics*, Cambridge: Cambridge University Press.

Hinsley, F. H. (1967), *Power and the Pursuit of Peace: Theory and Practice in the History of Relations Between States*, Cambridge: Cambridge University Press.

Hoffmann, Stanley (1965), *The State of War: Essays on the Theory and Practice of International Politics*, New York: Frederick A. Praeger.

Holsti, Ole R. (1972), *Crisis, Escalation, War*, Montreal: McGill-Queen's University Press.

Janis, Irving L. (1972), *Victims of Groupthink: A Psychological Study of Foreign Policy Decisions and Fiascoes*, Boston: Houghton Mifflin.

Jervis, Robert (1970), *The Logic of Images in International Relations*, Princeton: Princeton University Press.

Jervis, Robert (1976), *Perception and Misperception in International Politics*, Princeton: Princeton University Press.

Kaplan, Morton (1957), *System and Process in World Politics*,

New York: Wiley.

Keohane, Robert O. and Joseph S. Nye Jr. (1977), *Power and Interdependence: World Politics in Transition*, Boston: Little, Brown.

Knorr, Klaus and James N. Rosenau (eds), (1969), *Contending Approaches to International Politics*, Princeton: Princeton University Press.

Mansbach, Richard and John Vasquez (1981), *In Search of Theory: A New Paradigm for Global Politics*, New York: Columbia University Press.

Miller, J.D.B. (1981), *The World of States*, London: Croom Helm.

Modelski, George (1961), 'Agraria and Industria: Two Models of the International System', *World Politics*, 14, October, pp. 118-43.

Moran, Theodore (1974), *Multinational Corporations and the Politics of Dependence: Copper in Chile*, Princeton: Princeton University Press.

Morgenthau, Hans J. (1948), *Politics Among Nations: The Struggle for Power and Peace*, 1st ed., New York: Knopf.

North, Robert C. and Nazli Choucri (1975), *Nations in Conflict: National Growth and International Violence*, San Francisco: W. H. Freeman.

Organski, A.F.K. (1968), *World Politics*, 2nd ed., New York: Knopf.

Pentland, Charles (1973), *International Theory and European Integration*, New York: Free Press.

Reynolds, Charles (1981), *Modes of Imperialism*, Oxford: M. Robertson.

Rosecrance, Richard (1963), *Action and Reaction in World Politics: International Systems in Perspective*, Boston: Little, Brown.

Rosenau, James N. (ed.), (1969), *Linkage Politics*, New York: Free Press.

Rosenau, James N., Vincent Davis and Maurice E. East (1972), *The Analysis of International Politics: Essays in Honor of Harold and Margaret Sprout*, New York: Free Press.

Rummel, Rudolph J. (1968), 'The Relationship between National Attributes and Foreign Conflict Behavior', in J. David Singer (ed.), *Quantitative International Politics: Insights and Evidence*, New York: Free Press.

Russell, Frank M. (1936), *Theories of International Relations*, New York: D. Appleton-Century Company.

Schelling, Thomas C. (1962), *The Strategy of Conflict*, London and New York: Oxford University Press.

Schwarzenberger, Georg (1941), *Power Politics: An Introduction to the Study of International Relations and Post-War Planning*, London: Jonathan Cape.

Scott, Andrew (1983), *The Dynamics of Interdependence*, Chapel Hill, NC: University of North Carolina Press.

Singer, J. David and Melvin Small (1968), "Alliance Aggregation and the Onset of War, 1815-1945', in J.D. Singer (ed.), *Quantitative International Politics*, New York: Free Press.

Singer, J. David and Melvin Small (1972), *The Wages of War 1816-1965: A Statistical Handbook*, New York: John Wiley.

Snyder, Glenn H. and Paul Diesing (1977), *Conflict Among Nations: Bargaining, Decision-Making and System Structure in International Crises*, Princeton: Princeton University Press.

Snyder, Richard C., H. W. Bruck, and Burton M. Sapin (eds), (1962), *Foreign Policy Decision-Making: An Approach to the Study of International Politics*, New York: Free Press.

Spiro, Herbert J. (1966), *World Politics: The Global System*, Homewood, Il: Dorsey Press.

Tanter, Raymond (1966), 'Dimensions of Conflict Behavior Within and Between Nations', *Journal of Conflict Resolution*, 10, March, pp. 41-64.

Waltz, Kenneth N. (1959), *Man, the State, and War*, New York: Columbia University Press.

Waltz, Kenneth N. (1964), 'The Stability of a Bipolar World', *Daedalus*, 93, pp. 881-909.

Waltz, Kenneth N. (1979), *Theory of International Politics*, Reading MA: Addison-Wesley Publishing Company.

Wilkenfeld, Jonathan (1968), 'Domestic and Foreign Conflict Behavior of Nations', *Journal of Peace Research*, 5, pp. 56-69.

Wright, Quincy (1955), *The Study of International Relations*, New York: Appleton-Century-Crofts.

Zinnes, Dina A. and Jonathan Wilkenfeld (1971), 'An Analysis of Foreign Conflict Behavior Of Nations', in Wolfram F. Hanrieder (ed.), *Comparative Foreign Policy*, New York: David McKay.

9. The Comparative Analysis of Foreign Policy: Some Notes on the Pitfalls and Paths to Theory

This volume is important because, aside from offering the first focussed comparative analyses of all the countries in Southeast Asia, it provides an opportunity to evaluate progress in an area of inquiry that, according to James Rosenau,[1] is neither a fad nor a fantasy, but is an established subfield of political science and international relations. My purpose is not to present a review of the field, as others have already done this.[2] Rather, I would like to examine critically some of the problems that have appeared in attempts to develop a coherent, cumulative, comprehensive, and comparative field.

One way to approach the problem is to ask what should be the essential contours or requirements of a field of inquiry. It would be presumptuous for any individual to suggest that his or her preferred criteria are authoritative or exhaustive. The comments below are therefore suggestive, open to argument, and neither exclusive nor exhaustive. Whatever their merit, however, I believe it is important to think about them because they will at least provide benchmarks against which to measure progress, and perhaps offer a sense of direction for future research. I would list the following among my set of preferences:

1) a consensus on critical questions to ask (the criterion of centrality):
2) agreement on major analytical categories and how to connect them (the criterion of conceptual consensus):
3) examination of a sufficiently large number of cases (countries' foreign policies), over time (the criterion of representativeness); and
4. using concepts, categories and typologies that foster rather than hinder comparative analysis (the criterion of comparability).

Most disciplines converge around, or are derived from, a few critical normative and/or scientific questions. In the case of international relations, for example, most work can be traced to questions about the sources of war and the conditions for peace/order, and stability. Questions of equity, justice, and distribution of welfare values and public goods are at the core of international political economy.

It is not clear that foreign policy analysis of the comparative sort has a central intellectual puzzle to solve. Presumably we want to describe how states, typically and untypically, act toward the external environment, and somehow to account for both patterned and highly idiosyncratic behaviors. But it is easier to state that this is *the* core problem than to demonstrate that we have made much progress in elaborating sets of independent and dependent variables around such key concerns. Because we do not have a consensus regarding the problems that should animate research, individual studies are likely to be idiosyncratic and hence not easily amenable to comparative analysis. We have studies of decision-making, bureaucratic politics, cognitive dissonance and 'information-processing', but few formal links between these and this elusive thing we call foreign policy.

Do we have a reasonable consensus on key analytical categories and concepts? In foreign policy analysis the literature reveals considerable convergence around such concepts as decision-making, bureaucratic politics, capabilities, crisis, deterrence, compellance, and coercion. We can isolate decisions and actions, and researchers have developed an extensive list of their sources. But the critical question of what we are trying to explain remains contentious. There is no consensus on what the concept of foreign policy includes or excludes, or what are its essential and non-essential indicators. As in the numerous studies on international integration so popular in the 1960s, our field lacks a carefully delineated dependent variable.

The problem of bias, parochialism, and unrepresentativeness plagues the field, although there are welcome signs of improvement. The majority of studies that have some theoretical and comparative content are authored by Americans, and implicitly or explicitly use the United States as a model for others. I will not document this assertion because it should be obvious to anyone familiar with the field. However, we can anecdotally discuss some illustrations. For example, the model of bureaucratic politics[3] supposedly of universal applicability, derived from an experience of the United States in a crisis situation. To what extent can this situation be considered typical? As Kim Nossal has pointed out, the Westminster model of a parliamentary system has important implications for foreign policy-making in other countries.[4] We certainly need to be alert to the possibility that policy is the result of bureaucratic pulling and tugging, but in no sense can Allison's model claim to provide a 'paradigm' of foreign policy in general.

192

The Foreign Policy Course Syllabus Project of the International Studies Association's Comparative Foreign Policy Section has collected a number of syllabi of undergraduate and graduate courses in American universities. Even those labelled 'Comparative Foreign Policy' include almost no non-American authored works, and the comparative content is almost non-existent. A course syllabus 'Foreign Policy Decision-Making' at the University of Texas lists 123 different required and suggested readings for the students. Of these, only nine are authored by non-Americans, seven of whom are Canadian. The course examines foreign policy decision-making in only two countries, the United States and Israel. The problem of parochialism and bias is acute and needs to be addressed seriously before we can claim that the subfield meets the criterion of representativeness.

While dependency theory provides some highly suggestive insights of a non-American perspective, and while no doubt persisting economic structures do provide constraints and limit some nations' freedom of action, the theory is unsatisfactory as a comprehensive guide for comparative foreign policy analysis because it cannot account for the great variations of foreign policy practice that prevail in the Third World. On most important indicators, Burma's foreign policy, for example, is fundamentally different from Egypt's; Kenya, Zambia, and Tanzania have demonstrated significantly different orientations, roles, and actions over the past decades, although each shares the various characteristics of the dependency syndrome. Moreover, reducing political choices and actions to economic phenomena is to overlook a host of essentially non-economic issues that create a variety of foreign policy problems for all states in the system.

There is, of course, no dearth of excellent country studies that contain theoretical content, but most of these are not cast in frameworks that easily lend themselves to comparative analysis.[5] The self-consciously comparative efforts are mostly of recent vintage.[6] It remains to be seen if they can serve as models for the work of others.

The fourth desideratum is employing concepts, categories, and typologies that foster rather than hinder comparative analysis. Since academia in North America appears to place considerable emphasis on novelty, this is a difficult criterion to meet. Each researcher is likely to develop a vocabulary and roster of concepts for his or her own work, not mindful of the desirability of using concepts and categories that others have used, and which can be used in future work. Aside from the vocabulary associated with the decision-making literature, our subfield is not characterized by easy transfer of concepts. The result is a predictable accumulation of country studies that are largely incomparable.

A book on Canada, for example, typically covers the nature of the major relationships Canada maintains, seen from a geographical perspective (Canadian-American relations, Canada and the Commonwealth, Canada and the United Nations, and Canada's commercial interests in the Pacific Rim). This descriptive account is then embellished with some discussion of policy-making structures, the role of public opinion and interest groups, and perhaps some words about the consequences of federalism on the development of external relations. A book on India, in contrast, is likely to feature a lengthy discussion of non-alignment (usually its virtues), relations with immediate neighbors, and perhaps a critique of American naval presence in the Indian Ocean. At both first and last glance, there is little to compare between the two books. It will not occur to the reader of both that there might be something worth comparing in the first place. And so the books will probably be read only by area experts, and they will soon be dated as the current events discussed in the chapters no longer capture the headlines.

Lest this listing of weaknesses and impediments in the field appear overly pessimistic, let me acknowledge that in the areas of individual behavior, as in decision-making studies and the techniques of influence, we have observed very substantial progress over the past decades. The works of Brecher, Jervis, George, Ole Holsti, Lebow, Stein, Steinbruner, Tanter, and others has been largely cumulative and self-critical. Models of decision-making have become increasingly complex, and an impressive array of historical and simulation researchers have uncovered many fascinating and significant findings. But there is one caveat: these are studies of how policy-makers come to decisions, or at least how they array their preferences, usually in crisis situations. The decisions are highly constrained in the sense that an immediate situation has to be dealt with on an emergency basis. These incidents, while of obvious importance, do not tell us much about the broader foreign policy purposes of individuals and governments. Foreign policy cannot be reduced to crises alone.

Comparative studies on the instruments of foreign policy and techniques of influence have been no less impressive. For example, the works by George and Smoke[7] and George, Hall, and Simons[8] employing an explicit methodology of 'focussed comparison' provide numerous generalizations about the employment of coercive and deterrent strategies in foreign policy.

The literature on a particular type of foreign policy - imperialism - has developed to the point where it has considerable theoretical content (the search for explanations), numerous case studies, and generalizations that transcend the particular activities of individual states. It is in this area, of course, that the Marxist tradition has made the greatest contribution. But that contribution has been predominantly in the form of insights. In the realm of logic and provision of testable hypotheses, regarding a general form of foreign policy behavior, the tradition has been the subject of telling criticism.[9]

What of the numerous quantitative studies employing events data? Here, too, we can see significant advances in terms of explicit theoretical works, rigorous methodology, and cumulation, all important hallmarks of a theoretical enterprise. But as an approach to the study of foreign policy, patterns of events have serious limitations. They are useful for mapping transactions between nations, usually classified in terms of typologies of cooperation, conflict, threats, rewards, and the like. They can also inform us of the ups and downs of hostility and friendship between governments. But events data are not a very good indicator of foreign policy, if by that term we mean purposive behavior directed toward changing or sustaining a particular state of affairs at home or abroad. We cannot infer motive, purpose, aspiration, and long-range objectives from discrete events and actions.

Sketches for a concept of foreign policy

The comments that follow concentrate on the persisting problem of the dependent variable - foreign policy. The literatures from international politics and decision-making suggest two models of man in the foreign policy milieu. He is, in the realist tradition, a power maximizer in the world of power-maximizing states. Foreign policy is thus reduced to the problems deriving from the 'security dilemma'. At the systemic level, foreign policy is seen predominantly as the activities states take to erect, preserve, or destroy balances of power. These activities are of only two types: mobilizing domestic capabilities, and forming alliances.

However adequate this view of foreign policy may have been as a shorthand description of diplomacy in the eighteenth and nineteenth centuries, it is clearly inadequate today. Although the model has the virtue of identifying a problem that *all* states may face - and hence encourages comparative analysis - it is overly simplistic and fails to acknowledge many other types of problems that concern governments in their foreign relations. It can account for uniformity, but not for diversity.

The second model sees the policy-maker as a goal-achiever. Governments have *objectives* which they seek to achieve. Foreign policy behavior is purposive behavior. It is also rational behavior in that governments typically attempt to fit ends to means, and make calculations about the relative costs, risks, and advantages of various policy options. Foreign policy, then, is the total of the decisions and actions taken to achieve stated objectives. The purpose of foreign policy analysis is to identify the objectives and the strategies and actions fashioned to maximize goal-achievement. This model has come to predominate a large part of the literature on foreign policy and international politics. It has the virtue of compensating for the simplicities of the power-maximizing school by suggesting that there are numerous things governments, through their policy-makers, aspire to, and that actions cannot be reduced to the mobilization of domestic capabilities and allies. The concepts of objectives, strategies, and actions are not difficult to operationalize, and they are certainly comparable. The notion of 'orientations' has similar virtues, although the links between these orientations and actions are not always clear.

The model of the goal-achiever, however, overlooks the reportedly large amount of activity that does not seem to be specifically goal-related. What about 'muddling through', procrastinating, policies that seem more habitual than problematic, responses to crisis situations not of a country's making, but to which it has to respond? Also, how can we categorize goals and objectives if there are so many different types? I am not certain about the answers to these questions, but to speculate about them leads one to ask two questions that are, in my view, fundamental to the development of a coherent subfield of comparative foreign policy. The questions derive from both the power-maximizing and goal-oriented models: what 'problems' do all governments share *vis-a-vis* the external environment? and what sorts of problems are unique to each state?

A third model of foreign policy can thus be one that takes the perspective of *problem-solving* as its base, and adds to it elements of the goal-oriented model. I believe there are four clusters of problems that all governments face, irrespective of size, location, technology level, population and many other attributes. They are (1) autonomy; (2) welfare; (3) security; and (4) regime maintenance. For many developing countries, a fifth category is state creation, including ethnic unity. This list is not exhaustive, nor are the categories mutually exclusive. The dividing line between them is obviously fuzzy and, as I have suggested in Chapter 5, the 'guns versus butter' dichotomy is not always clear-cut. The links between security and autonomy are even closer.

Every state faces some sort of problem about its autonomy. One meaning of autonomy is the ability to monitor and control foreign penetration and/or transnational processes. At least since the nineteenth century, when technological innovations and ideological or religious cleavages transcending national frontiers rendered the state increasingly permeable, governments have sought to prevent or control external intrusions of various kinds. The problem, however, is not equally acute for all states. It is a continuum, in which, for example, the United States has much less to worry about than does Canada or the Ivory Coast. Foreign policy analysis can, on a comparative basis, examine how states try to maximize autonomy. These can range from highly exclusionist policies, such as those of Albania, Burma, or Iran, to rules and decisions that exclude only certain kinds of foreign penetration (e.g., American regulations about foreign ownership of defense-related industries and support for the domestic computer chip industry). Autonomy may also refer to the many ways governments facing serious external constraints on their freedom of action seek to reduce these. I assume that, within the context of both voluntary constraints (as in treaties) and imposed constraints, governments always seek to maximize their latitude of choice. How they go about this can be an interesting object for comparative analysis.

Until the nineteenth century, national welfare was often synonymous with the welfare of dynasties. Indeed, even some regimes in the twentieth century have appeared to place a much higher priority on the aggrandizement of ruling families than on the welfare of the average citizen. The names Trujillo, Somoza, Duvallier, and perhaps Marcos, come to mind. These of course are exceptions. Most governments are committed to enhancing and protecting public welfare, often defined in terms of employment, income, health, production levels and the like. Since most economies are entrenched in global productive, financial, and trade networks, the provision of welfare goods is highly dependent upon global trends and decisions made abroad. Every government must seek to maximize opportunities abroad, and to limit the impact of injurious policies by others. The second major problem of foreign policy, then, is to promote, guide, steer, monitor and control those processes and decisions that relate to national welfare. And in so far as some regimes make explicit ties between commercial and political questions, the welfare problematic can be closely linked to issues in the autonomy and security domains. National trade policy, for example, can be a significant component of national security policy. But for analytical purposes, they can be kept distinct. On the assumption that governments seek to maximize welfare values, comparative analysis can focus on constraints and opportunities, and on the particular mix of externally-directed policies governments choose to deal with the problem. These can include, for example, support of the NIEO (New International Economic Order), plans for economic integration, construction of free trade regimes, emphasis on autarky, and many others.

Every state has a security 'problem'. There is of course no solution in the sense that any particular set of policies will make the problem go away. But by manipulating such variables as the size, location, deployment, and armaments of military forces, and/or alliance commitments governments try to minimize externally-derived, actual or potential, threats. Some (fortunate) states do not appear to face any immediate danger from abroad, but even these commit valuable resources to the creation and maintenance of armed forces, either for reasons of internal security and regime maintenance, or as insurance for the future.

Presently available textbooks and monographs on defense policies generally eschew comparative analysis, focussing instead on the particular dispositions of forces, hardware, and strategic doctrines of the governments they cover. Few have approached the subject from the point of view of a comparative 'problem' that must be coped with, if not solved.[10] A concern for describing the properties of various weapons systems - particularly ballistic missiles - in the Soviet-American competition has monopolized much of the postwar literature on defense matters. Let us start with the assumption that all states have an actual or potential security problem, and then compare how they cope with it, placing hardware questions in that larger context.

Our final problem common to all states is regime maintenance, that is, the various ways that governments seek to maintain constitutional orders, parties, and personnel in place. Many governments, of course, do not see this as a foreign policy problem, but the literature on linkage politics suggests that domestic political issues and foreign policy concerns cannot be neatly separated.[11] Just as foreign trade policy is often linked to security policy, so domestic political arrangements are heavily influenced by events and trends in the external environment. Some governments, particularly in Africa, earn more than ten percent of their GNP through aid transfers. A regime may well survive or collapse depending on whether it can augment or sustain such levels of foreign largesse. Similarly, military sales, grants, and training by foreign powers may be a necessary condition for the survival of some governments. A comparative analysis would thus focus on the various ways that governments 'use' foreign policy issues and external relationships to help sustain themselves in office.

In seventeenth century Europe, wars created states, and states went to war to establish recognized boundaries, to create central administrative systems capable of extracting resources to fund further wars, and to create and sustain national and/or dynastic

198

political units. In the post-1945 world, liberation movements and international legislation have created a raft of new states, many of which lack the empirical ingredients of statehood (defined territory, government control, and *national* political community). Though the comparison is stretched, a number of the new states resemble fifteenth and sixteenth century European political organizations more than their twentieth century successors. Torn by secessionist movements, border disputes, minority rebellions, local warlords and the like, many of the new states are compelled to use foreign policy as just one of many instrumentalities for creating viable political orders that coincide more or less with the territorial boundaries bequeathed to them by the colonial powers. The attempt to overcome dependency, for example, cannot be divorced from efforts to transform weak, conditionally viable entities into genuine international actors. For some countries, then, foreign policy and state-building are inextricably linked.

These are, then, four universal problems of foreign policy. The fifth problem confronts mostly developing countries in Asia, Africa and the Middle East. All governments face these four 'problematics', although obviously not in equal degrees of importance or urgency. If this proposition is valid, then we have moved toward comparative analysis, because no state can be seen as having policies that are entirely unique and therefore incomparable. We can search for commonalities, describing policies not so much in their specifics, but as *types*. For example, on the autonomy problematic, policies can be characterized as exclusivist (Albania), adaptive (EEC countries), permissive and penetrated (Ivory Coast?), or compliant (Czechoslovakia). These of course are all matters of degree, as well as types. It should not be difficult to develop various measures and indicators to place states on the continua. For the security problematic, policies can be of the coalition-building types (alliances), non-alignment and neutrality, or isolation, buttressed by various configurations of military deployment. Viewed through the lenses of a problem-solving (or coping) approach, and a typology of policies, comparative analysis becomes relatively easy.

But as the goal-oriented model suggests, states *do* have unique aspirations; not all policy can be subsumed under the five problematics. Libya's commitment to the Palestinian cause has little to do with any of them; some would argue that the American government's fascination or obsession with the Sandinista regime was unrelated to American autonomy, welfare, security concerns, or maintenance of the Reagan presidency. Many other examples could be cited. They all point to the fact that many governments - though by no means all - develop sets of objectives as diverse as promotion of human rights abroad, imperialism on a regional or global scale, the creation of international arrangements to facilitate trade, commerce, transportation and many other forms of international activity. Comparative analysts should try to identify and classify as many of these as possible, and then ask questions why. A goal-oriented model describing objectives, strategies, decisions, and actions would seem most appropriate. Explanations in terms of the personal/ideological/perceptual and 'operational code' characteristics of key policy-makers are most likely to be typical, whereas if-then propositions would be few and probably trivial.

One final problem remains: change. Most monographic literature on foreign policy, even that small segment which is formally comparative, is static. A writer composes, in effect, a 'photo' of country X's foreign policy, usually within a prescribed time frame. This sort of descriptive account is obviously necessary to obtain the essential facts. But as suggested in our discussion of the four problematics, governments tend to experiment with different bundles of policies for each problem. Some work, some fail, in other instances circumstances at home and abroad change sufficiently so that the policies that are appropriate for one period become obsolete. Change is more than just keeping up with the latest facts. It entails a number of interesting questions. If country A and country B have similar foreign policies, why does one change, while the other does not? What constitutes significant change, and how do we measure it?[12] Does a change in regime, even a revolutionary change, result in significant modifications of foreign policy. If so, it suggests personalities matter; if not, it suggests situations are compelling.[13]

Conclusion

The thoughts in this essay do not constitute a solution or set of solutions to the many problems confronting the subfield of comparative foreign policy analysis. In this paper, however, I have identified several areas that require attention. The first priority must be to develop some conceptual consensus on the notion of foreign policy. Despite numerous attempts to come to grips with this problem[14] researchers continue to go their own ways, thus rendering comparison difficult. Second, individual country studies must be cast in frameworks that are inherently comparable. The concerns of the area expert, where facts and description are based on the sole justification of being 'interesting', should be expanded to include a theoretical justification. Third, researchers must be sensitized to the problems of parochialism. Models and frameworks implicitly or explicitly based on the experience of a single country must be approached with caution, and most importantly, we need to expand significantly the roster of countries whose foreign policy activities come under rigorous scrutiny. To date, the criterion of representativeness has not been met, although there are hopeful signs that the situation is improving.

The sketches I have provided, while no more than suggestive, might at least point us in a rewarding direction as regards some of the criteria. Models of foreign policy based on events and/or goals are appropriate for some types of analysis, but they fail to pick up certain kinds of behavior. An approach emphasizing problems that all governments face enhances comparative possibilities and provides numerous opportunities for those whose interests are both empirical *and* theoretical.

Notes

1. James N. Rosenau (1980), *The Scientific Study of Foreign Policy*, London: Frances Pinter.
2. Christopher Hill and Margot Light (1985), 'Foreign Policy Analysis', in Margot Light and A.J.R. Groom (eds), *International Relations: A Handbook of Current Theory*, London: Frances Pinter; M.A. East (1987) 'Assessing the Field of Comparative Foreign Policy', paper presented at the 28th Annual Meetings of the International Studies Association, Washington DC. 14-18 April.
3. Graham T. Allison (1971), *The Essence of Decision*, Boston: Little, Brown.
4. Kim R. Nossal (1984), 'Bureaucratic Politics and the Westminster Model' in R.O. Matthews, A.G. Rubinoff, and Janice Stein (eds), *International Conflict and Conflict Management*, Scarborough, Ontario: Prentice-Hall of Canada.
5. For example, J. Saravanamuttu (1983), *The Dilemma of Independence: Two Decades of Malaysia's Foreign Policy, 1957-1977*, Penang: Universiti Sains Malaysia.
6. Bahgat Korany and Ali Hillal Dessouki (1984), *The Foreign Policies of Arab States*, Boulder, CO: Westview Press.
7. Alexander A. George and Richard Smoke (1974) *Deterrence in American Foreign Policy: Theory and Practice*, New York: Columbia University Press.
8. Alexander A. George, David K. Hall and William R. Simons (1971), *The Limits of Coercive Diplomacy*, Boston: Little, Brown.
9. For example, Kenneth A. Waltz, *Theory of International Politics*, Reading, MA: Addison-Wesley; Charles Reynolds (1981) *Modes of Imperialism*, Oxford: M. Robertson.
10. An important general work on the problem is Barry Buzan (1983), *People, States, and Fear: The National Security Problem in International Relations*, Brighton: Harvester Press.

11. James N. Rosenau (ed.), *Linkage Politics*, New York: Free Press.
12. My proposed solutions to the problem are outlined in Chapter 4 of this volume. The work was originally published in 1982.
13. Joe Hagan (1987), 'Regime Change and Foreign Policy Restructuring: The Third World in the Postwar Era', paper presented at the 28th Annual Meetings of the International Studies Association, Washington DC, 14-18 April.
14. For example, Patrick Callahan (1982), 'Event Data and the Study of Policy' in Linda P. Brady and Margaret G. Hermann (eds), *Describing Foreign Policy Behavior*, Beverly Hills, CA: Sage Publications.

10. The Necrologists of International Relations

Mark Twain wrote to his audience that reports of his recent death had been vastly exaggerated. In the field of international relations, we are seeing an increasing number of obituaries which announce the demise of the nation-state, and of its corollary, the states system. But unlike most obituaries which are fulsome in praise of the recently deceased, the necrologists of international relations have little good to say about the main forms of national and international political organization. They sigh with relief when they see alternative forms of political life emerging. Technology and necessity have combined to kill off the old, and they have spawned at least the formative stages of some new era when the world will no longer be carved up into separate states. At the level of scholarly nomenclature, the necrologists are arguing that we must now rename our enterprise. International relations or international politics will no longer do, for these terms do not sufficiently convey the types of structures and processes that are re-emerging. We should now reconstitute ourselves as experts in transnational relations or in something more holistic, like 'global politics'.

Academics in the field of international relations have traditionally taken the political fragmentation of mankind as a given. Today, however, a number of theorists and researchers in the field question the continued existence of the states system, and of its component units, both on empirical and normative grounds. The claim, in brief, is that the nation state as a unit of social organization designed to provide a number of services for a distinct political community is no longer viable, and that given the enormous risks associated with war in a nuclear age, the system of states must give way to some other form of global political organization. In large part, the thesis reflects strong normative desires; but for some there is sufficient empirical evidence to warrant assertions that trends indicate the formation of a 'planetary human community'.[1] For example, Saul Mendlowitz has claimed that 'today we may be in the throes of an epochal change... away from particularistically based territorial settlements serving a variety of agro-industrial units upon which the nation-state system was based, on to a truly global society with a global economy and a global culture, and involving global governance'.[2]

While acknowledging that the state and the states system are hardly what they were a century ago, or even fifty years ago, we must ask why these observers are so convinced that fundamental changes are occurring. What sort of historical and contemporary evidence do they provide to substantiate their arguments? What new conceptual equipment do they bring to bear on the research that demonstrates the end of one great historical era - the era of the nation- state and of the states system - and establishes a trend toward a new type of world organization? While I have neither the data nor the space to elaborate a definitive challenge to those who proclaim novelty, I would like to fire at least a few warning shots, taking an undeniably conservative stance, but one which I believe is consistent with the main features of contemporary diplomatic life. In characterizing two bodies of literature that challenge the traditional approaches to international politics, I will undoubtedly fail to do justice to any particular author, nor will I present a full-scale literature review. Instead, I will try to draw a rough portrait of a tendency. I apologize to those whose views may be distorted by omissions and failure to elaborate; I mean not to criticize any individual scholar, but rather to challenge two general streams of thought about the world we live in, and about the directions in which it is tending.

The states system as a war system

The first body of literature looks backward. It examines the history of the states system from its formative years in the seventeenth century, until the present. It searches for patterns of warfare and for changes in the leadership roles of the major powers. It has used Kondratieff curves, related war to economic cycles, and sought to identify some sort of regularity in the upward and downward movement of the leading states. George Modelski, for example, has identified patterns of what might be called 'elite circulation', that interchanging of hegemonial roles among the Portuguese, Dutch, English, Germans and finally the Americans. Taking a healthy position that challenges the static models of many theorists, this literature focusses on the problem of change. The result is a power cycle theory, whose great intellectual prize is an increased understanding of the etiology of war and through that, a reasonable set of probabilities of what we might expect in future.[3]

Although the studies vary considerably in methodology, data bases and general approaches, they hold in common the conclusion that the ultimate source of war is differential capability growth rates among the major powers. At a certain configuration or constellation of power, hegemonic wars - to use Gilpin's term - are likely to ensue. Doran summarizes this body of work as follows:

> The general thrust of this evolving research is clear. Piece by piece, the elements of power cycle theory are receiving more theoretical attention and additional empirical validation. The works of Modelski, Thompson and Olson have contributed greatly to reinforcing the idea of the power cycle, the idea that states in the modern system have followed a pattern of ascendancy, maturation and decline. Moreover the works of Gilpin, Bueno de Mesquita, and Organski and Kugler give further support to the theoretical observation that change on the power cycle is causally related to the initiation of major war.[4]

While internal developments within states are the driving mechanism for expansion of interests, the power theory leaves the impression - and some argue it explicitly - that the states system is a war system.[5] If the diagnosis is correct - and much of the evidence is persuasive - the policy implication must be that the states system is not compatible with the continued existence of mankind. If there is indeed an automaticity to war, driven by differential growth rates, if there are cycles, and if hegemonies must inevitably replace each other through the device of major wars, then we are left with few possibilities for human intervention. They are reduced essentially to two: either we must stop differential growth rates, or we must organize the world on some basis other than that of the sovereign nation- state.

The leap from diagnosis to prescription does not look very promising. What government leader would accept either of these alternatives as a basis for electioneering or for conducting diplomacy? We have had enough difficulties organizing even ameliorist solutions to the problem of war, such as collective security organizations, deterrence, arms control, disarmament and recipes for conflict management.

But the literature to which I refer seldom enters the realm of policy analysis. In the tradition of international theory of the positivist mode, it is concerned primarily with understanding, not with drawing blueprints for peace. What is of concern, nevertheless, is the implication - and sometimes the explicit statement - that the states system is a war system. The external consequences of domestic economic development constitute the security dilemma. The causal link is inward to outward. But even differential growth rates are not a necessary condition for war. As Rousseau suggested in his parable of the stag hunt, collaborative efforts by separate states, even if in their long-term interest, inevitably lead to insecurity and defection, meaning war. The power cycle theory only substantiates with data that which Rousseau explained by logic. The states system, then, is the ultimate culprit, which leads to the inescapable conclusion that the only real solution to the problem of war lies in its transcendence.

Interdependence and the demise of the nation state

The second body of literature is more disparate, takes more forms, and rarely stands on a firm empirical platform. This is the argument of 'interdependence'. Its intellectual ancestors are the early nineteenth century liberals who drew a dichotomy between the interests of states (government), which usually lead to international conflict, and the interests of a 'society', which, taken collectively, are harmonious and complementary. Transactions, whether trade, travel and other forms of communication between societies, tear down prejudices, build mutual confidence and tolerance, and create the foundations for international peace. To the extent that public opinion can stifle governments' penchants for aggrandizement, one can have both a states system and peace. The liberals and their contemporary descendants firmly reject Rousseau's pessimism. They applaud all the indicators that suggest the increasing interconnectedness of the human family.

In its modern form, the thesis was developed in the literature on international integration and in the noted analysis by John Herz, who declared that air power and nuclear weapons have rendered obsolete the nation state as a unit of defence.[6] Many others have gone on to develop this perspective, judging that technological innovations that bring societies closer together ultimately have fundamental political consequences. The causal reasoning is always from technical change to political results, rather than the other way around. Alex Inkeles, for example, sees much evidence of the development of a global society because of the increased rates of transactions between peoples.[7]

Among contemporary political scientists, the discovery of 'transnational relations' has led some to see in this evidence of a fundamental structural change in the international system. James Rosenau, for example, has argued that human loyalties are increasingly transcending national frontiers and that governments have lost their ability to control transnational processes and to command the unalloyed obedience of their citizens and subjects.[8] Mansbach and Vasquez have written a lengthy treatise which purports to demonstrate that the 'realist' model of international politics - the model which has underlain virtually every serious

206

study of international politics since the Treaty of Westphalia - is conceptually misguided, empirically deficient and theoretically biased.[9] The better-known writings of those associated with the World Order Models Project (WOMP) have of course long argued that the days of the nation-state are numbered. Lurking behind almost all of these statements is the assumption that changes in transaction rates between societies must have some substantial impact upon both domestic and international political orders.

Before proceeding, let us admit that these kinds of statements range considerably in the sweep of their judgments. Many of those who have recently discovered 'transnational relations' claim only that the 'realist' model of international politics is incomplete and that non-state actors' behavior has to be taken into account in understanding the nature of political-strategic relations between states. They have not yet reached the position that the states system is in the process of a structural transformation, or that national governments can no longer provide their citizens with essential services. Others are puzzled because on the one hand we appear to have a global economy, but on the other we continue to be separated into distinct national communities.[10]

At the other end of the spectrum, we have those who see a fundamental transformation occurring, a new epoch emerging. They tend to be technological determinists, as suggested. Because events in one corner of the world influence attitudes, opinions and actions elsewhere; because social, economic and ecological problems have the characteristic of migrating across national frontiers; because an increasing number of people speak English, or because mail, tourism, trade, investment, athletics, international non-governmental organizations, and diplomatic conferences are all increasing at astonishing rates, somehow all of this indicates (or, more forcefully, proves) that we are indeed on the road to some sort of new global political organization.

What are we to make of these two bodies of literature? What do they tell us about the nature of the states system and of its component units? What do they indicate about the normative dimension of international relations as a field of study? For purposes of argument, I would like to analyze the states system separately from its constituent units, although I realize this procedure is methodologically suspect.

War and the states system

War, of course, persists. The fundamental stratagems and problems of international relations today are not dissimilar to those examined by Montesquieu, Rousseau or Kant. We still have alliances, balances of power, arms races and expenditures on defense that threaten to bring havoc to many economies. Whatever the purposes and rhetoric about peace among armchair and think-tank specialists, or the names ascribed to weapons systems (MX as the 'Peacekeeper'), planning in most ministries of defense is geared toward the fighting and winning of wars. All of this indicates, as the power cycle theory suggests, that little has changed. But is this really the case?

Today we have more than 160 states compared to 51 in 1945, and only about 18 in post-Napoleon Europe. It should come as no surprise that the incidence of organized state conflict has increased. The more traffic, the greater the possibility of accidents. This would certainly seem to be an artifact of the states system. But there is other evidence that suggests certain qualifications to the conclusion. Singer and Small provide data indicating that when we control for the number of states in the system, the incidence of war has declined, albeit not significantly.[11] More recent evidence also shows that the incidence of great power conflict has declined.[12]

There are other qualifications. Although they are not so systematic, they are more than fleeting impressions gained from diplomatic history.

Since the World War II, we have had more than four decades of peace between the major powers. This is historically unprecedented. While the first two decades of the Cold War were characterized by a series of crises, whether real or mock (Quemoy-Matsu), there has been no direct confrontation since 1962 and only a single potential crisis surrounding the 1973 Middle East war. There is considerable evidence that both sides have learned important lessons from earlier clashes, and that capabilities and skills for conflict-management have developed substantially.[13] Since Malenkov was relegated to obscurity for having admitted publicly that there could be no winner in a nuclear war, the leaders of all the major powers have repeatedly renounced nuclear war as a means of settling international conflicts. This is also historically unprecedented. We are left with the problem of accidental or inadvertent war, and escalation, so one cannot be overly optimistic. But perhaps, as a minimum, there is some validity to Kant's prediction that man would not deal practically with the overriding problem of war until he had experienced certain levels of costs and miseries. The two world wars have certainly been important learning events, as have Korea and Vietnam.

Public attitudes toward war have also changed fundamentally in the last two or three generations. War is no longer seen as a normal instrument of foreign policy, to be employed to defend or advance state purposes ranging from minor questions of prestige, frontier disputes and settling irredentist claims, to more important issues such as major tracts of territory or gaining imperial domains. The major powers have, it is true, intervened against small states, or for or against revolutionary movements, but as the aftermath of the Vietnam agony has suggested at least illustratively, a major intervention involving prolonged combat is not going to be undertaken lightly. We could speculate that in the 1990s someone in the Politburo or Central Committee will argue the line, 'No more Afghanistans!' In the 1920s Europe experienced a number of small wars (Poland vs Lithuania, Greece vs Bulgaria and the like) that arose over relatively minor issues. In contrast, the Soviets and Chinese moved quickly to mute the conflict generated by the Ussuri River incident in 1969. Fifty years earlier, a similar incident would likely have led to general war.

Despite some evidence that Kant's learning hypothesis does not hold,[14] my impression is that diplomatic practice and thought since the World War II have changed fundamentally. Certainly the literature on international political economy has proven satisfactorily that the whole range of welfare issues on the international agenda will be dealt with by means other than the threat or use of force. Military hardware is irrelevant to tariff questions, the broad range of issues comprising the 'north-south' dialogue, monetary stabilization, debt relief, the law of the sea and many other concerns. In other words, many of the types of issues that in previous centuries led to the use of force (for example, access to markets and sources of supply) no longer can be dealt with in that fashion, even when the stakes are high.[15] Kant's hypothesis may not be the entire explanation for the decreased likelihood of major war, but it is at least one avenue that needs comparative and systematic exploration.

I am suggesting, then, that the patterns of the past are not necessarily a good predictor for the future. While cycles of growth and decline of nations may continue, we must carefully scrutinize any deterministic or even probable assertion that hegemonic wars are the most prominent outcome of certain 'inflection points' or constellations of power. There have been fundamental alterations in the costs, risks and attitudes of war. Our intellectual furniture about the problem of war has also changed;[16] the realm of ideas and attitudes must count as much as past patterns of practice. The inference from these comments - if they are plausible - is that whatever the historical experience, the contemporary states system is not necessarily a war system, and certainly not a system which will inevitably generate hegemonic wars.

If one examines not only the aggregate statistics about war incidence, but the nature of the issues underlying conflicts since 1945, one is struck by the extent to which most wars have had little to do with the operation of a traditional states system, that is, with balances of power, spheres of influence, claims for strategic territory, and the like. A surprisingly high proportion of the conflicts have been associated with the birth of states. We are witnessing, in fact, the formative years of a global international system, not its transcendence. Indonesia, the Arab-Israel conflict, Cyprus, India-Pakistan, the Congo - these and many more are or have been essentially conflicts over who will become new members of the states system, when, and how. These wars have few parallels in the eighteenth century, and they certainly challenge the idea that today we have a 'global village'. They have everything to do with the pronounced aspiration of peoples to achieve statehood. War and instability occur not because of some inherent fault in a politically fragmented world, but because we have an immature system populated in part by all sorts of infant states, unborn states (the Palestine Liberation Organization [PLO]), weakling states and a few aborted states (Lebanon). The chronicle of wars since 1945 has not included a hegemonic war, a war over a balance of power, or any of the types of major wars identified in the power cycle theories.

What, exactly, is a hegemonic war? According to Gilpin, it is a war 'that determines which state or states will be dominant and will govern the system'.[17] Gilpin does not use the term 'govern' in the way it is commonly rendered in political studies. It does not mean the governance of an empire, but rather holding the pre-eminent position in the states system and thereby determining a number of major rules and regimes of the system. In this sense, governance is not inconsistent with the idea of political anarchy, which is the essential characteristic of a states system. While since the fifteenth century there have been numerous 'governors' of the system, the system has not undergone any fundamental structure change. The argument of the power cycle theories, then, is that wars were fought primarily to see who would hold these top positions, but always in the context of maintaining and sustaining the states system. The fundamental rules of the system, as enunciated in the Treaty of Westphalia, in other words, are not challenged by the circulation of elites. Has this been the case?

I would argue that the great wars of the system were not a consequence of its normal operation, and therefore the states system cannot be characterized as a war system. In fact, the great wars were caused by individual leaders or small elites who wanted to destroy the system. Most of them did not seek hegemony. They sought empire. They sought to deny to other states the right to exist, and in so doing they trampled the fundamental rules of the states system, namely sovereignty and legal equality. Charles V, Louis XIV, the French Revolutionary armies, Napoleon, possibly Kaiser Wilhelm and definitely Adolf Hitler warred for much more than hegemony. They did not accept the rules of the states system and they did not play the game of diplomacy as it was meant to be played. They were not concerned with minor adjustments, righting balances or creating new alliances. Their model of Europe's political organization was a genuine Holy Roman Empire, a French Empire or a New Order in Europe under the direct administration of the Thousand Year Reich. They did not seek a redistribution of power, but a monopoly of power.

The system could accommodate all sorts of significant change, as in the case of Bismarck or the emergence of the United States as a great power, because they sought only limited gains, including acceptance into the club. Thus, when the system operates with all major actors accepting its fundamental norms and contours, it does not produce hegemonic war, or at least does so with little frequency. Hegemonic war occurs precisely when one of the system's members chooses to destroy it. Redistributions of power are more the results of these wars than their cause. In brief, we are ill-advised to condemn the states system rather than those who sought to destroy it. The system can maintain reasonable stability and peace, as the nineteenth century, and possibly the post-1945 period, have revealed.

International pluralism has been at least an important contributory factor to the incredible achievements in public welfare, the arts, science, literature and the like. As Robert Wesson[18] has argued, it is perhaps no accident that the greatest periods of intellectual and economic advancement were associated with states systems, and not with empires. Despite wars and instability, Western civilization's greatest achievements came in fourth century BC Greece, fourteenth and fifteenth century Italy (the city states), and nineteenth century Europe. While it may be overstating the case to argue that international pluralism accounts for such progress, the implication of the power cycle theory, namely that the states system breeds only war and mayhem, needs to be scrutinized much more carefully. Behind the aggregate statistics lies evidence of a different nature, leading to different conclusions about the states system.

In fact, most states most of the time are not engaged in war. Many have not been at war for decades, some not for centuries. We have learned a great deal from previous follies. Today, we have huge zones of peace, incorporating North America, a large part of Latin America, Western Europe, Scandinavia and arguably parts of Africa. I am not ready to concede that the poor reputations of the Middle East antagonists, the Soviet-American arms race, the great powers' proclivities for regional interventionism, or the posturings of the Ayatollah or Colonel Qadaffi warrant the conclusion that we can no longer 'afford' the states system, or theoretically that it is the system which is the sufficient and necessary explanation for all war.

Technological determinism and theories of interdependence

No one can deny the dramatic increases in transactions between societies, the ability of communications media to penetrate to the most remote backwaters of the world, and the vast increases of human contacts made possible through airplane travel and the development of numerous transnational organizations. There is convergence occurring everywhere, as family structures become more similar, government welfare policies copy each other, and as industrialization helps create modern bureaucratic structures.[19] We do indeed have the makings of a global economy, at least in the sense that individuals and investors respond to opportunities around the world, and that major economic trends in the world's largest economies often have significant impact abroad.

What does all of this mean for the viability of the state and of the states system? Do the diverse trends add up to a fundamental change in the sense that the political fragmentation of mankind, a characteristic of all human history, is about to undergo a transformation?

Arguments to the effect that national governments can no longer meet the needs of their citizens, that governments can no longer control transnational processes, and that loyalties are shifting to other types of jurisdictions have an air of wishful thinking and a rather naive view harkening back to the nineteenth century liberals. This is the view that more profuse transactions between societies are necessarily a force for peace. The argument that interdependence (however defined) causes the disintegration of the state and ultimately of the states system also makes inferential leaps. The data on convergence and transaction growths are widely available and well-known. But trends do not necessarily lead to structural changes.

Increases in ownership of automobiles have transformed some aspects of our lives; they have influenced family bonds, the shape of cities and priorities of government expenditures. But automobiles have not eliminated families, cities or governments. The same can be said of a host of technological innovations. They have numerous consequences in practice, but their impact on institutions that have deep historical roots is problematic, not predictable. The state as a political unit is surely one of those institutions.

Most political analysis assumes a pre-existing social community. The ideal polis for the Greeks was strictly limited in size. The good life was to be achieved in the context of a distinct and circumscribed political jurisdiction that could provide a variety of public goods ranging from welfare, justice and order, to group security. The alternative was seen in the Roman Empire, a universalist order that provided achievements and benefits to many, but not one devoid of war, slavery, oppression and violence. More recently, ideas such as federalism have been developed partly in recognition of the necessity of limiting political jurisdictions to some size principle. Universalist theories, such as those of Dante and the Marxists, follow in the line of the Stoics in presuming a governable global community; but in failing to recognize the ubiquity of the limited political community, they have suffered intellectually and, in practice, their ideas often have led to various forms of imperialism.

In the nineteenth century, the notion of self-determination, which today continues as a major international norm, was based on the thesis that political jurisdiction must reasonably coincide with the social, ethnic, language and religious distinctions among humanity. Although impossible to apply strictly - as the world leaders learned in the 1920s - the idea persists and animates numerous separatist movements in both the industrial countries and the Third World. The Middle East problem is basically one where, as the Palestinians insist, there is a 'people', but not a state. The Zionist movement took exactly the same position, as have the Karens and Chins in Burma, the Puerto Ricans and many others. In other words, while the data about growing interdependence may point to the formation of a single world economy, at the political level the prime datum is the continued quest for the creation of distinct political communities. The forces of political fragmentation, which are manifested in real life struggles, constitute more impressive evidence about the real state of the world than do theories of the transcendence of the state, the decline of national loyalties, or the hypothesis that the state is obsolete because in a nuclear age it can no longer provide security.

If the theories of some international relations scholars have any validity, why should political scientists be resurrecting an interest in the state? Why should the International Political Science Association have made the role of the state the theme of its Congress in Paris in 1985? Why should the numerous criticisms of behavioralism focus on its relative disinterest in the institutions

213

of the state? The reasons are many, but surely one of them is that the state - no matter how defined - continues to be one of the most salient factors in our lives. Indeed, the available evidence suggests not the 'withering' of the state, but its continued growth.

Richard Rose[20] and Klaus von Beyme[21] have chronicled the growth of government activities, as measured by a number of different indices. The evidence is overwhelmingly against the argument that the state is withering in the face of transnational phenomena. While these studies contain few indicators of state authority or legitimacy, that is, no data that could test Rosenau's contention that the exclusive loyalties of citizens toward their state are eroding, it is hard to believe that governments could be expanding their functions and their ability to extract taxes in the face of massive shifts of loyalty.[22] Thus, whatever the growth of international transactions and transnational organizations, we cannot assume that those developments are in any way antithetical to the continued viability of the state.

But what of Herz's argument that the techniques of modern warfare have rendered the state incapable of providing for the citizens' security - presumably one of the premier functions of all political organization? When written in the 1950s, this thesis seemed persuasive. Nuclear weapons and air power were relatively new, some states did indeed seem more permeable than they had been previously, and we could all agree that in a state of nuclear war, few governments could provide protection. But that is just the problem. Herz writes about the role of the state in a condition of total war, not in time of peace or even in a condition of limited war. Just like so many postwar military strategists, Herz was dazzled by the experience of World War II, assuming that future wars would also be total. But the destructiveness of nuclear war has not rendered the nation state obsolete. It has just made it (at least those armed with such weapons) more prudent in its diplomacy.

All the wars fought since 1945 have been at the conventional level. No state, with the possible exceptions of South Vietnam and East Timor, has been obliterated by war. Air power, as the United States demonstrated in Vietnam, can indeed inflict massive damage (against friends as well as foes), but if anything, bombing enhances the authority of the target government. (There is some evidence, for example, that the authority of the government of North Vietnam over its citizenry was greater in 1975 than a decade earlier.) In the Iran-Iraq war, air power was used cautiously and in a limited fashion - in part because supplies of aircraft were limited, and in part because of the fear of retaliation. Conventional wars illustrate that sophisticated weapons systems do not necessarily revolutionize the nature of warfare. Herz's analysis, while highly insightful, suffers from the common malady of social observers, the assumption that everything new renders old forms of doing things, including fighting wars, obsolete.

There is also the common fault of ascribing to all international relationships the characteristics of just a few of the major powers. Only five of 160 states possess nuclear weapons (six if we include India). Assuming that no nuclear power would use such weapons against a non-nuclear state, there are only ten hypothetical dyads for nuclear war; in diplomatic reality, there are only two (USSR vs the West; USSR vs China). In contrast, there are 11,781 possible dyads for conventional war, not counting nuclear power states which could use conventional means only. In diplomatic reality, the figure would be considerably lower, confined in most cases to contiguous states. But even here, since most states have on average 2.5 neighbors, there are well over a thousand possibilities. In brief, the Herz thesis does not even pinpoint a trend because it does not discuss the realities of most states most of the time.

There remains the argument that states are not able to control transnational processes and that, therefore, their authority has withered. Examples often cited include huge amounts of capital suddenly flowing across national boundaries, the inability of governments to fashion national economic policies - interest rates are a key example - that are distinct from, or contrary to, the policies of the economic giants, and the impossibility of protecting national cultures from global demonstration effects, unwanted cultural intrusions, and the mores and fads of other societies.

There is considerable merit to these observations, but it is easy to ask, so what? Is any of this really new? And even if so, does it signal some mortal weakness in the nation state?

Transnational activities and processes are, of course, nothing new. Today we have terrorist groups with international linkages. In the late nineteenth and early twentieth centuries, they were anarchist groups, also with transnational connections. Today we have drug runners. In the seventeenth and eighteenth centuries and even later, there were pirates. Admittedly, massive capital transfers can take place within a few hours, in contrast to the nineteenth century when everything moved more slowly. But if they really constitute serious assaults on national authority, governments have instruments to control them. We have all sorts of governments 'interfering' in each others' internal affairs by hiring lobbyists and other groups to influence domestic legislation. Washington and Ottawa are full of them, as are Bonn, Tokyo, Paris, London and other national centers. They operate relatively freely for the prime reason that they do not constitute a threat to the authority of national governments. Were they to do so, they could be easily excluded, as many authoritarian regimes have demonstrated.

National governments are not passive actors facing the onslaughts of undesirable foreign imports, whether goods, ideas or people. They have at their disposal a variety of mechanisms to monitor, control and sometimes to exclude unwanted or threatening foreign influences. Our own experience during the Trudeau years reveals very well how a government can fashion various policies to enhance or protect autonomy. Pluralist societies by choice remain relatively open to foreign goods, ideas, people and fashions. Those countries, like Burma, Albania, and China in the 1960s that genuinely fear transnational processes can effectively build moats around themselves, although the cost may be very high in terms of economic efficiency and other values.

The conclusion that governments have lost their authority in the face of transnational processes is thus a major inference drawn from raw data demonstrating only that interconnectedness is growing. But we cannot infer from these data that there is an erosion of governmental authority. We could only prove the case if we could demonstrate that most governments wanted to control those processes, but were unable to do so, even at a high cost. To use Rosenau's alliteration - but not his intent - the state is certainly not withering; nor is it merely weathering. The evidence seems to indicate that it is, on the contrary, waxing. Those who like to use Lebanon as an example of what fate awaits all states should really look for a more representative illustration.

There is also something ethnocentric in the arguments of those who proclaim the demise of the nation-state and, ultimately, of the states system. The trends they observe are most evident in the transactions and relationships between the Western industrial states; they therefore cannot predict to some global structural change. While there have been dramatic increases in trade, tourism, communications of various kinds and capital flows, all of these are highly patterned and concentrated, not dispersed. The majority of tourists go from Western industrial country to Western industrial country. The same is true for trade, investment, cultural contacts, radio and television programming and publications. More than 99 per cent of Russians, Chinese, Indians, Zambians and dozens of other nationalities will never go abroad, will never talk to a foreigner, will never read a book written by a foreign author, and will have virtually no knowledge of any country other than their own, save for a few negative stereotypes of national enemies. Even among those who travel, a very large proportion will learn little of the politics, social problems, economics and cultural life of their destinations. The idea that most travellers go abroad 'to get to know the people' is one of the great fictions surrounding tourism. This is even more the case when we examine the nature of connections between people in industrial and developing countries.

Among themselves, the populations of the developing countries (and probably among the socialist countries as well) are connected only by miniscule elites. Trade and investment among them, while growing, remain a very minor proportion of all trade. Chadians do not watch Brazilian movies, and Ecuadorians do not listen to the favorite pop songs of Yugoslavia. Artists in Kampuchea have no contacts with, and are unaware of the artistic fashions in Tanzania. There are relatively few transnational organizations in which leadership positions are held by representatives of the Third World. The realities behind aggregate figures of international transactions can lead only to one conclusion: while contacts are increasing, the political fragmentation of the world is largely duplicated at the social level. The cliches of 'spaceship earth' and the 'global village' are little more than that; they distort more than they reveal, and what germs of truth they do contain pertain primarily to the interconnectedness of the Western industrial states.

My argument, to summarize, is that while there are certain suggestive trends that must have some impact on the state, the realities are often hidden behind aggregate figures. And even if the realities and the figures coincide, we cannot make the inferential leap that these trends have a demonstrable effect on the capacity of government to wield authority, to provide a range of public goods and services, and to engage in foreign relations. Questions of war and peace, of economic development and welfare and of justice and order remain almost exclusively within sovereign jurisdictions. The exceptions are primarily cases where the governments in question are barely viable to begin with, where authority barely extends beyond the national capital, and where foreigners have set up puppet regimes. Such states are weak not because of transnational processes, but because they were not initially founded on a cohesive community. The governments are weak because they were born weak, not because they are declining in authority. Many persist not because they have been successful in developing an underlying community, but because others in the international community support and legitimize them. As Jackson and Rosberg have argued, 'The global international society... has been generally successful in supporting the new state jurisdictions of independent Africa; thus, the survival of Africa's existing states is largely an international achievement'.[23]

The international community, through transfers of aid, technology and brain-power, has sought to create more viable states in Africa and elsewhere. Contrary to those who see such transnational processes resulting in the declining authority of the state, the African post-colonial experience demonstrates exactly the opposite: they have the explicit or unintended consequence of helping to create 'real' states.

How do we characterize the states system?

First, we must recognize, as Stanley Hoffmann has pointed out, that international politics is not a single game, but many games.[24] It has elements of the 'realist' view of international life, taking its main outlines from Rousseau and his modern heirs. Some states constantly face a security dilemma, and they view the growth of power of their adversaries as a direct threat to their own well-being. They have difficulty in understanding that major global reforms, even if involving some short-run costs and risks, are better for all in the long run. They are particularly unwilling to accept any risks in the area of military security. Arms control and disarmament measures, while eminently beneficial to all concerned, fail to be negotiated because each side either seeks a unilateral advantage, or because one or both insist on one hundred per cent security with no risk of non-observance. Lack of trust and/or unwillingness to recognize the legitimacy of adversaries prevents negotiated settlements to distinct issue conflicts. The world of diplomacy between such adversaries is indeed Hobbesian. Because the media insist on reporting mostly the sensational aspects of international like, it is easy for the average person to believe that all of international relations must be like these cold wars.

But anyone who wishes to look further than the daily headlines will see another side of the coin, namely peaceful and often col-laborative relations among states. Western Europe, Scandinavia, North America, most of Latin America, the antipodes and even a good part of Africa are zones of peace, where relations are predictably non-violent, if not entirely free of diplomatic conflict.

This second side of the coin is characterized by problem-solving approaches to issues that touch upon welfare rather than security questions. Outcomes of bargaining tend to extend the interests of both or all parties. Stakes are distributive rather than win-lose. Pressures tend to be subtle, threats are relatively uncommon, and the manipulation of military capabilities to influence outcomes is rare. Here we have a type of politics with some characteristics similar to those found within the liberal democracies. In these domains, transnational relations flourish, non-state actors play roles in diplomacy, both major and minor states set the agenda and, as Keohane and Nye have convincingly argued, outcomes are seldom determined by the power capabilities of the players.

In this area, politics can also be creative in the sense of establishing a host of rules, standards, norms and even binding regulations to allocate values, to regularized procedures and to manage resources. Today we call such activities 'regime-creation', suggesting that even in a system characterized by anarchy, major and minor actors can come together to create the network of law that is necessary for order, predictability and even justice.

But there is yet a third side to international politics, one that is more subtle than the domain of regimes or the very explicit rules and norms that successfully regulate transactions between states. The late Hedley Bull argued persuasively that the states system is more than just a collection of entities.[25] It is, following in the traditional view expounded by Grotius, a society of states. Despite the seeming anarchy, the prevalence of war, and the lack of a central authority, this society in both subtle and forceful ways, like a club, regulates the major forms of behavior of its constituent units. Some of the regulation derives from international law. Perhaps more important is the consensus among a majority of states as to what is acceptable and what is unacceptable. The fundamental rules of the states system, as enunciated in the Treaty of Westphalia, set down criteria regarding membership in the club. Today, many states are created and sustained by the community of states, as much as by their own efforts, as Rosberg and Jackson have shown in the case of Africa. The PLO can never head a state until a majority of states recognize it as such. Many national liberation movements are bound to fight in frustration, knowing that even if they win the plum of statehood through successful insurgency, they will not receive recognition from the international community, and hence they will be states in name only.

The pressures of the community effectively restrain behavior in many realms. We need only mention a few to make the point that anarchy and order are not incompatible and that despite occasional wars, the states system is not an inevitable 'war system'.

The pressures of the community came to bear on Iran, whose government was unanimously censured by the United Nations General Assembly during the 1980 hostage incident. Iran had broken one of the fundamental norms of international life: the sanctity of the diplomatic mission. The careful scrutiny of the international community probably prevented Iran and Iraq from adopting certain military measures, including the use of poison gas. After Iraq did use such weapons, the outcry was probably sufficient to make it reassess the policy. Technically, we have a non-proliferation 'regime' embedded in the Non-Proliferation Treaty, but one should ask whether it is the treaty or the anticipated reactions of the international community that prevent more states from developing nuclear arsenals.

I need not stretch out the examples, since Bull did so in such a masterly fashion. But we can emphasize that war, too, can be a sanction of the international community. This was recognized by theorists of the balance of power in the eighteenth century, who argued that the ultimate protection of the states system may be war through a coalition of states banding together to prevent their elimination by those who aspire to empire.

I hope the analysis has at least planted seeds of doubt about the theses regarding the viability of the nation-state and the impending transformation of the states system. Behind the aggregate statistics that demonstrate power cycles lie important diplomatic-historical realities that cannot be overlooked, namely that it is not systems that breed war, but particular individuals and regimes that have sought to destroy the states system in their search for empire. General war, while incredibly costly in lives and destruction, has been in most instances an appropriate response for those who believe, for whatever reasons, that nationhood, sovereignty, and independence are values worth fighting for. While we can certainly sympathize with the need for better international coordination of policies, for a better awareness of the general good, and for a modicum of trust and civility between the superpowers, there is scant evidence that fundamental transformations either in the actors of the system or in the system itself are underway or in the offing. The arguments about demise or transcendence appear to be born of hope rather than of scientific inquiry.

Notes

1. Zdenek Masoput (1985), 'Global Problems of Humankind', *International Political Science Review*, 6, p. 458.
2. Saul H. Mendlowitz (1977), 'The Program of the Institute of World Order', *Journal of International Affairs*, 31, p. 261.
3. Compare with George Modelski (1978), 'The Long Cycle of Global Politics and the Nation State', *Comparative Studies in Society and History*, 20, pp. 214-235; C. F. Doran and W. Parsons (1980), 'War and the Cycle of Relative Power', *The American Political Science Review*, 74, pp. 947-65; C. F. Doran

(1983), 'War and Power Dynamics: Economic Underpinnings', *International Studies Quarterly*, 27, pp. 419-41; Robert Gilpin (1981), *War and Change in World Politics*, Cambridge: Cambridge University Press.

4.   Doran, 'War and Power', p. 428.

5.   Albert Bergesen (1985), 'Can the World Economy Produce Nuclear War?', paper presented at the 26th annual meeting of the International Studies Association, Washington, DC, March.

6.   John H. Herz (1959), *International Politics in the Atomic Age*, New York: Columbia University Press.

7.   Alex Inkeles (1975), 'The Emerging Social Structure of the World', *World Politics*, 27, pp. 467-95, and (1981), 'Convergence and Divergence in Industrial Societies', in Mustafa Attir, et al. (eds), *Modernization Theory, Research, and Realities*, Boulder, CO: Westview Press.

8.   Rosenau addresses a number of problems arising from growing interdependence in his (1980), *The Study of Global Interdependence*, London: Frances Pinter.

9.   Richard Mansbach and John Vasquez (1981), *In Search of Theory: A New Paradigm for Global Politics*, New York: Columbia University Press. Some similar ideas which have largely gone unnoticed in the literature are developed in Hebert Spiro (1966), *World Politics: The Global System*, Homewood, IL: Dorsey Press.

10. Compare with Eric Kierans (1984), *Globalism and the Nation-State*, Toronto and Montreal: CBC Enterprises.

11. J. David Singer and Melvin Small (1972), *The Wages of War, 1816-1965: A Statistical Handbook*, New York: John Wiley.

12. Thomas R. Cusack and Wolf-Dieter Eberwein (1980), 'International Disputes: A Look at Some New Data', Berlin: Institute for Comparative Social Research.

13. Christer Jonsson (1984), *Super Power: Comparing American and Soviet Foreign Policy*, London: Frances Pinter.

14. David Garnham (1980), 'Predicting Belligerency Cycles of Nations: State Bellicosity and Pacifism', paper presented at the annual meeting of the American Political Science Association, Washington, DC. However, another study shows that in the nineteenth century 15 per cent of the major power disputes escalated to war, while in this century the figure has declined to 10 per cent. Of course, there have been no intra-great power wars since 1945. See Melvin Small and J. David Singer (1979), 'Conflict in the International System, 1816-1978', in J. David Singer, et al. (eds), *Explaining War*, Beverly Hills, CA: Sage.

15. The standard work is Robert O. Keohane and Joseph S. Nye (1977), *Power and Interdependence: World Politics in Transition*, Boston: Little, Brown.

16. F. H. Hinsley (1981), *The Fall and Rise of the Modern International System*, Canberra: Canberra Studies in World Affairs, the Australian National University.

17. Gilpin, *War and Change in World Politics*, p. 15.

18. Robert G. Wesson (1978), *State Systems: International Pluralism, Politics, and Culture*, New York: Free Press.

19. Inkeles, 'Convergence and Divergence in Industrial Societies'.

20. See (1983), *Understanding Big Government*, London: Sage.

21. See (1985), 'The Role of the State and the Growth of Government',

International Political Science Review, 6, pp 11-34.

22. The problem, of course, is that loyalties need not be exclusive. As the Europeans have proven, one can be a good Frenchman or Dutchman and a strong supporter of the European Community at the same time. For a theoretical discussion see Harold Guetzkow (1955), *Multiple Loyalties: Theoretical Approach to a Problem in International Organization*, Princeton: Princeton University Press.

23. See Robert H. Jackson and Carl G. Rosberg (1982), 'Why Africa's Weak States Persist: The Empirical and Juridical in Statehood', *World Politics*, 35, p. 22. The comments in this paragraph echo the general thesis developed by Jackson and Rosberg.

24. See (1978), *Primacy or World Order: American Foreign Policy Since the Cold War*, New York: McGraw-Hill.

25. See (1977), *The Anarchical Society*, London: Macmillan.

11. International Theory: National or International?

More than forty years have passed since the first rounds of the great debate between 'behavioralism' and 'traditionalism' in the study of international politics took place. The arguments continue in many guises, but it may be accurate to claim that a somewhat mellowed form of scientific inquiry in international politics has become the norm, at least in North America and a few other regions of the world. As is often the case in initial debates about the merits and shortcomings of different methodologies and general approaches to a field, claims were exaggerated on both sides. The most zealous among the behavioralists demanded more rigor, empirical verification and cumulation than they and their successors could possibly deliver, while the traditionalists exalted too vigorously the quality of knowledge gained primarily from insight, intuition and the lessons that could be learned from a close reading of diplomatic history. Today, most would agree that the firm dichotomization of paths to knowledge overlooks areas of commonalty: traditionalists do measure, while much 'hard' science is launched on the basis of insights that do not derive from adhering to strict canons of scientific method.

Many of the early proponents of scientific methods - especially those who developed formal deductive models, operationalized concepts, 'tested' hypotheses against data, and measured precisely - made extensive claims and predictions about the superior results of their methodologies. Among them were greater reliability and cumulation, results which by and large have been achieved. The most ambitious claimed, furthermore, that a science of international politics could lead to a general theory, accurate 'laws', and predictions. If we were to judge the field today in terms of such claims, the mark assigned would be low. Most investigators have recognized that while formal scientific modes of inquiry hold many virtues, the subject of study inherently limits most results to more or less significant associations, correlations, probabilities and trends. Those statements which have had the qualities of 'laws' have on the whole been too trivial to stimulate research agendas or knowledge.

My purpose, however, is not to evaluate all the debates about the philosophy of science, the claims made by leaders of various methodological schools or even the position which holds that 'scientism' buttresses the *status quo*. These issues have received extensive attention elsewhere. I will confine my comments to a problem that has received much less exposure. This is the problem of parochialism. It is in part a problem created by national perspectives on international relations. But it is not only an issue arising out of differences in geography, history, language and culture. There is also a habit among some theorists of international relations that might be called conceptual or methodological parochialism. This is the stance, prominent among more than a few scholars in our field, that there is only a single legitimate approach, model, methodology or theory of international politics. The quarrels about behavioralism versus traditionalism, among many other debates in the field, clearly revealed this position. This form of parochialism is really an argument for intellectual orthodoxy and, as such, contradicts the scientific spirit which emphasizes exploration, novelty and innovation. I do not suggest that this form of parochialism is always a conscious decision on the part of analysts to accept or reject certain approaches to a field. Rather, it reflects a trait of many scholars in international relations, namely an unwillingness to confront directly the relationship between our personal values, including political perspectives, and the subject we study. I would like to examine briefly some of the roles values play in the development of international theories, because understanding of this problem may help us locate some sources of parochialism.

Values and research

We have tended to be prudes about the relationship between personal values, theoretical activity and research agendas, either pretending it does not exist, or claiming that if it does, we can handle it quietly and effectively by a methodological quick fix. In most discussions the issue is posed as essentially a technical one: how to develop research tools that will sensitize investigators to their value biases; the effect of interviews and polls on subsequent behavior; developing 'unobtrusive measures'; 'squeezing' unwarranted inferences from data; and the like. But from its origins, the study of international politics has been critically influenced by normative and philosophical concerns. We study a subject not because 'it is there', but because we are morally concerned about it. We should acknowledge and, like some peace researchers, even celebrate this. For it is these concerns that basically determine *what* we study and deeply influence *how* we study it.

Let me illustrate this assertion by examining briefly three main theoretical approaches to international relations: 'realism' and its modern versions; dependency theory; and world society models. I want to emphasize the extent to which normative concerns underlie these approaches to the field.

The classical theory of international politics, of which realism constitutes just one version, developed coincidentally with the formation of the European states system. One of the fundamental characteristics of that system was war, a phenomenon, according to Rousseau, which was an inevitable consequence of a system of sovereign, independent states with no central authority to regulate their mutual relations. The early theorists of the states system condemned war from a variety of perspectives. For some, it was wasteful and destructive. For others, war was an instrument of ruling dynasties to perpetuate their monopoly of power and to suppress the rising tide of republicanism. And, for those who saw virtues in the system of independent states, war was the evil instrument which imperially-minded rulers could use to unite Europe into a single imperium, that is, an instrument to destroy the states system. Various writers of the era, from Grotius and the Abbe Saint-Pierre, to Rousseau, Kant and Bentham thus had a common moral concern: to identify the etiology of war and, having done that, to outline the necessary and sufficient requisites for peace.

Since the eighteenth century, these questions have remained the theoretical cores of our discipline, and no matter what our preferred solutions to the problem, we all call ourselves scholars of international relations because ultimately we have a moral and ethical concern with the problems.[1]

Studies on transnational relations have generated neither major theoretical statements nor a body of cumulative knowledge about international relations. Why? Certainly not because there is an absence of empirical data, or because transnational relations are declining. It is, I believe, because descriptive studies of transnational relationships are for the most part far removed from the war-peace problematic. The main streams of contemporary theoretical work converge on issues such as crisis decision-making, the requisites for effective deterrence, patterns of bargaining in international conflicts, the sources of international cooperation, the problem of mis-perception and miscalculation in foreign policy-making, and the like. All of these are intimately related to the core ethical concerns of our field. But a large proportion of transnational relations have not yet been empirically linked to the causes of war and the conditions of peace - although someday they may be. To study systematically all phenomena that involve communications across national borders would lead to the amassing of great quantities of data; but as yet, these have not been directed toward the solution of any important moral puzzles.

Transnational relations, focussed on the connections, for example, between a Japanese prefecture government and state governments in the United States; or the politics of the International Olympic Committee; or between the cities of Strasbourg and Munich, might be of some interest just to demonstrate the interconnectedness of societies. But we are unlikely to build a field of international politics around such studies, because they are not derived from the war-peace problem. In brief, we earn our identity as scholars of international politics because, ultimately, we are all concerned with the causes of war and the conditions of peace, order and security.[2]

Dependency theories, a second major perspective on international relations, have different normative and ethical concerns. These are the causes of inequality and exploitation and the conditions of international justice, as measured essentially by economic equality and opportunity. Questions of war and peace are not central concerns; indeed, most dependency writers treat them as mere epiphenomena of basic economic structures, as instruments used by the center, or industrial countries, to control the developing countries. There can be no solution to the problem of war until there is a restructuring of the world capitalist system. In the meantime, major intellectual concerns have to focus on the condition of poverty and the steps necessary to end exploitation and domination. Justice, conceived in economic terms, is the goal; and concern or outrage about inequality propels theoretical and empirical analysis. Dependency theorists disagree on many critical methodological, conceptual and empirical problems, but they are united in their ethical and moral concerns. The ultimate test of dependency theories will be an empirical one: to what extent do the various hypotheses and generalizations coincide with the real world. We cannot reject them on the grounds that their central normative concerns are unimportant.

World society theories also reflect strong normative concerns. War and peace are important problems, but to them they have added questions of equality and justice, pollution, the depletion of resources and a whole host of other global problems. The basic argument, perhaps rooted more in wishful thinking than in demonstrated fact, is that the genesis of all of these problems resides in the continuation of the states system. Decisions and management that optimize the global good cannot ensue from bargaining between 160 or more nation-states, each pursuing its short-run self-interest. The solution to global problems, all of which are integrally linked, can only come from centers of authority or leadership that have the interests of the human family in the forefront of their concerns. This would require some sort of restructuring or transcendence of the states system. Some writers

226

see evidence that this is already occurring, as the interconnectedness of societies continues to grow; others are more skeptical, and suggest that structural systems of domination and dependency will have to be overcome - that is, all 160 states will have to become genuinely independent and autonomous - before there can be any sort of world authority. Like the proponents of dependency theories, world society modelers have intense internecine debates, but their essential normative concerns are similar. There is an ethical core to scholarly research and analysis.

Unlike many of the physical sciences, all of these major surviving approaches to international relations are driven by more than just curiosity. Ethical concerns are at the center of our activities, and yet we often hear the argument that values are nothing more than a slight intrusion into 'objective' work. All we need to do, it is to claimed, is to be aware of our biases and to make certain that our methodologies are as neutral and 'scientific' as possible. And many of the critiques of these major theoretical approaches are based more on our political distaste for them than on grounds of logic or empirical adequacy. We do not often admit this, but if pressed, one could make at least a moderately persuasive argument in support of the assertion.

One implication is that we will never have a theory of international politics, for the simple reason that our ethical and moral concerns are different. We can only have different approaches to the field, none of which is inherently superior to others because no one can argue that the problem of war (excluding of course nuclear war, because it is truly the ultimate problem) *scientifically* takes precedence over the problem of justice or inequality. I will return to this question when we examine briefly the second form of parochialism.

That values animate much of our research and analysis I hope is by now reasonably clear and established. But values play a much more subtle role as well. They determine or influence not only what we study, but also how we approach a particular subject. Here, we may be essentially unaware of how exactly our personal views of the world, our ideologies, political preferences, and assumptions about the human interactions intrude upon our otherwise scientifically correct concepts and methodologies. It is a problem of what kinds of questions we ask, and how we ask them. Unfortunately, I cannot state a generalization, but perhaps one example will illuminate the point.

The body of literature known as integration theory was among the first to employ non-ideographic research approaches. Much of the literature was formally scientific, and many of the generalizations were assumed to be of universal validity. But the whole enterprise was based on some very traditional liberal views on the diplomatic consequences of interaction between societies. Indeed, we could argue that integration theory was less a scientific exercise about international politics than a research agenda exploring the consequences of inter-state relations of a liberal economic order. While the research often employed formal measurement devices, and thus satisfied some of the criteria of science, the whole enterprise was fundamentally concerned with liberalism. This political preference determined not only the problem to be explored, but how certain research questions could be asked.

Much of the research stressed the positive effects of increasing transaction flows between societies. The experience of the EEC in the 1950s and 1960s seemed to bear out optimistic predictions about such trends, predictions that had been voiced in one form or another since the time of Jeremy Bentham. The ultimate value of integration was not enhanced economic welfare - as most policy-makers saw it - but peace. While some of the integration theorists acknowledged their normative concern with peace, they seldom subjected the precondition of increased transactions to critical scrutiny. They never entertained the opposite hypothesis, enunciated by Rousseau, that increased transactions increased the likelihood of conflict.

Researchers often fail to contemplate what I would call counterintuitive hypotheses. Suppose that they had started off from the assumption that integration is a 'bad' thing. Had they held such a view, and the questions they might have asked - for example, why has there not been more opposition to integration - would lead us to view the problem of integration from an entirely different angle. I am not proposing that arms races, imperialism, international crises, mis-perception and many other phenomena are in fact good, but the integration of normative preferences and scientific methodology will continue until we are willing to confront directly a variety of counter-intuitive hypotheses *before* we outline research designs. Sensitivity to the role of values and political preferences in theoretical and empirical work can help produce more reliable knowledge. It can also help reduce the two forms of parochialism - national perspectives and the demand for orthodoxy - that are characteristics of our field today.

Parochialism I: international theory as a national enterprise

One keystone of a scientific enterprise is the search for generalizations, associations and correlations that transcend temporal or spatial location. Although there is no *a priori* reason to believe that patterns of behavior are changeless or that highly idiosyn-

228

cratic behavior never exists, a bias of the study of international politics has been to go beyond the reporting of current events, as if they were unique, to look for patterns and to explain variations in classes of events. The problems of alliances, mis-perception, bargaining, integration and the like, though usually explored in specific historical-geographic contexts, are not assumed to be germane only to these contexts.

If we grant the assumption of regularity, or patterned behavior, then science cannot be 'national', in the sense that the methods of inquiry in one place are unique to, and different from, those of scholarly communities located in other countries. There cannot be American, Japanese or Latin American schools of international politics, although obviously there are different substantive studies of these areas. We would expect those who examine international politics in general - those concerned with the traditional questions - to have a pronounced global outlook as far as questions asked, data sources and research procedures are concerned. The notion of national 'schools' of thought, whether theoretical or methodological, is inconsistent with the requirements of reliable knowledge.

If the claims about the superiority of knowledge gained through universally-valid scientific procedures are correct, we would expect that a significant proportion of scholars working in the field today adhere to similar canons of enquiry. And, we would also expect that by now there would be at least the nucleus of a global community of scholars, each member producing knowledge, each aware of the works of others in far corners of the world, and all acknowledging important breakthroughs and findings, no matter where their location. A global community of scholars implies some degree of symmetry in production and consumption of knowledge, as distinct from a situation of intellectual dependency, where scholars of just a few nations produce, while a large proportion on the peripheries consume the new ideas, models, findings and data sets but otherwise contribute nothing original into the communications network. Moreover, theories of international politics should be uncontaminated by national or parochial distortions. For example, case studies should come from a variety of geographic and historical locations; aggregate data should come from reasonable samples of countries, over time. And innovative models supposedly of universal validity should not be mere distillations of a single country's diplomatic or organizational experience. What has been the record of achievement over the past thirty years in terms of developing a genuine global community of scholars, and a field of inquiry that is largely liberated from parochial habits rooted in geography?

Most of the evidence available to answer this question is unsystematic and impressionistic. I acknowledge this fundamental weakness in the comments that follow. To lend some credence to the observations, however, one can call upon an initial exploration of this question published by Frederick H. Gareau[3] five years ago; in addition, I have data from my own recent work that provide at least a few clues.[4] Both these sources suggest that the early expectations are not being achieved, or achieved only very slowly. There are significant residues of parochial habits, and considerable evidence that American scholars, in particular, are significantly uninformed about work going on in other areas of the world. This overall conclusion is surprising given the recent growth of international scholarly infrastructural organizations.

Opportunities for scholarly exchanges have grown rapidly over the past few decades. Organizations such as the International Studies Association, the International Peace Research Association and the International Political Science Association have organized varied and numerous facilities to bring academics together; conferences, workshops, newsletters, research groups and the like. I am certain the number of conferences and meetings of specialists, coming from various areas of the world, have also grown significantly in number. Most journals in the field are published in English or other major languages, and numerous works in minor languages are eventually translated into English. There is, then, no overbearing physical or language impediment to scholarly communication on a global basis. But there is no community of scholars defined by reasonably symmetrical patterns of production, awareness and acknowledgement of knowledge and research.

Evidence about the awareness and acceptance of scholarship in various areas of the world can be obtained from reviewing citations in scholarly articles and reference or bibliography sections in textbooks on international politics. Gareau has already drawn our attention to the fact that North American academics rarely cite, in journal articles, the research and publications of foreign authors. In part of another study, I have identified the nationalities of authors cited in the reference and bibliography sections of American (and other) textbooks since 1948. While acknowledging some difficulties in using such data as indicators of scholarly globalism or parochialism (an American textbook author is not likely to recommend a work in German or Russian to an undergraduate student), on the whole they are useful because they reflect the authors' explicit judgements about works which are important contributions to the field. The figures emerging from the research are startling. In a sample of six textbooks published in the United States between 1948 and 1968, almost 69 per cent of the bibliography entries or recommended readings were to American authors. For the 1970-1982 sample (also six volumes) this figure had increased to more than 79 per cent. In the latter sample, bibliography entries to American and British authors combined reached almost 87 per cent, which leaves only slightly more than 13 per cent for all other nationalities in the world. The increase over time toward greater concentration of references to authors of one's own nationality is hardly consistent with a model of an international community of scholars whose members are aware of, or acknowledge any significant work, regardless of the authors' nationality. The American pattern, though duplicated in less stark numbers in some other academic communities, is distinct from countries such as Canada, Australia and India, where there is increasing recognition of scholarship being done abroad.

There may be several types of explanation for the data summarized here. Questions of quality, the comparative numbers of academics in the field in various regions of the world, the general tendency of many scholars outside the English-speaking countries not to be interested in theoretical questions, language, the nature of the publishing industry and the like come to mind. But the fact remains that as the scholarly communications infrastructures proliferate, and as international politics becomes established as an organized teaching field in more countries (and hence the entire pool of IR scholars increase), the trend for bibliography entries and suggested readings becomes increasingly concentrated towards national colleagues. Patterns of intellectual dependence - identified as one-way flows of awareness and acknowledgement - are also visible in England and Korea, so the American experience is not unique. Hence, we have a puzzle in the sociology of knowledge. The predictions of the increased 'globalization' of the field of international politics have in some important respects not been borne out by subsequent practices. Characteristics of parochialism remain significant and in some countries are increasing.

Some rough impressions about research developments support the findings reported above. The selection of case studies, development of models and use of data often reflect limited historical experiences. For example, although there has been significant new work comparing crisis behavior across many different countries and eras, until recently much of the literature derived from only two experiences: the Cuban missile crisis and the origins of World War I. Second, the bureaucratic politics model, also developed initially on the basis of the Cuban experience, has numerous references to American practices that may not be particularly germane to the analysis of foreign policy in small countries, parliamentary systems, or in many authoritarian regimes. Third, interdependence is often described as a relatively new characteristic of the world, whereas in fact it may be new only to the United States, which until recently was not a major trading nation. Interdependence is also proclaimed to be a global characteristic, whereas it is a rather poor descriptive or explanatory concept when applied to a majority of states in the world. Other examples could be cited, but the three mentioned here may be sufficient to sensitize researchers against the habit of projecting on to others the characteristic practices and problems of one's own government, or of globalizing generalizations derived from a single historical experience.

A final example of parochialism I is less impressionistic, but more personal. While it may not be entirely typical, it certainly illustrates the nature of the problem. An anonymous American reader of a book-length manuscript I completed several years ago offered a severe criticism for having chose Bhutan as one of several countries in a comparative examination of foreign policy change. The charge was that Bhutan is no more important in international politics than Monaco or San Marino. Whatever the merits of the other criticisms of the manuscript, I could not accept this one. To an American, Bhutan is indeed remote and virtually unknown; it is not therefore surprising that there are few specialists who have an interest in the country. But to an Indian, just to take one example, Bhutan is extremely important in terms of that country's security interests. Indeed, in many ways, it is more significant and theoretically interesting than El Salvador, a small remote country to most American political scientists until a few years ago. The anonymous reader's reaction was typically parochial in that he or she defined the importance of the case study only in terms of American foreign policy interests. The implication was that unless the United States is directly engaged in a country, it is not a subject worthy of inquiry.

Parochialism II: the demand for theoretical and methodological orthodoxy

The debates between behavioralism and traditionalism of the 1950s and 1960s had much of the flavor of an intellectual crusade, the purpose of which was to win and to convert. Behavioralists dismissed the traditionalists as purveyors of superstition and anecdotes, incapable of producing genuine knowledge. Those pigeonholed into the category of the quantifiers were characterized by their protagonists as illiterate and obsessed with measurements of things that inherently cannot be measured. Happily, the debate has largely subsided and the extreme claims made by both sides have been muted. Perhaps more worrisome about the debate than the particular issues that it raised was the demand for orthodoxy, the idea that there can be only a single method of analysis in our field.

This trait has reappeared in many of the theoretical debates that have surrounded our field during the past decade. The attack on realism, for example, has not been confined to pointing out some of the discontinuities between the realist version of the world, and the world as it actually is and operates. It has been, rather, to destroy realism (and its successor, neorealism) totally, replacing it with something else. Some prominent critics of realism have not sought theoretical amendment, reconciliation, synthesis or development. They have sought instead an intellectual knockout, the victory of a new paradigm or world view.[5]

The demand for orthodoxy which is, I suggest, a form of parochialism, may have the deleterious consequences of compartmentalizing and fragmenting the field into separate schools or approaches, the members of which then develop their separate journals, institutes, newsletters and scientific organizations. These institutionalized aspects of the field then help perpetuate narrowness and exclusiveness, the exact opposite of what a true community of scholars requires, namely contacts and mutual learning. In other words, intellectual parochialism becomes institutionalized.

A more charitable interpretation of the demand for orthodoxy - the view that only a single approach or methodology is the appropriate path towards reliable knowledge - is that it is a necessary step for ultimate synthesis, and for refashioning our field to fit with political, economic and technical developments in the world. Just as the hard-line debates between behavioralists and traditionalists ultimately led to the dismissal of the most absurd positions, and to an eventual mutual respect and even mutual learning, so it could be argued that initial statements in favor of a particular paradigm or methodology have to be laced with exaggeration and an aura of exclusivity if they are to make a point vigorously. At a minimum, polemics such as Ashley's critique of realism and neorealism, may be useful because they force adherents of those schools to re-examine their assumptions, to uncover hidden values, and to find new ways of reconciling their views of the world with the main trends and changes in the real world. Perhaps conventional wisdom needs a shock, a fundamental challenge, to become renewed. Synthesis, restructuring, and addition, it could be argued, can come only if those comfortable with a body of knowledge are forced to undergo an exercise of self-examination. In other words, intellectual knockouts, even if intended to replace one orthodoxy with another, may have the consequence of developing knowledge.

I am not certain which interpretation is correct. Certainly the strident tones of many of the debates, and the extent to which we have developed theoretical ghettos, whose members are barely aware of each other's work, is a cause for concern. I do not think, for example, that a student of international relations of the more conventional schools can consider him or herself well-grounded in the field until he or she has made a reasonably strenuous effort to understand at least the major points of dependency theory. Similarly, dependency theorists who simply dismiss strategic theory and the areas of great power politics that resemble the main propositions of realism as a mere facade for western imperialism in the developing countries, cannot be complete theorists in the field. Reliable knowledge would seem to depend upon a healthy pluralism rather than the all-too-prevalent view that a particular school or approach is either right or wrong.

I believe we should be at least sensitive to the possibility that theoretical parochialism renders a disservice to knowledge and to the progress of our field. Pluralism and intellectual development should not be inconsistent. We should not require exclusiveness and theoretical ghettos as the price for progress. Reliable knowledge should come from intellectual persuasion and superior empirical work, rather than from polemics, denunciations and political preferences masquerading as science.

Conclusions

The year 1956, when the Japan Association of International Relations was founded, constituted an important date also for the development of the field of international relations. Publications by Quincy Wright and Karl Deutsch provided fundamental stimulus to the movement to make international politics a more disciplined and theoretical enterprise.[6] Their works demonstrated that a healthy blend of systematic empirical methodology with theoretical questions posed in the classical literature of our field could produce knowledge of a very high order. Since that year, we have seen much progress in developing the discipline in both scope and depth. If we do not have a grand theory of international politics - which is probably a chimera - at least we have bodies of fairly reliable knowledge, knowledge that transcends time, location, and personality. Many of the hypotheses about international diplomatic life proposed by Thucydides, Machiavelli, Rousseau, Bentham and others have been either confirmed, disproved or at least highly qualified. Our habit of making assertions of opinion and passing them off as facts has been largely overcome. Those who write textbooks in our field are more careful to specify when they are proposing a hypothesis, a hunch, or an established fact or trend. We have learned, too, to distinguish between political preferences masquerading as analysis and genuine scholarly research. I am certain all of us could extend this list of accomplishment. Taken together, they suggest that our discipline has matured in many ways. It is fitting that the JAIR would choose to celebrate its 30th anniversary with a special conference, because those thirty years coincide with the greatest period of intellectual development of our field.

Yet as my comments suggest, we have some way to go before we can claim that ours is a discipline characterized by an international community of scholars, and by a healthy respect for innovation *and* older approaches that still tell us important things about the essential characteristics of the world of diplomacy and war. My own situation is symptomatic of the first type of parochialism. In order to stay abreast of my field, I try to read several dozen books and many more journal articles annually. I am aware that Japan has a vibrant community of international relations scholars, and yet I probably read annually not more than one or two articles authored by Japanese scholars. For a variety of reasons, most of which ultimately have to do with language and the social structure in which academics operate - that is, the various needs to write to a *national* audience - I do not have adequate access to the work of most Japanese scholars. Until I can say with certainty that I am as familiar with the research and theoretical efforts of my colleagues in Japan, India, the Soviet Union, Germany and many other countries, as I am with my Canadian or American colleagues, we will continue to face the problem of national parochialism.

The development of a genuine international community of scholars in our field is a very long-range endeavor. International scholarly organizations help, but they are by no means sufficient as an instrument for overcoming the problem. Indeed, as I have shown elsewhere, there is evidence that as our international scholarly organizations have developed, academics in the United States and Great Britain have become even more parochial than they were thirty years ago. A re-emphasis on language training as part of our graduate programmes is just one of the many essential steps toward eventual progress.

The second form of parochialism bedevils all of us. Its roots are in the human character rather than in social institutions or graduate training. The demand for theoretical orthodoxy, the claim that every insight is a new paradigm, and the wholesale rejection of traditional modes of analysis simply because they do not conform to the fads of the moment betrays forms of intellectual intolerance. Sometimes a vigorous challenge to old ways of looking at the world is healthy; indeed, it may be a necessary step towards intellectual development and renewal. But many of the debates of the last thirty years have not been conducted in the spirit of mutual learning or the desire to amend, synthesize, or to do whatever is necessary within a healthy pluralism, to develop more reliable and extensive knowledge. We seem more prone to seek theoretical or methodological victories, to prove that our colleagues are wrong while we are right, that a single (and therefore partial) view of the world is correct while all others are incorrect. I am not certain what can or should be done about this problem. A starting point, however, might be to point out that it exists, and that it is not consistent with the scholarly enterprise. Beyond that, we might acknowledge that we will never have a single theory of international politics, that different perspectives on the world are probably a reasonable expression of the complexities of real life and of different value preferences. We may not feel comfortable with those complexities, but surely ambiguity, grey areas and uncertainty are preferable to intellectual orthodoxy.

Notes

1. The developing field of international political economy must be excluded from this statement. Its value concerns are primarily distributive, with the core problems of wealth maximization - usually within societies - and equity or reciprocity between societies. Concerns of efficiency are also prominent. The links between wealth maximization and security considerations have not been explored systematically. For a case study of the relationship, however, see K.J. Holsti (1986), 'Politics in Command: Foreign Trade as National Security Policy', *International Organization*, 40, pp. 643-71.

2. Waltz is critical of studies of transnational relations on other grounds, principally that they have not demonstrated that such relationships fundamentally alter the essential properties of international systems, which are their structures, units and capabilities. Hence, transnational relations cannot be a variable in a parsimonious theory of international politics. (Kenneth N. Waltz (1979), *Theory of International Politics*, Reading, MA: Addison-Wesley, ch 5). Neither my comments nor those of Waltz imply that it is impossible to make theoretical statements about transnational relations, but they would be theories of transnational relations, not of war and peace.

3. Frederick H. Gareau (1981), 'The Discipline of International Relations: A Multinational Perspective', *Journal of Politics*, 43, pp. 779-802.

4. K.J. Holsti (1985), *The Dividing Discipline. Hegemony and Diversity in International Theory*, London: Allen & Unwin.

5. For particularly sharp critiques of realism and its modern successors see, for example, Richard K. Ashley (1984), 'The Poverty of Neorealism', *International Organization*, 38, pp. 225-86; John Vasquez (1983), *The Power of*

Power Politics: A Critique, New Brunswick, NJ: Rutgers University Press.

6.   Quincy Wright (1955), *The Study of International Relations*, New York: Appleton-Century-Crofts; Karl Deutsch (1954), *Political Community at the International Level*, Garden City, NJ: Doubleday.

12. Mirror, Mirror on the Wall, Which are the Fairest Theories of All?

How are we to choose the best selections in the expanding menu of theoretical offerings in international relations? Should we accept the post-modernist argument that no body of knowledge is intrinsically superior to others? What are the virtues and drawbacks of theoretical pluralism? What do we mean by 'theoretical growth'? And why, at this time, is there such a profusion of theoretical activity? My comments are directed to three interrelated questions: the purposes of theoretical pluralism, the nature of theoretical progress, and the sources of theoretical activity in the field. I state my position clearly at the beginning: the ultimate purpose of theoretical activity is to enhance our understanding of the world of international politics, what Lapid[1] terms the phenomenic axis of scientific knowledge. That is primary; the analytical and thematic axes are valuable not in themselves, but in the ways they can increase our knowledge of the real work by helping guide research and by interpreting data. We add to knowledge primarily when we render reality more intelligible by seeking generalizations of empirical validity, remaining alert to significant unique and deviant phenomena. I confess that this position is not friendly to some (but not all) of the post-modernist views on epistemology, the author-reader relationship, and the meaning of time, location, and personality.

The purposes of theoretical pluralism

There is no intrinsic virtue in theoretical pluralism. If the world were relatively simple - as in an international system comprised of only two intermittently interacting tribes or city-states - one could probably develop a single set of explanations for understanding the essential characteristics of 'international' institutions, structures, processes, and outcomes, and of changes in them. In such a situation, an accumulation of theories, discourses, and research programs could add to knowledge, but more likely they would produce confusion and intellectual cacophony.

Our world is complex and growing more so. It is therefore unlikely that any single theory or perspective, much less their derivative research programs, could adequately reveal all of its

239

essential characteristics, explain them, and account for change. The first significant purpose of pluralism is thus to alert us to oversimplification. In fact, the 'third debate' in international relations theory is largely the result of oversimplifications found in realism.

Pluralism also guards against the hazards of 'intellectual knockouts', those attempts to disown past methodologies and theories, on the assumption that they are entirely wrong, only to replace them with a new orthodoxy. This was a major shortcoming of the most extreme pretensions of behavioralists and of some recent efforts to demolish realism and its variants. Theoretical pluralism is the only possible response to the multiple realities of a complex world. Any attempt to establish an orthodoxy of a particular perspective or methodology can only result in oversimplification and lost opportunities for expanding knowledge.

Theoretical pluralism is also an expression of the diverging intellectual roots of our discipline. Contested visions of the world and of its political dynamics go back at least to the Greeks. Attempts to demolish those roots are likely to lead to vertical parochialism - ignorance of our past - and to rediscovery of theoretical wheels. Some aspects of the 'third debate' bring to mind the contemporary emphasis on novelty and disdain for continuity (an example of this practice is provided in the International Studies Association's 1989 annual meeting program, where one panel was entitled 'International Theory: Out with the Old and In with the New'). We have witnessed in North America the rise and decline of research programs, some lasting a few years, others for a decade or more, and then disappearing, only to be resurrected decades later with a new terminology and some new concepts. Comparative international systems, international integration, subsystems, interdependence, regimes (what used to be called international law and organization) have all come and gone, but the realities that they illuminated are still with us. Academics apparently get bored with them and then begin looking for new theoretical fields to till. We are even seeing the rebirth of interest in international institutions after this subject was declared passé by the leaders of the behavioral revolution three decades ago. It is relatively safe to predict that integration studies will reemerge shortly, albeit under a new name. International theory does not seem immune to the merchants' and couturiers' habit of claiming that the new is 'In' and the old is 'Out'. Theoretical pluralism helps to prevent this style of academic innovation. It confirms and guarantees our intellectual roots and it provides us with a proper skepticism against fashion.

The most obvious and important function of pluralism is based on our Socratic belief that the validity of ideas is enhanced through challenge, debate, and the development of alternatives. The whole edifice of intellectual activity since at least the fifteenth century has been based on the assumption of progress through the conflict of ideas. The criteria for assessing the validity and reliability of knowledge are many and remain contested, but the one belief that unites all, including the post-modernists, is that knowledge does not emerge from authority, whether that of fashion (the triumph of the ephemeral), religion or government. But is intellectual progress measured solely by the accumulation of theories, a pluralism without purpose?

Problems of defining intellectual progress

The purpose of theoretical innovation in some versions of the 'third debate' is to demonstrate the extreme anomalies between older theoretical formulations and modern facts, and to replace them with more appropriate constructs.[2] Their philosophical and methodological strategies are those of *replacement*, substituting one vision, explanation system, or methodology with another. This conforms to the Kuhnian version of progress, one espoused vigorously by both 'strict' and 'loose' positivists. They have assumed that there is already an existing reality out there, a fixed quantity of facts, awaiting discovery and exploitation, like nuggets in a mine. If one uses the right (new) methodological tools, if we engage in sufficient theoretical dialogue, if we eliminate blunted theoretical instruments, and if we throw out the tailings - old knowledge and perspectives - we will discover those nuggets of knowledge.

For the sake of argument, I would suggest another view of intellectual progress in our field, one that is based on its history and practice, rather than on the pronouncements of philosophers of science or those who proclaim that suddenly all is new and 'in'. Knowledge has progressed additively and dialectically, and not through sudden replacements of 'knowledge-producing units' (to use Lapid's term). Unlike the natural sciences, knowledge in our field is not like a mine filled with pre-existing, unchanging facts, just waiting to be discovered. A more appropriate analogy would be a very slow-motion explosion. For us, knowledge generally *succeeds* facts. Intellectual progress is largely keeping up with the facts - describing, categorizing, comparing, and explaining new or previously hidden associations, regularities, or significant deviant facts. Some facts and patterns of international politics have persisted throughout recorded history; others are new. But whether old or new, they are usually interconnected.

We cannot throw away paradigms (or what passes for them)

241

like natural scientists do, à la Kuhn, because the anomalies between realities and their theoretical characterization are never so severe in international relations as they are in the natural sciences. None of the thinkers of the past portrayed the world of international (or world) politics in so distorted a manner as did some analysts of the physical universe prior to the Copernican revolution. We do not read Thucydides, Aristotle, Rousseau and many others as historical curiosities. We may and do add to them, and often criticize them, but we do not replace them. Long before the behavioral revolution, Aristotle claimed that generalizations about political life can be derived from the empirical data of sense and historical experience, and that these generalizations can be treated in terms of cause and effect. Thucydides' hypothesis on the causes of preemptive war is as germane today as it was in 431 BC. Rousseau's insights about the sources of war and the difficulties of cooperation in a condition of anarchy command our attention as much today as they did when first published. No amount of meta-theoretical debate, or perspectivism, or postmodern relativism renders their work less theoretically useful. We cannot discard them because they explain some things about politics at the international level that have persisted throughout recorded history.

Does this mean that we rely simply on the knowledge and insights of the past? Certainly not, because our intellectual ancestors did not describe and explain all the significant realities of international life, either those of their own day or those of our times. Others have shown how their analyses were incomplete and partial or how, by shifting assumptions, different questions and answers could be generated. Statement and counter-statement have proceeded dialectically. At no time has a single paradigm commanded the field as a whole, replacing all others, although some have been predominant in various periods. Lapid suggests (p. 243) that perspectivism has become 'massively internalized as a foremost characteristic of the third debate in international relations theory'. I would argue that it has always been a characteristic of our field. How otherwise would we account for the antinomies of Rousseau and Bentham, of von Gentz and Deutsch, or of Wilson and Gilpin, unless there had been perspectivism at work?

We can analyze international theorists according to at least six dimensions:

1) atomistic anarchy - community as visions of the world;
2) pessimism - optimism in terms of the outcomes of processes;
3) immutability - mutability in terms of the possibilities for change and improvement in the human condition;
4) static - dynamic models;

242

5)   zero-sum - positive sum outcomes of interactions; and
6)   hierarchy - equality of structures.[3]

When we observe any particular theorist inhabiting the ends of four or more of these dimensions, a stream of thought invariably develops to challenge that position. The new 'revisionist' stance will probably contain its own excesses, thus prompting further revision. But in each case some essential truths or explanatory systems remain; they are not replaced. As examples: early nineteenth century liberal thought seriously challenged Rousseau's descriptions and explanations. In our time, the excesses of some versions of realism have been successfully challenged in studies of international integration and in more recent regimes analyses. All of the denizens of the left or right (on the extremes of the dimensions, not politically) remain in our bodies of theory not because they had the whole answer but because they proposed insights and generalizations that accorded and remain reasonably consistent with significant facts and patterns of diplomatic, strategic, and commercial behavior at the international level.

Progress is thus not measured by unlimited accumulation of perspectives, paradigms, models, or methodologies any more than it is by the replacement of 'units of knowledge'. Some perspectives, models, and the like have and should have higher intellectual claims than others. The ultimate test is what light they shed on, and how elegantly and comprehensibly they describe and explain the *important* persisting, new, and developing realities. Higher claims also belong to those theoretical perspectives that define what *is* important, and why - ultimately a question of values. Realism claims to explain the persistence of war and balances of power, and outlines some necessary conditions for peace. In some ways it has lived up to those claims; in others it has fallen short. What, exactly, are the claims of some of the replacements of realism remain unclear.

As the world becomes more complex, the need for theoretical activity increases, but we necessarily follow in the footsteps of diplomats, military men, non-governmental organizations, and all the other actors and activities that make up the subject of investigation. But until there is a Copernican revolution in the way men behave diplomatically, strategically, and commercially, there is not likely to be a theoretical one. A plethora of 'themes' and 'paradigms' is an expression of greater international complexity. But it may also result from other sources, some of which are far removed from the real world. I remain skeptical of the 'liberation of theory from data' or as Halliday[4] has put it, a 'rejection of empiricism in favor of a theoretical approach that accepts the place of data in a subordinate position'. Theoretical proliferation that is not rooted in realities may lead to fashion rather than to knowledge.

The sources of theoretical innovation

Lapid suggests that the main source of the recent growth of theoretical debate in the field lies in the unfulfilled expectations of the behavioral revolution. For many, the demands of strict positivism became an intellectual strait-jacket rather than a fillip for creative speculation and theorizing. This observation is probably correct; it is also incomplete. Theoretical innovation results from at least five sources: (1) events in world politics; (2) facts; (3) other theories, or what Lapid terms 'perspectivism'; (4) values; and (5) meta-theoretical debates. Many of the positions taken among the diverse participants in the third debate derive from a mixture of these sources.

Event-driven theory

Singular events have inspired attention to particular aspects of international relations and foreign policy analysis. The Cuban missile crisis, the origins of World War I, and the OPEC embargo have acted as critical sources of theories of decision-making, crisis management, power relations, and international political economy. Parts of the literatures have served as sources of hypotheses and comparative analysis. Thought-provoking events have also spawned research programs, themes, sets of new questions, and perspectivism (e.g., evidence of information-reducing psychological mechanisms and mis-perceptions challenge the rationalist premises of realism).

Fact-driven theory

Facts refer to actors, persisting patterns of behavior, trends, institutions, structures and/or processes in international relations. They transcend a particular time, location, and personality. Some of the current debates revolve around the claim that there are anomalies between the important facts of international relations and their interpretation and explanation in realist models of international politics. Prominent examples would include essays by Burton, Nye and Keohane, and Puchala and Fagan.[5]

Theory-driven theory

This category refers to the development of new or additional research programs through critical examination of the assumptions, premises, and major generalizations of existing theories and models. This is the essence of 'perspectivism'. Since 1945, we have had one spectacularly successful example of theory-driven theory. Karl Deutsch[6] took the classical problematic of realism and changed it slightly to generate a new research program. Instead of asking, as had most of his predecessors, what are the causes of war and the conditions of peace (thereby focussing on the antecedents of war and a hypothesized set of non-existing conditions for peace), he asked what are the sources of peace *in fact*? By this re-arrangement of a traditional question, he, and later with his colleagues[7] produced a corpus of theoretical and empirical work that stands as a monument of creativity that has successfully challenged major elements of the realist tradition. We emphasize again, however, that the body of literature did not assume authority until the empirical work was completed.

Value-driven theory

Some of the contemporary theoretical ferment arises not so much from fact - theory anomalies or perspectivism, but from personal disenchantment with the current state of the world. Criticism of realism, in particular, is often rooted in value positions. The argument is that the states system and the governments who play the realist game have got us into a terrible mess, in part because leaders are familiar with the normative elements of realism and attempt to apply them as guides to policy. The anomalies are not between facts and theories, but between a particular rendering of the facts and some conception of a better world. This position sometimes takes the form of an argument from desperation.

There are also more subtle ways that values drive theory. Here we may overlap with perspectivism, but it is generally the assumptions we make when we formulate research questions. Deutsch organized his research around classical liberal assumptions that communications enhance mutual understanding and that integration is in general a desirable approach to peace. Had he asked somewhat different questions reflecting, for example, the political value of *autonomy*, he might have organized the research in a different manner, asking instead what are the sources of opposition to integration, or is autonomy or isolation a better path to peace?

Meta-theoretically-driven theory

Finally, the third debate, and particularly recent post-modernist innovations, arises from philosophical differences over questions of ontology, epistemology, the definition of 'subjects' and the like. I pass over problems raised in this sort of discussion for lack of qualifications, but note with some sympathy Theda Skocpol's[8] comment that such debates (may) lead to dead-ends because they fail to result in enhanced understanding of our subject matter.

Conclusion

I have argued that our enterprise shows signs of maturation. Why? Not just because there is debate, or because the limitations of the strict positivist position have been acknowledged, or because today there is a more honest awareness of the role of values in guiding inquiry. The reason is that the substance of the field has begun to catch up with the realities. It no longer focusses on the Cold War and the security policies of the superpowers. It no longer assumes that the limits of wisdom are to be found in the practices and malpractices of the Soviet Union and the United States. Today we have theories (admittedly limited ones) of conflict and war based on impressive bodies of data spanning centuries; theories of dependency and hegemony that better reflect the unique characteristic of inter-state and intersocietal relations between north and south; research programs that focus on the critical issue of international cooperation; important insights into the changing bases of power and influence. We know more than we did previously about the predicaments of small states (the Melian dialogue did not state the final word on the subject), the role of economic issues in international politics, and many other areas. Some of the knowledge remains descriptive and unintegrated into higher-order statements, but it is there nevertheless to check impressionistic generalizations and broad-range theories that seem far-removed from the realities.

The field is maturing because there is an increased recognition and acceptance of multiple realities, and hence of multiple theories. Hoffmann[9] pointed out more than a decade ago that there are many different games of international politics - which was not the case when Machiavelli or Rousseau wrote - and the third debate is partly a recognition of this fact. The other sources of theory are important, but in my view there is no foundation of theory that is superior to a keen understanding of the facts of international relations, past and present. We are indeed condemned - happily - to live a life of theoretical pluralism for the

246

reasons elaborated above. If we keep our eyes on what is actually happening in the world and on the requirements of reliable knowledge[10] we may be able to avoid the dangers of the replacement syndrome, faddism, and extreme theoretical and methodological relativism, that is, of an intellectual life without standards.

Notes

1. Y. Lapid (1989), 'The Third Debate: On the Prospects of International Theory in a Post Positivist Era', *International Studies Quarterly*, 33, p. 255.
2. R.W. Mansbach and J.D. Vasquez (1981), *In Search of Theory*, New York: Columbia University Press; James Rosenau (1988), 'Patterned Chaos in Global Life: Structure and Process in the Two Worlds of World Politics', *International Political Science Review*, 9, pp. 327-64.
3. Three of these dimensions are noted in R.W. Mansbach and Y.J. Ferguson (1986), 'Values and Paradigm Change: The Elusive Quest for International Relations Theory', in M.P. Karns (ed.), *Persistent Patterns and Emerging Structures in a Waning Century*, New York: Praeger.
4. F. Halliday (1985), 'A Crisis in International Relations?', *International Relations*, November, p. 412.
5. J.W. Burton (1972), *World Society*, Cambridge: Cambridge University Press; R.O. Keohane and J.S. Nye (eds), *World Politics and Transnational Relations*, Cambridge: Harvard University Press; D. Puchala and S. Fagan (1974), 'International Politics in the 1970s: The Search for a Perspective', *International Organization*, 28, pp. 247-66. See also the works of Mansbach and Vasquez and Rosenau cited in note 2 above.
6. K.W. Deutsch (1954), *Political Community at the International Level: Problems of Definition and Measurement*, Garden City, New York: Doubleday.
7. K.W. Deutsch et al. (1957), *Political Community and the North Atlantic Area*, Princeton: Princeton University Press.
8. T. Skocpol (1987), 'The Deadend of Metatheory', *Contemporary Sociology*, 16, p. 12.
9. Hoffmann (1978), *Primacy or World Order: American Foreign Policy Since the Cold War*, New York: McGraw-Hill, pp. 106-45.
10. J. David Singer (1985), 'The Responsibilities of Competence in a Global Village', *International Studies Quarterly*, 29, pp. 245-62.

Index

161-2

252